**The urban informal sector
in developing countries**
Employment,
poverty and environment

The urban informal sector in developing countries
Employment, poverty and environment

Edited by S.V. Sethuraman

International Labour Office   Geneva

ISBN 92-2-102591-8 (limp cover)
ISBN 92-2-102590-X (hard cover)

First published 1981

ILO publications can be obtained through major booksellers or ILO local offices in many countries, or direct from ILO Publications, International Labour Office, CH-1211 Geneva 22, Switzerland. A catalogue or list of new publications will be sent free of charge from the above address.

Printed in Switzerland

PREFACE

One of the unique, and perhaps disturbing, features of development in the Third World during the second half of the present century is the unprecedented growth of population and labour force in urban areas, notably in large cities. The share of urban population in total in developing countries rose from under 7 per cent in 1920 to 13 per cent in 1950; it is expected to rise further to 43 per cent by the end of the century. The projected trend is disquieting, for the cities in the Third World are already experiencing the pressure of population on the available shelter and other basic urban amenities. Besides posing a threat to the urban environment it also raises questions about the quality of life, the cost of providing shelter and urban services in a man-made environment and unbalanced spatial development to mention only a few.

Policies for de-concentration, promotion of rural farm and non-farm employment and improvement in the quality of life in rural areas, besides measures to contain population growth, no doubt constitute the key elements of a long-term strategy designed to meet the goals of ecodevelopment. This book is however concerned with the implications of urbanisation to urban employment, poverty and environment in developing countries. Few believe that migration toward urban areas can be arrested in the foreseeable future. The sheer magnitude of the urban population in these countries and its concentration in reproductive age groups suggests that the problems resulting from urbanisation can no longer be swept under the carpet.

The substantial increase in urban population and labour force, some half of it due to internal migration, is no doubt partly a response to concentration of investment and incomes in large urban centres, notably in the modern sectors including government. Yet since employment in these sectors has failed to keep pace with the urban labour force growth, the process of urbanisation has elevated the concern for urban employment, underemployment and unemployment. Much of the additions to the urban labour force are seeking refuge in what is known as the "informal sector" in which they create their own employment to the extent the capital and skills at their disposal would permit. An array of labels have been coined and used to describe the activities encompassing this sector. To some they consist of illegal, criminal or marginal activities and hence parasitic; and to others they represent productive, small-scale self-employed activities and hence serve as a source for promoting growth, employment and equity objectives. It is not therefore surprising that the informal sector subject has aroused a passionate controversy in recent years. Some view it as an effective means for redistributing income and opportunities while others are sceptical. More importantly the nature, range and extent of interventions necessary to promote employment, equity and basic needs through the urban informal sector are gaining increasing importance in the debate on development issues. To the ILO it raises additional questions concerning the future role of the sector in labour absorption, the conditions of work and the like.

Though the informal sector has been in existence in many countries in one form or another it is only during the last decade that it has drawn the attention of policy makers and researchers, notably from the point of view of opportunities for participation in, and reaping the benefits of, development. Following a series of city case studies on Calcutta, Jakarta, São Paulo, Abidjan, Bogotá and Lagos supported by a generous grant from the Federal Republic of Germany, the Urbanisation and Employment Research Project under the World Employment Programme of the ILO turned its attention to the urban informal sector, for it seemed to provide anywhere between a quarter and a half of employment in cities of the Third World. Three survey studies were carried out on the subject in Calcutta, Dakar and Bogotá. It was at this point that the scope of the research project was widened to include a number of other cities and to assess the links between employment promotion in the urban informal sector and improvement of the urban physical environment. A generous grant from the United Nations Environment Programme in 1975 facilitated this task and led to survey studies in Freetown (Sierra Leone), Lagos and Kano (Nigeria), Kumasi (Ghana), Colombo (Sri Lanka), Jakarta (Indonesia), Manila (Philippines), Cordoba (Argentina) and Campinas (Brazil). The present volume is the end product of this research.

Even though the informal sector seems to have emerged as a major source of urban employment it is not clear under what conditions labour is being absorbed in this sector. Nor is it clear how productive these activities are and what opportunities they offer for upward mobility. One of the objectives of the studies in this volume has therefore been to throw light on these issues. Another aim of the volume has been to explore the scope for combining policies for employment creation in this sector with measures to improve the urban environment in the Third World. Given the dual nature of the urban systems, informal sector promotion does raise questions for development policy, notably with regard to interdependence between the formal and the informal sectors. It also has implications for migration policies, urban labour markets, human resources development, regional development, growth, poverty alleviation and satisfaction of basic needs. The book therefore addresses itself to these issues as well.

Both the very small-scale nature of these activities and their wide range undoubtedly pose problems in terms of concepts and measurement and research methodology. The studies reported in this volume are therefore necessarily exploratory in nature; both the quality and coverage of data vary across studies. Though the studies were carried out during the 1975-76 period, since the focus was on the problems and policies rather than on quantitative estimates of absolute magnitudes, much of the findings reported here have not lost their validity. Since the studies presented here refer to cities of varying size the word "urban" essentially means large urban centres. Notwithstanding the fact that the volume is based on data from some 16,000 small-scale units in the informal sector and draws on evidence from a number of other related studies on the subject, it represents no more than a first attempt to look at the informal sector in developing countries. Perhaps the book raises more questions than answers.

The studies reported in this volume are drawn from the respective full-length versions which appeared earlier as a series of World Employment Programme Research Working Papers under the Urbanisation and Employment Research Project (WEP 2-19). Though some of the authors prepared chapter-length summaries based on their respective reports it was often necessary to recast them with a view to including other relevant evidence, ensuring complementarity and comparability between different chapters and keeping the length of the book to a reasonable size. In other cases it was necessary to prepare a summary based on the respective working papers. Though the authors were provided with an opportunity to look through the relevant chapters in a draft form and to ensure proper representation of their factual findings, in an edited work of this nature they may not necessarily subscribe to some of the interpretations. Finally, the views and opinions expressed in this volume do not necessarily reflect those of the ILO or the UNEP.

Thanks are due to Dr. Harold Lubell, who was in charge of the Urbanisation and Employment Research Project until August 1978 and Dr. A.S. Bhalla, Chief of the Technology and Employment Branch of the ILO for providing advice and encouragement in the preparation of this volume. The Editor would also like to acknowledge the valuable comments received from the UNEP and the members of the Reading Committee within the Employment and Development Department of the ILO.

TABLE OF CONTENTS

Page

Preface v

PART I The role of the urban informal sector
S.V. Sethuraman

Chapter 1. Introduction 3

Chapter 2. Concepts, methodology and scope 10

Chapter 3. The urban informal sector and
development policy 28

PART II Evidence from Africa, Asia and Latin America

Chapter 4. The informal sector in Freetown: Opportunities
for self-employment
D.A. Fowler 51

Chapter 5. Human resources and the Lagos informal sector
O.J. Fapohunda 70

Chapter 6. The informal sector in a small city:
The case of Kano
A.L. Mabogunje and M.O. Filani 83

Chapter 7. The informal manufacturing sector in Kumasi
George Aryee 90

Chapter 8. Informal sector without migration:
The case of Colombo
Marga Institute, Colombo 101

Chapter 9. Occupational mobility and the informal
sector in Jakarta
Hazel Moir 109

Chapter 10. The Manila informal sector: In transition?
G.M. Jurado et al. 121

Chapter 11. The informal and quasi-formal sectors
in Córdoba
Carlos E. Sánchez et al. 144

Chapter 12. The urban informal sector and industrial
development in a small city: The case of
Campinas
Manuel Tosta Berlinck et al. 159

Page

Part III   Implications for environment and
             development policies
             S. V. Sethuraman

Chapter 13. The informal sector and the urban environment ..   171

Chapter 14. Summary and conclusions: Implications for
             policy and action   188

Appendix tables 209

Sources 215

Informal sector: selective bibliography 217

LIST OF TABLES

Page

Chapter 4 Table 1 Distribution of sample enterprises by main activity 52

Table 2 Capital-labour ratio by main activity .. 59

Table 3 Gross value of output per worker by main activity 60

Table 4 Net revenue to the entrepreneur by main activity 63

Chapter 5 Table 1 Distribution of enterprises by main activity groups 70

Table 2 Distribution of enterprises by value of capital equipment and by activity ... 77

Chapter 6 Table 1 Distribution of informal sector participants by level of income 85

Chapter 7 Table 1 Size distribution of enterprises by activity 93

Table 2 Distribution of enterprises by capital . 95

Table 3 Capital, output and value added per enterprise and per worker in selected activities 96

Table 4 Output, value added and capital per worker by size 97

Table 5 Value added and employment per unit of capital, by size of enterprise 97

Chapter 8 Table 1 Distribution of enterprises by type of clientele and by activity 105

Chapter 10 Table 1 Distribution of enterprises with full-time wage workers by minimum and maximum daily wage paid to males and females ... 122

Table 2 Distribution of enterprises by gross value added per week 124

Table 3 Value added and employment per unit of capital, by size of enterprise 125

Page

Table 4   Backward linkages: Distribution of
           sample enterprises by sources of inputs
           and by sectors   127

Table 5   Forward linkages: Distribution of
           enterprises by sectors   127

Table 6   Distribution of enterprises by weekly
           earnings of entrepreneurs in trade   132

Table 7   Distribution of enterprises by size of
           fixed capital owned   133

Table 8   Capital, value added, earnings and
           wages in the informal service sector ...   139

Chapter 11 Table 1   Distribution of immigrants between
           quasi-formal and informal sectors by
           duration of residence in Córdoba   146

Table 2   Distribution of heads of enterprises
           by occupation   148

Table 3   Distribution of informal and quasi-
           formal units by activity   149

Table 4   Distribution of the sample units by
           size and activity   151

Table 5   Distribution of heads of enterprises by
           income level and skills   153

Table 6   Distribution of heads of enterprises by
           income level and sex   154

Table 7   Distribution of enterprises by activity
           and age of business   155

Chapter 12 Table 1   Distribution of sample units by activity
           and capital size   160

Table 2   Distribution of sample units by amount
           of capital and monthly income per unit .   162

Table 3   Distribution of enterprises and wage
           workers by size of enterprise   163

PART I

The role of the urban informal sector

S.V. Sethuraman

CHAPTER 1.   INTRODUCTION

The urban population nearly tripled in the developing countries in a short span of 25 years from 275 million in 1950 to 794 million in 1975. During the next 25 years over 1,300 million more are expected to be added, bringing the urban population in these countries to over 2 billions.[1] The rate of increase in the Third World urban population seems to have accelerated in recent years, notably in the poorest developing countries. As compared to a rate of 4 per cent per year during the four decades following 1920,[2] the rate of increase during 1960-70 seems to have been around 5.4 per cent per year in low-income developing countries (i.e. under US$250 per capita) and 4.8 per cent per year in middle income developing countries (i.e. per capita income above US$250).[3] Consequently the share of urban population in total has risen from 6.7 per cent in 1920 to 12.9 per cent in 1950[4] and 27 per cent in 1975; it is expected to rise further to 43 per cent by the end of the present century.[1]

The phenomenal growth in urban population is no doubt primarily due to the over-all growth in total population in the Third World countries. From under 0.5 per cent per year during the last century, total population in these countries increased at 1.1 per cent per annum during the first half and at 2.4 per cent per year during the third quarter of the present century and this trend is expected to continue over the next few decades.[5] What is more striking is the accelerated pace of urbanisation implied by the diverging rates of growth of urban and rural population. The pace at which urbanisation is taking place in the Third World countries now is far in excess of the rate experienced in the developed world during their comparable stage of development.[6] Differential rates of growth of population no doubt explains much of this phenomenon. The consequences of such a rapid urbanisation are however much more far reaching owing to the absence of conditions under which population growth and urbanisation occurred in the developed countries during the nineteenth century.

The developing world of today does not have the opportunities for territorial expansion which the developed countries had during the last century. Between 1800 and 1900 the geographical area of

----

[1] United Nations: _World population trends and prospects by country, 1950-2000: Summary report of the 1978 assessment_ (New York, 1979), and other unpublished materials from the United Nations. More developed regions include Europe, North America, the USSR, Japan, Australia and New Zealand.

[2] Paul Bairoch: _Urban unemployment in developing countries_ (Geneva, ILO, 1973), table 6, p. 19.

[3] World Bank: _World Development Report, 1978_ (Washington, 1978), p. 100.

[4] Bairoch, op. cit., table 7, p. 20.

[5] ibid., table 1, p. 8.

[6] ibid., pp. 20-21.

developed countries increased from 10.5 million km² to some 43 million km².[1] Neither does the former have the opportunities for growth and labour absorption through trade coupled with industrial development to the same extent.[2] The Third World countries, under the circumstances, have been forced to look inward and absorb as much labour as possible within the rural areas, particularly in agriculture. In the 50 years between 1920 and 1970 the number of persons engaged in agriculture in these countries practically doubled increasing from 240 million to some 450 million, even though the land available for cultivation (including multiple cropping) increased but little. For example, between 1950 and 1970 the area of agricultural land in these countries increased by about 25 per cent, while the number engaged in agriculture rose by 50 per cent.[3] With the exception of Latin America, the rate of expansion of cultivated land has slowed down in most developing countries. Notwithstanding migration from rural to urban areas, rural population growth on the other hand has tended to increase. As compared to 1.9 per cent per year during 1950-60, the rate of rural population growth in 1960-70 period in developing regions (Latin America, East Asia and Middle East and Africa) was 2.1 per cent per year.[4] Though there is scope for absorbing more labour through technological change, investment in infrastructure and structural changes, there are indeed formidable difficulties.[5] Consequently the growing pressure of population on agriculture would seem to have increased the extent of rural poverty.

Given the disparities between incomes in agriculture and non-agricultural activities and between rural and urban areas, the shift of population from rural to urban areas is not therefore surprising. Notwithstanding the recent advances in agricultural technology the increasing pressure of population on land would seem to echo the Malthusian prediction of surplus population. Better employment and income opportunities in the urban areas (notably primate cities) coupled with increasing and cheaper transportation and communication facilities would seem to have played a major role in the urbanisation process. Location of industries, expansion of government administration in the wake of independence, and concentration of opportunities for acquiring education and skills, to mention only a few, have played an important role too in attracting migrants.[6] Whatever may be the reason the fact remains that migration has played an important, and in some countries even dominant, role.

----

[1] Bairoch, op. cit., p. 10.

[2] ibid., p. 23.

[3] ibid., pp. 13-14.

[4] World Bank: The assault on world poverty (Baltimore, 1975), pp. 240-241.

[5] ibid., especially chapters on rural development and land reforms.

[6] See for example, ILO: Why labour leaves the land (Geneva, 1960); Paul Bairoch, op. cit., Chapter 2. See also United Nations: The Determinants and Consequences of Population Trends (New York, 1973), Vol. I, Chapter VI, for an excellent summary and review of the relevant literature.

In most developing countries nearly a third of the increase in urban population during the 1960s is estimated to be due to migration from rural areas. In some countries like Ghana, the Republic of Korea and Tanzania, it accounted for over 60 per cent of urban growth and in a few like the Ivory Coast and Uganda, even higher - over 70 per cent.[1] On the average, nearly half the increase in urban population in the less-developed region seems to have been the result of migration. In some countries, for example, in South-East Asia, however, the role of migration in urban population growth is diminishing.[2] Nevertheless, the rate of growth of urban population is expected to remain substantial since most of the migrants are young and hence in the reproductive age groups.

Consequences and concern

One of the disturbing features of the urbanisation process or what some would prefer to call "the urban explosion" is the growing concentration of urban population in large cities. The number of cities with a population of one million or more in the developing world in 1975 was estimated to be 90 and it is expected to increase to 300 by the year 2000. Of the urban population in cities (one million plus) in the world, the share of developing countries has increased enormously from 33 per cent in 1950 to 48 per cent in 1975. By the year 2000, over two-thirds of the population in big cities (one million plus) in the world will be in the developing region. In other words, the population in big cities of the LDCs has been increasing at 5.8 per cent per annum.[3] Big cities absorbed about half of the urban growth in the less-developed regions during the 1920-60 period.[4]

The major source of concern emerging from the above pattern of urbanisation relates to quality of life. The proportion of city population living in slums and squatter settlements in many developing countries ranges anywhere from 25 to 90 per cent, the figure being higher in cities growing more rapidly.[5] This is indeed a natural consequence; besides the magnitude of population increase, most of the urban migrants are too poor to afford anything better. Land is scarce and housing costs more in urban than in rural areas. "Urban housing is more dependent upon the man-made environment than upon the natural environment." It is not therefore an exaggeration to call the proliferation of slums and squatter settlements as an

----

[1] World Bank: World Development Report, 1979 (Washington, 1979), p. 55; see also United Nations: World Housing Survey, 1974 (New York, 1976), p. 152.

[2] United Nations: Economic Bulletin for Asia and the Pacific, No. 1, June 1978, p. 107.

[3] The evidence is based on the latest estimates from unpublished United Nations sources.

[4] R.M. Westebe: The urbanisation problem in the less-developed countries: Causes, impacts and policy implications for the Bank Group (unpublished manuscript, 1970), p. 11.

[5] United Nations: World Housing Survey, 1974, op. cit., tables 48-49, pp. 159-172.

invasion on vacant public and private lands in the cities. This
process has inevitably led to "a rapid increase in living densities
in central, low rental, low income areas, extending and intensifying
slum conditions".[1] And the trend continues; "in as much as slums,
with one third of the city population, account for the city growing
at a rate of 4 per cent, they themselves are growing at a rate of 12
per cent."[1] In the urban areas where water must be paid for,
disposition of solid and liquid waste must be paid for, growing
population densities in such settlements necessarily pose a greater
threat to health and environment. And yet, shortage of basic urban
services and inadequate access to them by the urban poor continue to
pose a challenge to the urban authorities concerned. In many cities
urban services have been stretched to the point of a breakdown.[2]
Needless to add much of these problems are compounded by the limited
capacity of the urban poor to pay for the urban services besides the
limited response of the urban authorities to the emerging problem.

Growth of incomes in the urban areas has generally exceeded
the corresponding rates in rural areas even though urbanisation is
taking place in many developing countries ahead of
industrialisation. And yet income inequalities in urban areas are
significantly above that in rural areas in many countries.[3] Further
as can be seen from Appendix table 3, the bottom 50 per cent of the
urban households mostly received under a quarter of the total income
generated. These findings are also consistent with the data on
distribution of consumer expenditures in Tanzania, Tunisia,
Indonesia, Pakistan and Mexico.[4] While it seems plausible that the
process of urbanisation has been accompanied by an increase in the
absolute number of urban poor and a greater inequality in the
distribution of urban incomes, further data are required to
substantiate this hypothesis.[5]

Another source of concern has been the swelling rates of urban
unemployment, often twice or more the rate prevailing in rural areas
even though between 1950 and 1970 urban employment increased faster
(160 per cent) than total employment (60 per cent) in developing

---

[1] United Nations: World Housing Survey, 1974, op. cit., Chapter
IV, p. 30.

[2] See, for example, Barbara Ward and René Dubos: Only one earth:
The care and maintenance of a small planet (1972), Chapter 12.

[3] H. Chenery, et al.: Redistribution with growth (Washington,
1974), p. 21. See also Appendix tables 1 and 2.

[4] W. Van Ginneken: Rural and urban income inequalities in
Indonesia, Mexico, Pakistan, Tanzania and Tunisia (Geneva, ILO,
1976).

[5] There are however many pitfalls in interpreting the income
distribution statistics. Besides varying quality, concept and
coverage, it is possible for example to raise the share of income
accruing to the poor without improving, or even worsening, the
distribution of income. For more details on measurement and
interpretation of urban poverty, see Richard Webb: On the
statistical mapping of urban poverty and employment, World Bank
Staff Working Paper No. 227 (Washington, Jan. 1976).

countries.[1] The rates however have to be interpreted with caution owing to different population bases in rural and urban areas; the evidence nevertheless clearly suggests that a substantial part of the urban labour force, particularly among youth, is jobless. Though open unemployment is a source of concern from a socio-political point of view the wide prevalence of underemployment is perhaps even more serious since few urban poor in these countries can afford to remain openly unemployed for long periods of time and many of the unemployed are young dependants of better-off households. Notwithstanding these and other problems, urbanisation continues and few are willing to leave the cities suggesting that urban areas provide better income opportunities among other things.

Yet another concern pertains to the unrestrained growth of cities themselves. Does the growth of cities in absolute terms contribute to inefficiency as well, besides generating income disparities between regions and within the cities themselves? Though some would argue in favour of restricting the size of cities on the grounds of diseconomies of scale, the available evidence is far from conclusive.[2]

Coping with the problem

The brief summary above of the urbanisation process taking place in the Third World and its consequences coupled with the projected rates of urbanisation already poses a number of questions as well as a challenge to the countries concerned. In the view of Malthus, the first economist to be concerned with the question of over-population and its implications for poverty and employment, the "surplus" population or the unwanted poor should perforce be gone from "nature's mighty feast".[3] Subsequent economists, however, were not so pessimistic; they saw a wide range of solutions. While those in the Marxian tradition saw the need for a change in the social order, others in the classical and neoclassical tradition were hopeful of technological change, expansion through trade, capital accumulation and migration of labour.[4] The reality, however, is somewhere in between the range of solutions envisaged above.

Development experience in the Third World shows that, "During the 1960s national income per head grew exceptionally fast by

----

[1] Bairoch, op. cit., Chapter III.

[2] P.M. Townroe: "Employment decentralisation: Policy instruments for large cities in developing countries", in Progress in Planning, No. 2, 1979, pp. 94-95; Paul Bairoch: Emploi et taille des villes (Geneva, ILO, 1976; mimeographed World Employment Programme research working paper; restricted).

[3] Ian Bowen: "Nature's feast today", in Finance and Development, No. 4, Dec. 1973, pp. 13-17.

[4] United Nations: The Determinants and Consequences of Population Trends, op. cit., Chapter III, for a survey of the literature.

historical standards in most developing countries."[1] "However, the recent growth in the developing countries has often tended to be concentrated in relatively limited parts of the economy, mostly those using capital-intensive techniques and having few linkages with the traditional rural sector or the urban informal sector, which between them account for by far the greater part of the total employment in most developing countries."[1] A number of factors including the existing economic structures, patterns of pricing and allocation of investment resources and choice of production technologies and product mix would seem to have contributed to uneven patterns of development in developing countries. Whatever may be the reason, economic development failed to generate adequate employment and income opportunities, notably in the modern sector which received the bulk of the resources, to cope with the problem of labour-force explosion.

Under the circumstances the surplus population or the labour force has been forced to generate its own means of employment and hence of survival. Writing more than a century ago about the surplus population resulting from industrial revolution in England, Engels noted: "... the 'surplus population' of England, which keeps body and soul together by begging, stealing, street-sweeping, collecting manure, pushing hand carts, driving donkeys, peddling or performing occasional jobs. In every great town a multitude of such people may be found. It is astonishing in what devices this 'surplus population' takes refuge."[2] While similar conditions exist in many developing countries even today, it is also true that a new class of petit-bourgeois engaged in a variety of more productive activities (e.g., small-scale manufacturing and repair services) has emerged all of which are included in what is now called the "informal sector".[3] The share of urban labour force in the Third World cities engaged in the informal sector ranges anywhere from 20 to 70 per cent, the average being close to half or more (Appendix table 4). The contribution of the urban informal sector to urban regional income also seems quite substantial; for example in Asunción (Paraguay), San Salvador (El Salvador) and Lima (Peru) it was estimated to be 33, 25 and 30 per cent respectively.[4] In Ahmedabad (India), it seems to be 28 per cent.[5]

The present volume is an attempt to understand the urban informal sector in developing countries and its role in employment

----

[1] ILO: Employment, growth and basic needs: A one-world problem (Geneva, 1976), p. 16.

[2] F. Engels: Conditions of the working class in England in 1844 (London, 1920), p. 85.

[3] See next chapter for a more detailed discussion.

[4] P.R. Souza and Victor E. Tokman: "The informal urban sector in Latin America", in International Labour Review, Nov.-Dec. 1976, p. 357.

[5] T.S. Papola: The informal sector in an urban economy: A study in Ahmedabad (Lucknow, 1978), p. 74. Similar conclusions seem to hold for Africa too. See W.F. Steel: Small scale employment and production in developing countries (1977), Chapter I; and Georges Nihan et al.: "The modern informal sector in Lomé", in International Labour Review, Sep.-Oct. 1979, p. 634.

generation, poverty alleviation and urban environment. Following a brief presentation of the concept, methodology and scope of the research undertaken in the field of the urban informal sector in Chapter 2, some of its implications for various development objectives are discussed in Chapter 3. Chapters 4 through 12 in Part II present a summary of findings emerging from the informal sector survey studies in Freetown (Sierra Leone), Lagos and Kano (Nigeria), Kumasi (Ghana), Colombo (Sri Lanka), Jakarta (Indonesia), Manila (Philippines), Córdoba (Argentina), and Campinas (Brazil). Implications of the evidence emerging from the above studies for improving the urban environment in developing countries are discussed in Chapter 13. The last chapter provides a summary of evidence and the scope for policies and action in the field of the urban informal sector.

CHAPTER 2. CONCEPTS, METHODOLOGY AND SCOPE

Notwithstanding the growing recognition of the role played by the informal sector and the need to consider it explicitly in the formulation of development plans, the concept has remained as elusive as that of unemployment and underemployment. It is not, therefore, surprising that one of the first questions frequently encountered is: what is the informal sector? Though the question is very simple, the answer is far from it; it is like asking: what is an underdeveloped country? The concept of the informal sector cannot be defined without going into some details about its history and evolution. The chapter therefore presents a brief review of the development of the concept and then spells out the concept underlying the various studies included in this volume.

Development of the concept[1]

Dualism in the urban economy

The dualistic nature of the urban economy in developing countries has been recognised in the development literature for some years now.[2] The concept of dualism as applied to developing countries has been attributed various meanings by different social scientists ranging from social anthropologists to economists depending on the particular aspect or aspects they chose to study and emphasise. In the discussion below however attention is focused on dualism in the production system in so far as it has implications for employment, development and equity.

The two sub-systems of production have been labelled in different terms that are not necessarily identical: "capitalistic" and "peasant forms of production";[3] "firm" centred and "bazaar" economies;[4] "upper" and "lower" circuits,[5] to mention only a few. While such efforts described the two sub-systems and sought to
- - - - - - - - - - - -

[1] S.V. Sethuraman: "The urban informal sector: Concept, measurement and policy", in International Labour Review, July-Aug. 1976.

[2] Besides the references cited below see also Georges Nihan: Le secteur non structuré: Signification, aire d'extension du concept et application expérimentale (Geneva, ILO, 1979; mimeographed World Employment Programme research working paper; restricted); and Markus Reichmuth: Dualism in Peru: An investigation into the interrelationships between Lima's informal clothing industry and the formal sector (Oxford, 1978), Chapter 1 for further discussion on dualism and the informal sector.

[3] T.G. McGee: "Peasants in the cities: A paradox, a paradox, a most ingenuous paradox", in Human Organisation, Summer 1973, pp. 135-142. See also the works cited therein.

[4] C. Geertz: Pedlars and princes: Social and economic modernisation in two Indonesian towns (Chicago, 1962).

[5] Milton Santos: L'espace partagé: Les deux circuits de l'économie urbaine des pays sous développés (Paris, 1975).

explain the factors that contributed to their origin and significance, another study,[1] looking at the sectors of economic activity brought out, perhaps more explicitly, the implications of dualism to labour absorption currently taking place in many developing countries. It characterised dualism in terms of traditional (trade-service) and modern (industrial) sector. Another study focused on Africa,[2] approaching the problem from the point of view of growing imbalance in the urban economy, came to the conclusion that a substantial part of the growth of the urban population and labour force is being absorbed not in the "enumerated" sector consisting of well-organised enterprises but in the "unenumerated" sector consisting of small-scale self-employed activities. The author chose to characterise the structural imbalance in terms of "rich" and "poor" sectors where the former is alien to the traditional societies in so far as it relied on imported capital, skills and technology. Yet another empirical study,[3] focusing on migrants in urban Ghana (Accra) highlighted the existence of a variety of new income-generating activities particularly in the trade and service categories. By virtue of the fact that most of them were in the unorganised sector and fell outside the purview of the existing statistical data-collection machinery they were labelled as "informal" income-generating activities or the informal sector.

Following this trend in thinking relating dualism in the urban sector to employment generation, the ILO/UNDP employment mission report on Kenya[4] carried this development further and sought to promote specific policies for employment and income generation in the informal sector. The formal-informal sector division of the urban sector had thus made its appearance.

The brief discussion above describes in a nutshell the evolution of the concept of dualism as it relates to the urban economies of the Third World. Several ideas are implicit in the above approaches to dichotomisation. First, they generally refer to economic activities. Second, the distinction between the two sub-systems of production has been generally based upon one or more of the following factors: mode of production, mode of organisation and scale of activities. Consequently, urban dichotomy in these countries has also been described in terms of "technological dualism"; or more frequently in terms of "organised" and "unorganised" sectors or simply large and small-scale activities. Third, in describing the coexistence of the two sub-systems of production, considerable emphasis is placed on one of the two sub-

----

[1] Lloyd G. Reynolds: "Economic development with surplus labour: Some complications", in Oxford Economic Papers (New Series), Mar. 1969.

[2] John Weeks: "An exploration into the nature of the problem of urban imbalance in Africa", in Manpower and Unemployment Research in Africa, Nov. 1973.

[3] Keith Hart: "Informal income opportunities and urban employment in Ghana", in Journal of Modern African Studies, Feb. 1973.

[4] ILO: Employment, incomes and equality: A strategy for increasing productive employment in Kenya (Geneva, 1973).

systems, be it labelled as "peasant form of production" or "bazaa
type of economy" or "lower circuit" or "informal sector". Th
emphasis on this sub-system rather than the other seems to originat
from the notion that it is alien to the urban sector in some sens
and is primarily the consequence of urban population growth. Th
mode of production, organisation and/or the scale of activitie.
characterising this sub-system is rationalised in terms of certai:
basic traits of its participants and/or the constraints o:
opportunities available to them. Finally, it should also be note«
that the traits of individual participants (e.g., rural/urba:
origin, ethnic or cultural background, age, sex, level of educatio:
and skills and the like), would also seem to explain th«
differential values, attitudes, behaviour and motivations observe«
in the two sub-systems.

Growth of urban population, however, is not the only factor
that has contributed to dualism (as described above) though it
sharpened the dichotomy and brought out its significance for
employment generation more explicitly. Factors derived from
colonial heritage, patterns of trade and foreign aid, patterns of
allocation of resources with an urban bias, presence of
multinational corporations and international transfer of
technologies, to mention a few, seem to have played an important
role too in sharpening the dichotomy between the two sub-systems in
so far as they led to the promotion of large-scale activities with
modern modes of production and organisation that are alien to these
countries. Whatever may be the reason, the existence of dualism
with significant implications for employment cannot be denied.

Following the Kenya employment mission report, the two sub-
systems of production in the urban economy are here labelled as the
formal and informal sector.[1] Leaving aside the question of
definition for a later discussion, the two sectors may be
distinguished in terms of the mode of production, organisation and
scale of activities: formal sector consisting of activities using
modern modes of productions and organisation comparable to the
developed world and hence are larger in scale of operation as
compared to those of the informal sector. The rationale behind the
choice of this terminology stems from its neutral connotation. Most
other equivalent terminologies assume what remains to be proved.
For example the modern-traditional sector terminology implies a
distinction based on the type of goods produced and technology used;
obviously, as the study on urban Ghana showed, many non-traditional
items are produced in both the sub-systems of production. Also the
term "traditional" sometimes carries a negative connotation implying
an absence of dynamism or inferior production technologies.[2] Though
the informal-formal terminology may not appear as satisfactory from
every point of view, the fact that it has gained wide currency in
the development literature and in the development plans and
programmes of some developing countries would seem to suggest that
it has come to stay.
----

[1] Though the government sector (including local authorities) is
in many ways similar to the formal sector from an employment point
of view, the formal-informal sector dichotomy in this volume refers
to the private sector of the urban economy.

[2] Louis Emmerij: "A new look at some strategies for increasing
productive employment in Africa", in International Labour Review,
Sep. 1974; and John Weeks: "Policies for expanding employment in the
informal urban sector of developing economies", ibid., Jan. 1975.

Towards a definition of the informal sector

The term informal sector has gained wide currency in recent years. And yet the concept has remained somewhat obscure and even caused confusion in some quarters. Attempts to clarify the concept have also come under attack;[1] according to this view, endless preoccupation with the definition of the term must come to an end and attention should be focused on the results and implications of dualism. As will be shown below, the term informal sector has acquired various meanings according to the researchers and their objectives. Consequently the findings and policy prescriptions attributed to the informal sector are not always comparable; often they contradict too. It is therefore necessary to discuss briefly the rationale and approach underlying the studies presented in this volume.

Much of the above state of affairs can be attributed to the following. Though many would subscribe to the existence of dualism and its implication for employment and development there seems to be little agreement on what the two sub-systems of production should consist of. Essentially there are two problems: one is the choice of the unit; and the second, how to determine the boundary separating the two sub-systems.[2] These are discussed below.

Choice of unit

One of the first problems encountered in trying to define the informal sector is the choice of an appropriate economic unit. Should it be defined in terms of individuals? Households? Or enterprises? The evidence cited earlier generally referred to economic activities as the basis for distinguishing the informal from the formal sector. Since dualism is defined in terms of activities, it is however possible to focus either on the individuals engaged in these activities or the enterprises in which they participate. Consequently the informal sector has been subject to different interpretations.

One approach focusing on the individuals has been to divide the urban labour market into formal and informal segments where the latter is defined to include workers in the "unprotected" sector.[3] According to this view, "employment in the formal sector is in some sense or senses protected so that the wage level and working conditions in the sector are not available, in general, to the job seekers in the market unless they manage to cross the barrier of entry somehow". This kind of "protection" may arise from the action

----

[1] Chris Gerry: Petty producers and the urban economy: A case study of Dakar (Geneva, ILO, 1974; mimeographed World Employment Programme research working paper; restricted), p. 5.

[2] Many would question such a dichotomisation. See a critique of the approach presented below.

[3] A.C. Harberger: "On measuring the social opportunity cost of labour", in International Labour Review, June 1971.

of trade unions, of governments, or both acting together¹ as a
result of institutional practices. In other words the informal
sector is equated with the unprotected segment of the labour market
where free entry exists owing to high labour turnover; and wages are
significantly lower than in the formal sector. By extension of this
approach, the informal sector is sometimes defined to include
workers earning below the legal minimum wage.² Or alternatively
attempts have been made to divide the urban workers in terms of the
individual characteristics such as their education and skill,
occupational and employment status (i.e., wage worker or self-
employed).³ And in some cases, the informal sector is defined not in
terms of individuals but in terms of households to which they
belong.   Perhaps the choice of households as a unit can be
rationalised on grounds of operational considerations viz., the
existence of household survey data and sampling frames in many
developing countries.   In so far as such an approach focuses on poor
households or those located in slums it would seem to imply that
urban dualism can be interpreted in terms of the sick and the poor.
Obviously the "urban poor" and the "informal sector" are not
coterminus; many studies show that urban poor could belong to either
of the two sub-systems of production. Thus, the informal sector has
been attributed different meanings at different times — urban poor,
low-income households, urban population living in slums and squatter
areas and so on.

     The selective and brief discussion above nevertheless
explains, at least partly, the confusion prevailing in this area.
No doubt the various definitions emerging from the above have much
in common. Presumably each definition can be justified on its own
grounds taking into account the purpose on hand. The ILO,
recognising the merits of alternative approaches, decided to use
activities/enterprises as the basis for defining the informal sector
in the studies reported here.⁴

     The reasons for choosing the activity (or enterprise) rather
than the individual or household as the basic unit for defining the
informal sector are many.   First, following from the initial
----

¹ D. Mazumdar: "The urban informal sector", in World Bank Staff
Working Paper No. 211 (Washington, July 1975) (reprinted in World
Development, Aug. 1976). See also J. Breman: "A dualistic labour
system? A critique of the informal sector concept", in Economic and
Political Weekly, Vol. 11, No. 48, pp. 1,870-1,875; and No. 49, pp.
1,905-1,908 and No. 50, pp. 1,939-1,944 (1976).

² P.R. Souza and V.E. Tokman: "The informal urban sector in
Latin America", in International Labour Review, Nov.-Dec. 1976, pp.
355-365.

³ See for example John Friedman and Flora Sullivan: "The
absorption of labour in the urban economy: The case of developing
countries", in Economic Development and Cultural Change, Apr. 1974,
pp. 385-413.

⁴ Even though criminal activities and the like, in so far as
they provide employment and incomes, are often considered as part of
the informal sector they are excluded from the purview of this
volume on the ground that they fall outside the realm of socially
desirable economic activities.

discussion on dualism, the ILO's interest has been on the dual production systems and their implication for employment. Consequently it was felt that the focus should be on production units. Second, by focusing on the production units, it is possible to isolate the development policies that have a bearing directly on the dualistic nature of the urban economies and hence on employment promotion and income distribution. In other words such an approach stresses the conditions under which employment and income generated in the urban areas of the developing countries. Third, it could faciliate the task of assisting the informal sector activities/enterprises directly and indirectly by providing the necessary assistance. In other words it is possible to help the enterprises to help themselves and improve the conditions under which income and employment in this sector are generated. Needless to add such efforts need not necessarily focus on this sector exclusively, ignoring the over-all setting in which they operate.

It should be noted however that such a choice in favour of activities or enterprises does not deny the usefulness of other approaches based on individuals or households briefly mentioned above. In fact they are highly complementary. For example, attempts to focus on particular groups of workers or segments of labour market are highly desirable since they provide insights into the problems of specific groups and the functioning of the urban labour markets in developing countries. They could therefore suggest appropriate remedial measures notably in the field of labour market policies, social security and labour legislations, unionisation and the like. Likewise it may be useful to isolate certain classes of wage workers or occupations as target groups for specific policies and assistance. Similar arguments can be made in favour of choosing households as the unit. Finally, the choice of enterprise/activity as the unit for dichotomisation does not preclude the possibility of learning about the individuals engaged in it or their households.[1]

Clarifying the informal sector concept

The choice in favour of activity or enterprise as the basic unit for dichotomisation implies that the urban economy is viewed as a continuum of enterprises engaged in the production of goods and services. The studies cited earlier on dualism provide some indication about the types of enterprises that belong to each of the two sub-systems. They suggest that the activities (or enterprises) can be sorted out on the basis of one or more of the characteristics: mode of production, organisation and the scale of operation.

The ILO/UNDP employment mission report on Kenya, in an effort to distinguish the informal from the formal sector, suggested the following: the informal sector is one where free entry to new enterprises exists; enterprises in this sector rely on indigenous resources; they are family owned and small scale; they use labour-intensive and adapted technology; their workers rely on non-formal
----

[1] As a matter of fact, many studies presented in this volume do throw considerable light on the individuals and households even though the informal sector was defined in terms of activities/enterprises.

sources of education and skills; and finally they operate in unregulated and competitive markets. Correspondingly the formal sector enterprises possess characteristics obverse to the above - entry for new enterprises is difficult; the firms rely frequently on overseas resources; they are generally subject to corporate ownership and large-scale operation; they use capital-intensive and often imported technology; their workers possess education and skills acquired through formal sources, and they are often expatriate; and finally they operate in protected markets (through tariffs, quotas and trade licences).[1] In other words, the Kenya report would seem to have made explicit what some of the earlier authors had implied in their writings. Not surprisingly the mission's attempt to characterise the informal sector in specific terms mentioned above has come under criticism from some quarters even though it was a step in the right direction. Part of the criticisms was however unjustified in so far as the above criteria were interpreted in a wider and general context even though they were proposed in the specific context of Kenya. It must however be admitted that the characteristics spelled out above do not add up to a definition of the sector; perhaps it was never the intention of the mission. But the report did come somewhat closer to providing a definition inasmuch as it tried to crystalise ideas about the two sectors.

Notwithstanding the above refinements the informal sector universe remains vague because of the multiple criteria; each criterion can be used to define a universe of its own. Consequently one is not certain about the universe to which the term informal sector refers. It is therefore useful to explore the possibility of defining the informal sector in more precise terms. Perhaps the distinguishing feature of the informal sector enterprises is that they made their appearance, not so much in response to investment opportunities as in the neoclassical sense but out of necessity to create one's own employment. Thus the accent was on employment generation and not on seeking suitable investment opportunities for the sake of realising a return on investment. The individuals or "entrepreneurs" associated with the informal sector enterprises are not capitalists in the classical sense of the term seeking investment outlets. Since many of them are migrants to urban areas in search of employment and since few possess substantial capital or education or skills, the key characteristic of the informal sector would seem to be that the enterprises emerged in spite of the lack of necessary capital and skills.

The above line of reasoning suggests that the so called enterprises in the informal sector are not really enterprises in the conventional sense of the word; perhaps it is more appropriate to call them production units (or micro business as it is sometimes called) still in the process of evolution; they are yet to acquire the status of an enterprise as the term is commonly understood. As one study put it, the evolution implies a change whereby a technician with managerial responsibilities becomes a manager with technical responsibilities.[2]

----

[1] ILO: Employment, incomes and equality ..., op. cit.

[2] ILO: Human resources for industrial development: Some aspects of policy and planning (Geneva, 1967), p. 138.

Besides entrepreneurial skills, many of those entering the informal sector also lack the necessary technical skills and possess little or no capital of their own. Given the limitations on the scope for raising capital through borrowing,[1] a means normally available to firms in the textbook sense, they have little command over resources. These features in turn would seem to explain not only the choice of activity to be pursued but also the mode of production, organisation and scale of operation actually observed in this sector.

Much of what is said above is perhaps implicit in the writings cited earlier and hence not new. It nevertheless facilitates clarification of some of the ideas and issues. The informal sector enterprises can be interpreted as belonging to the lower end of the urban continuum of enterprises. The informal sector units can therefore be expected, in principle, to overcome the capital and skill constraints over time and thus assimilate themselves with enterprises; the extent to which they succeed in breaking such barriers in practice is however an empirical question and depends on a number of factors.[2] Viewed in this framework, the term "small enterprise" as commonly used can be interpreted as belonging to the middle of this continuum; it uses a mode of production and organisation somewhat similar to the formal sector enterprise but on a relatively smaller scale. It is therefore sometimes labelled as the intermediate sector.[3] Perhaps the distinguishing feature between the informal sector unit and the small enterprise is their orientation; whereas the former is motivated <u>primarily</u> by employment creation, the latter is concerned <u>primarily</u> with profit maximisation.

The framework presented above suggests the following definition of the informal sector. <u>It consists of small-scale units engaged in the production and distribution of goods and services with the primary objective of generating employment and incomes to their participants notwithstanding the constraints on capital, both physical and human, and knowhow</u>. Such a definition of the informal sector would also seem to provide the justification for focusing employment and development policies on this sector.[4] It emphasises, as did other writers, the significance of urban population growth to the emergence of the informal sector. It also implies that dualism manifested in the form of different modes of production, organisation and scale of operation is simply a reflection of the varying circumstances under which enterprises in the two sectors come into existence and operate.

The exposition above of the informal sector concept does no more than to spell out, perhaps in a more general way, what was already noted. More importantly, it would seem to pave the way for

---

[1] See Chapter 3 for further discussion on limited access to capital and its implications.

[2] See Chapter 3, the section on evolutionary or involutionary growth.

[3] Steel: <u>Small scale employment and production in developing countries</u>, op. cit.

[4] See Chapter 3.

formulating a definition with analytical significance. Since the output of a firm can be postulated as a function of capital (both physical and human), labour and technology, one can hypothesise that the value added per worker reflects the mode of production, organisation and scale.

The informal sector concept elaborated above suggests that the production units are motivated by employment generation and that they have little capital (and skills) at their disposal. These features imply that they are relatively more labour intensive and that they have relatively low value added per worker, as compared to the formal sector firms. The concept also implies that these units use relatively simple technologies of production partly because of the capital constraint and partly because of their limited access to technical knowhow. All these factors suggest that the informal sector can be characterised by a single measure viz., value added per worker.[1]

Dualism, as described above, then implies a significant discontinuity in labour productivity across the enterprises. To put it crudely, the formal sector can be described in terms of a high labour productivity while the informal sector is characterised by a low labour productivity.[2] Dualism is then defined in terms of the coexistence of a high and a low productivity sector. It is therefore tempting to describe dualism in terms of high-low wage sectors; but it would be erroneous to do so for two reasons: first, the bulk of those engaged in the informal sector is self-employed and not working for a wage; and second, the labour market imperfections and rigidities in wage structures are common features in many developing countries.

Even though the use of labour productivity as a measure to distinguish the two sub-systems within the urban economies is highly appealing it does pose a couple of problems. The first relates to empirical evidence; for example it is not obvious that there are visible discontinuities in the labour productivity across the firms. It is possible that labour productivity increases gradually as one moves along the urban continuum of enterprises from one end of the scale (informal sector) to the other end (formal sector) owing to the existence of firms in between the two extremes. Or alternatively, it is possible that labour productivity rises from a low level, moves into a transitional phase and then reaches a high plateau as one moves along the continuum. In other words the distinction between the two sectors is a matter of empirical evidence.

The second problem pertains to the use of labour productivity measures from an operational point of view. In the light of what is stated above it may be necessary to choose a level of labour
----

[1] S.V. Sethuraman: <u>Towards a definition of the informal sector</u> (Geneva, ILO, 1974; World Employment Programme unpublished research), p. 7.

[2] See for example R.C. Webb: "Government policy and the distribution of income in Peru, 1963-1973", in Lowenthal (ed.): <u>The Peruvian experiment</u> (Princeton 1975); and Reichmuth: <u>Dualism in Peru: An investigation ...</u>, op. cit., pp. 85-88 for some related evidence.

productivity as a cut off point to determine the boundary of the informal vis-à-vis formal sector. This could introduce an element of arbitrariness and pose the problem of comparison between different situations. It may however be possible to minimise such a bias by choosing a standard criterion: for example one might choose the level of legal minimum wage as the cut off point since it is likely to reflect the national socio-economic objectives; or alternatively the level of per capita income or the poverty line defined on a national or regional basis. More importantly, the labour productivity criterion can only be an expost measure since it cannot be assessed until after the data are collected from all enterprises in the urban economy. In other words the labour productivity measure could serve as a policy goal once the data are collected and evaluated. It is in this sense the problem of defining the urban informal sector is akin to the problem of defining an underdeveloped country. Any definition of this sector can only be interpreted in a relative sense, relative to some arbitrarily chosen norm; the informal sector can therefore be defined as large or as small as one wishes by so choosing the labour productivity measure. The merit of this approach however lies in drawing attention of the policy makers to the question of resource allocation and income distribution.

A critique of the dualistic approach[1]

One of the basic criticisms of the dualistic approach has been the validity of the assumption that the urban economy in developing countries can or should be divided into two - formal and informal - sectors even though the dual nature of such economies has been recognised in the literature and noted by several authors. Though there is considerable truth in this argument, it can at least partly be attributed to the mistaken notion that dualism denies the presence of interdependence between the two subsectors. According to this view, it is pointless to isolate the informal sector as a target group and suggest policies for employment promotion and income generation through its development in so far as much of its problems can be traced to its subordinate position in relation to the formal sector, which, for reasons of its own interest and survival, would like to maintain the status quo.[2] Focusing on the urban informal sector for purposes of employment promotion obviously does not necessarily imply, as already mentioned, denial of such interrelationships between the two sectors; nor does it imply a neglect of their implications for policy. Needless to add much depends on what information is collected from the informal sector and how it is analysed. For example, it is always possible to collect information on the nature of relationship between the informal and the formal sector by addressing appropriate questions to the informal sector.

Another criticism is related to the fact that the urban economy is after all a continuum however defined; why should it be

----

[1] Caroline O.N. Moser: "Informal sector or petty production: Dualism or dependence in urban development?", in World Development, Sep.-Oct. 1978, as well as other articles in this special issue.

[2] See Chapter 3 for more on these and other issues.

divided into only two subsectors?[1] The question is indeed relevant
and important and has implications for the informal sector concept.
As already suggested, it may well be necessary to divide the urban
economy into more than two subsectors. Indeed the Ghana study
referred to earlier did distinguish between various kinds of
informal activities. Only empirical evidence can tell how many
meaningful and analytically significant subsectors are worth
identifying in order to draw valid policy conclusions in the field
of employment and income generation. Thus, it is one of the
objectives of research on the informal sector. The studies
presented in this volume, as will be seen later, do throw some light
on this issue. The approach taken in these studies has generally
been to define the informal sector as broadly as possible leaving
open the possibility for further disaggregation and analysis
wherever the evidence warranted.

And finally some would argue that the dichotomous situation
observed in the urban sector of the Third World is perhaps a
temporary phenomenon.[2] The so-called informal sector, according to
this view, is just a "holding ground for people awaiting entry into
the formal sector" and thus is in a transition process;[3] in the long
run it will become a part of the formal sector too and thus
disappear. Perhaps so. But the emerging evidence seems to
contradict this view. As the studies presented in this volume will
show, most of the participants in this sector have spent many years
in their respective activities and few believe that they will be
absorbed in the formal sector; neither are many interested in
working for the formal sector.

The scope, methodology and objectives

One of the main objectives of the studies reported in this
volume has been to understand the conditions under which the
informal sector absorbs labour and generates income. Another
objective has been to assess the implications of promoting the
informal sector to urban environment. More specifically, the
studies try to delineate the interrelationships between this sector
and the rest of the urban economy with a view to determining the
extent to which such linkages are beneficial and hence desirable to
promote. The studies also aim at throwing light on the evolution of
the informal sector enterprises over time, notably on their ability
to overcome the barriers mentioned earlier. Since one of the
arguments in favour of informal sector development is its ability to
produce goods and services efficiently, an effort has been made to
shed light on this issue as well. In addition, the studies also
look at the issues pertaining to labour market and the like. The
main thrust of all this has been to identify the measures
appropriate to promote urban employment and environment on the one
hand and to improve the incomes of urban poor on the other.
----

[1] Guy Standing: "Urban workers and patterns of employment", in
Subbiah Kannappan (ed.): Studies of urban labour market behaviour in
developing countries (Geneva, International Institute for Labour
Studies, 1977), p. 37.

[2] Emmerij, op. cit.

[3] Tara Chana and Hunter Morrison: "Nairobi's informal economic
sector", in Ekistics 257, Aug. 1975, p. 122.

Identification of the informal sector enterprises

Though the conceptual basis outlined above dictated that the informal sector universe be confined to the lower end of the urban continuum, there was nevertheless the need to identify the enterprises that belonged to this universe in order to collect data. The ideal procedure would of course be to compile a list of all production units in a given urban area and classify them according to the conceptual criteria stated earlier and thus determine the ones belonging to the informal sector. This procedure, however poses two problems: (a) compilation of a list of all establishments; and (b) application of a set of criteria to each establishment to determine whether it belongs to the informal sector.[1]

In most developing countries a complete list of all establishments is not available; in particular smallest among them are either not registered with any official body and hence unknown to the statistical authorities; or they cannot be reached by the statistical authorities owing to an absence of information on their whereabouts, or because of their itinerant character or because of their ill-defined status; or the authorities have not been concerned about such data. Whatever the reason, it is generally necessary to compile such a list. While it may be feasible to undertake such a task in smaller towns (as some studies have done) it is ruled out in the case of large cities. Moreover, if the object is primarily to identify the informal sector enterprises as defined earlier (i.e. the lower end of the continuum) it is pointless to compile a list which includes firms that obviously belong to the formal sector. The approach generally followed in the studies reported here was therefore to eliminate the production units that clearly do not belong to the informal sector. Thus all government departments/agencies, public sector corporation, private joint stock companies, multinationals, formal institutions and the like were excluded from the outset since they do not satisfy the definition of the informal sector proposed earlier. In order to narrow down the scope further, it was decided to eliminate all enterprises with more than ten workers per establishment on the assumption that an enterprise of that size normally requires a significant amount of capital and managerial skills; further an enterprise above this size, though small, is unlikely to have the orientation of an informal sector enterprise noted earlier. To the extent the assumption above is not valid, it leads to an error in classification. In anticipation of such a possibility, additional criteria were employed to sort out such enterprises, as will be seen later.

As above, other a priori considerations were utilised in narrowing down the scope further. First, agricultural activities are relatively unimportant as a source of employment and income in the urban context; and given the high urban land value, agriculture cannot be a source of self-employment for the poor and jobless; it was therefore assumed that informal sector enterprises are absent in this activity. Second, following the one digit ISIC classification, sectors such as mining and quarrying, electricity, gas and water,

----

[1] Surveys of small-scale and household industries and employment generation in developing countries, Paper presented by the ILO at the ESCAP Seminar on Statistics of Small-Scale and Household Industries, Bangkok, 11-17 July 1977.

and finance, insurance, real estate and related services were
assumed to contain none of the informal sector enterprises since
they are generally dominated by formal (including public) sector
establishments.[1]

The search for the informal sector enterprises was thus
confined to the following: all enterprises with ten persons or less,
and engaged in manufacturing, construction, transport, trade and
service sectors. Though it is unlikely, such a procedure might lead
to the exclusion of at least some truly informal sector activities;
for example, it is conceivable that more than ten persons are self-
employed but operate in the same business premises or, as is common
in Africa, a master may have a number of apprentices working for
him. It was therefore necessary to apply a set of operational or
diagnostic criteria to such enterprises and thereby determine where
they belonged. These included: whether the enterprise was legal or
not? works on an irregular basis? located in temporary structures?
uses electric power? depends on formal credit institutions? relies
on a formal distribution network? most workers have fewer than six
years of schooling? Needless to add these are but a few suggested
criteria; and one could think of a number of other similar ones.
The rationale behind the choice was simply that most of them can be
applied without asking any questions, just by visual observation of
the enterprise. The essence of this additional measure was to
include enterprises even though they had more than ten persons
provided they satisfied at least one of the suggested criteria of
informality.

It should be obvious from the above that even though the
universe consisting of informal sector enterprises was narrowed
down, the sub-universe including the latter itself was not
identified. Adoption of any additional criteria would not only
introduce the researchers' own bias; more importantly their
application in the field would almost amount to carrying out a
survey with a full length questionnaire. It was therefore decided
to abandon the effort of further narrowing down; instead it was
decided to focus on the larger universe of which the informal sector
proper forms a part. This approach was also considered desirable in
the light of the criticism referred to earlier; that it would amount
to putting the cart before the horse. It was therefore decided to
allow the data to speak for themselves. Collection of data from a
universe larger than the informal sector itself leaves open the
possibility of analysing the data at a more disaggregated level; it
leaves open the possibility of defining the informal sector in
empirical terms as large or as small as one wishes.

Research methodology

It was apparent from the beginning that all empirical research
in this field must necessarily be exploratory not only because of
the problems of definition but also because of the lack of adequate
statistics. The research methodology followed in these studies is
therefore exploratory and it varied somewhat between different
----

[1] As with every rule, there are exceptions. Two examples of
informal sector activity in the excluded sectors: self-employed
fisherman; and self-employed persons engaged in collection and
delivery of water (e.g. Jakarta).

cases. The methodology involved the selection of enterprises on a sample basis from the universe referred to above and application of a questionnaire through personal interviews. In order to ensure comparability between various studies, a draft questionnaire was prepared in advance[1] and the various researchers were encouraged to adapt it to suit the local conditions and needs. Briefly stated, the questionnaires sought information not only about the enterprise but also about the heads of these enterprises and their households.[2] The scope of information collected was restricted somewhat, taking into account the cost considerations. More importantly, it was felt that unless one undertakes an in-depth study, it may not be possible to collect precise quantitative data on a large number of items owing to the small scale of operation, numerous retail transactions and the absence of records or accounts. Insights based on the studies presented here already suggest that there is considerable scope for improving the above.

Turning to the selection of sample enterprises, different studies followed different approaches, depending on the extent to which prior information was available (Annex II). Absence of a sampling frame precluded the possibility of a probability weighted sample in most cases. Generally speaking, the studies sought to cover several areas within the city/town on a sample basis and attempted to compile a list of enterprises described earlier before drawing a sample. The studies generally sought to include enterprises from the five sectors: manufacturing, construction, transport, trade and services.

Before concluding this chapter, perhaps a word of caution is in order. As already stated, it is perhaps inappropriate to call the units engaged in the production of goods and services and belonging to the informal sector as "enterprises". By the same token, the term "entrepreneur" as applied to the head of the informal sector unit is a misnomer. This is particularly true since the informal sector, as defined here, includes even the smallest units as well; for example, a shoe-shine boy, a self-employed vendor selling cigarettes on a street corner, a self-appointed building caretaker, a self-employed parking attendant and the like can hardly be called an enterprise. Notwithstanding the marginal nature of these activities, the terms enterprises, establishment, firm, activity and production units have been used in this volume interchangeably. Likewise the terms entrepreneur and head of enterprise have been used to connote the same meaning.

----

[1] S.V. Sethuraman: Survey instrument for a study of the urban informal sector: The case of Jakarta (Geneva, ILO, 1975; World Employment Programme unpublished research).

[2] See Annex I for further details.

Annex I

The informal sector survey questionnaire:
A brief description

The information sought in the questionnaire,[1] besides identification particulars, can be classified into three categories: (a) information pertaining to the enterprise and its linkages with the rest of the economy; (b) information pertaining to the head of the enterprises; and (c) information pertaining to the household of the head of the enterprise. Information sought about the enterprise included the following: (i) physical background-fixed/variable location, access to economic infrastructure and public utilities, permanent/temporary structure, commercial/residential location, legal status of the structure; (ii) structural background - detailed description of the main and subsidiary activities, structure of the markets, etc.; (iii) legal constraints such as licence requirements, registration, etc., and the nature of the relationship with the government, if any; (iv) history of the enterprise - age, changes in physical location, physical structure or the premises, the nature of activity, goods and services produced, quantity of output, employment, technology and the hurdles confronted in establishing the enterprise; (v) operational characteristics - capacity utilisation, extent of underemployment among labour, structure of employment (full time, part time and casual), use of unpaid family labour, availability of skilled and unskilled labour, sources of supply of labour, age, sex and educational structure of employees, the extent of labour turnover and reward for experience, training facilities and terms, data on wages paid and the extent of cash and kind payment, value of capital employed, sources of funds for acquisition of capital, extent to which building, machinery and the like are hired and the cost of doing so, the nature of backward and forward linkages, total revenue, value of inventories, taxes paid, etc. Besides the above, the enterprises were asked about imperfections in factor and product markets, difficulties in securing the necessary inputs including credit and in marketing the products. Further the enterprises were asked to list the areas of assistance needed by them in order to expand their activity; and their reactions to possible government policies and programmes were assessed as well.

The information sought about the head of the enterprise was largely confined to his personal characteristics - sex, age, formal and non-formal education, experience, job history, migration status, his parent's occupation, sources of non-formal education and training, his preference for self-employment as opposed to wage employment, job satisfaction, changes in his earnings over time, extent of employment and desire for more work, his attitude towards possible government policies such as training, alternative occupation, alternative location for his enterprise, etc.

Finally, the information sought about the entrepreneur's household included: proximity of the residence to place of work,

----

[1] S.V. Sethuraman: Survey instrument for a study of the urban informal sector: The case of Jakarta (Geneva, ILO, 1975; unpublished manuscript for the World Employment Programme).

other members of the household participating in the activities of
the enterprise, extent to which other members of his household
participate in the labour force, particularly in the informal
sector, the extent to which others contribute to the household
income, extent of unemployment, and details about the residential
structure in which the household is located and access to utilities.

Coverage and sampling procedures

A brief summary of the informal sector universe covered by various studies as well as the sampling procedures is presented below.

Freetown (Sierra Leone): A sample of 1,000 enterprises was selected and interviewed in January-February 1976. Based on a knowledge of the concentration of small-scale activities in inner Freetown, the city was stratified into five parts; within each stratum, enterprises belonging to the five sectors (manufacturing, construction, transport, commerce and services) were selected, the sample size being proportional to 1963 population in the respective area. In the absence of a sampling frame, an attempt was made to distribute the sample units geographically as widely and as randomly as possible.

Lagos (Nigeria): The sample survey was carried out in July-October 1976 and covered 2,000 enterprises. A two-stage sampling design was adopted; the city was stratified into 200 enumeration areas and 10 enterprises were selected at random from each of them. In the absence of a sampling frame the study chose to distribute the sample among various streets within each stratum.

Kano (Nigeria): The Kano study was based on a sample of 505 enterprises and was carried out during March-April 1976. Unlike in Freetown and Lagos, Kano study carried out a complete listing of enterprises in all the 583 enumeration areas before drawing a random sample of the informal sector enterprises. One of the interesting features of the procedure was to "overweight" the less important activities (e.g. carpentry) and "underweight" the most common ones (e.g. trade and services) and as a result the sample provided more information on less important activities as well.

Kumasi (Ghana): Unlike the studies mentioned above, the Kumasi study focused only on selected manufacturing and rapair activities (see Chapter 7). The study compiled a list of all small enterprises (under ten workers) in the selected activities in the town through a census carried out in August-September 1975 and took a 10 per cent random sample of them. The survey covered 300 enterprises and the field work was carried out during October 1975.

Colombo (Sri Lanka): The 47 wards of the city were stratified into 11 homogeneous strata, taking into account the housing and occupational patterns, infrastructural facilities, demographic data and the degree of commercial and industrial activity. In the second stage, a pocket or a cluster of informal sector activities was chosen from each stratum and a complete listing of small enterprises was drawn from this list and interviewed in early 1977.

Jakarta (Indonesia): This being one of the early studies, the procedure to identify the informal sector enterprises was still unclear. As a result it sought to identify the enterprises through a listing of households. Thus, in the first stage the city was stratified into five geographical areas. In the second stage a 10 per cent sample of the smallest administrative units (Kelurahans) was chosen. The third stage consisted of selecting 25 per cent of the household clusters (kekun tetangga) within each of the selected kelurahan through a systematic random sample. Finally, all households falling within the selected clusters were listed along with additional information on the source of employment for all workers in the household. Thus, a sampling frame of informal sector participants was constructed which was then used to select a sample. Information on the enterprises was collected through the informal sector participants. The sample covered 4,367 such participants engaged in the five one-digit ISIC groups. The survey was carried out in August-September 1975.

Manila (Philippines): The Manila study relied on a readily available sampling frame of small establishments (under ten workers) compiled by the National Census and Statistical Office. Since the listing was made in 1972, the effort was made to supplement the sample by including new enterprises that were added to the list between 1972 and 1975. A sample of 3,500 units was drawn on a random basis and interviewed in March-May 1976. One of the drawbacks of this approach seems to have been the exclusion of at least some enterprises, by virtue of their small scale of operations, that may have escaped the official listing and hence from the sample.

Cordoba (Argentina): The Cordoba study, unlike the ones mentioned above, covered all enterprises with five or less number of persons. Further, it sought to distinguish between high and low income activities, calling them quasi-formal or informal activities respectively. However, in order to draw the sample, the study relied on two sampling frames - one based on enterprises (with fixed location) and the other based on households (for self-employed workers without fixed location). The samples were drawn using a stratified random sampling procedure. The survey was carried out in early 1976.

Campinas (Brazil): The study on Campinas adopted a stratified random sampling procedure where the two were divided into 40 zones and the sample size of 500 was allocated to them according to the level of employment prevailing in 1975. The sample units, consisting of self-employed activities and small enterprises with ten workers or less, was distributed between industry, commerce and services in the proportion of 20, 40 and 40 per cent. The survey was carried out in 1976.

CHAPTER 3.   THE URBAN INFORMAL SECTOR AND
DEVELOPMENT POLICY

The urban informal sector in developing countries, almost by definition, is playing a major role in absorbing labour. Considering the circumstances under which the sector has emerged it is clear that the sector plays an important role too in generating incomes for the poor.[1] Given the projected rates of growth of urban population and labour force in these countries the need to assess the future role of this sector in labour absorption cannot be overemphasised. Since the formal sector in developing countries has a small base both in terms of output and employment a simple calculation will show that employment in this sector must grow at an incredibly high rate - say 10 per cent per year or more - in order to absorb the future additions to urban labour force. This implies that output must grow even faster since employment in this sector increases less than proportionately in relation to output.[2] But in reality the formal sector seems to be absorbing only a fraction of the increase in urban labour force.[3] In other words the burden on the informal sector to absorb more labour will continue to grow unless other solutions including the development of rural non-farm activities and spatial decentralisation of growth are envisaged.

Development of the informal sector with a view to increasing its employment and productivity levels however raises a number of issues including the basic one - whether it should be developed at all. Besides growth and equity, its development has implications for urban development and environment, migration and conditions of living and work and labour market, to mention only a few. This chapter is devoted to a brief discussion of these issues and their short- and long-run implications.[4] Though the informal sector includes marginal activities that fall somewhere on the border between productive and unproductive (or economic and non-economic) activities much of the discussion below excludes them from the purview. In so far as such truly marginal activities are simply a reflection of the prevailing opportunities (or the lack of them) elsewhere the discussion below nevertheless has significant implications for their development.

----

[1] The link between the informal sector and poverty is discussed later.

[2] Morawetz, D.: "Employment implications of industrialisation: A Survey", in Economic Journal, No. 335, Sep. 1974.

[3] In Nairobi, for example, formal sector employment seems to have grown at only 3.2 per cent per annum even though the city's labour force increased at 9.1 per cent per year during the 1964-72 period. See William J. House: "Nairobi's informal sector: An exploratory study" (Nairobi, 1979; unpublished manuscript), p. 2. See also P.R. Souza and Victor E. Tokman: "The informal urban sector in Latin America", in International Labour Review, Nov.-Dec. 1976, pp. 358-359.

[4] Many aspects of the problems discussed below have been dealt with by different authors in greater detail. In particular see idem, ibid.; and Santos: L'espace partagé: Les deux circuits de l'économie urbaine des pays sous-développés, op. cit.

Resource allocation

Equity considerations apart, one of the basic arguments for promoting the informal sector as a group of activities would seem to rest on resource allocation. It was postulated in the last chapter that the informal sector enterprises emerged not in search of lucrative investment opportunities but out of necessity to create one's own employment in spite of the lack of investment resources. Accumulating evidence from various informal sector studies also suggests that virtually none of these enterprises have access to capital from formal sources of credit; they primarily depend on own savings and to a lesser extent on borrowings from friends, relatives and other indigenous sources. The implications of capital constraint are many fold.

First, capital shortages lead to sub-optimal levels of output and employment. Second, lack of access to capital from formal sources of credit at reasonable rates of interest often forces the informal sector enterprise to seek other sources of credit. It could take the form reliance on "middlemen" or intermediaries such as money lenders, implying that the cost of capital is generally higher than the rate at which capital is accessible to the formal sector.[1] But more frequently capital market imperfections, it is argued, lead the informal sector enterprises to depend on formal sector enterprises; often it means subordination of the informal sector itself.[2] For example the informal sector enterprise may have no option but to surrender all or part of its output at prices predetermined by the lender. Alternatively, it may have to give up its independence and operate as a dependent unit serving the interests of the formal sector engerprise.[3] Thus, even though the informal sector enterprise operates like an independent unit, it may

----

[1] Development of informal sector in Java, Indonesia, ILO/UNDP Technical Report 1 INS/72/030 (Geneva, 1976), p. 11, suggesting annual interest rates of over 40 per cent. See also R. Bromley: "The street traders of Cali, Colombia", in World Development, No. 6, 1978, pp. 1,161-1,171, which reports that the daily rate of interest varied between 5 and 10 per cent, for example; and yet the participants in these activities seemed to earn an income well above the national minimum wage.

[2] See for example A.N. Bose: Calcutta and rural Bengal: Small sector symbiosis (Calcutta, ILO, 1978), Chapter IV; and Chris Gerry: Petty producers and the urban economy: A case study of Dakar (Geneva, ILO, 1974; mimeographed World Employment Programme research working paper; restricted). See also R. Bromley and C. Gerry (eds.): Casual work and poverty in third world cities (1979), for evidence and discussion on these and related issues, particularly Chapter 3.

[3] See for example Bromley: "The street traders of Cali ...", op. cit. In some cases the enterprises may voluntarily choose to work on a subcontracting basis; one study shows that such dependence does not lead to lower incomes. See Reichmuth: Dualism in Peru: An investigation ..., op. cit., p. 136.

in fact be working for "wages" at sub-optimal levels of remuneration.[1]

Thirdly, in many cases, the informal sector enterprises may not have access to any capital at all or in an effort to retain their independence, avoid dependence on financial intermediaries. One of the consequences of such shortages, notably in working capital, is to make the inputs dear. Unable to buy in sufficient quantities, small enterprises may be driven to rely on "middlemen" rather than the original source and thus end up paying higher prices. Such a situation could arise, perhaps more frequently, even in the absence of capital shortage owing to scarcity of local and imported inputs, lack of direct access to imports by small enterprises and market imperfections.[2] Fourthly, non-availability of capital often forces the informal sector enterprises to choose remote and poor physical locations restricting their direct access to markets for their goods and services. Many enterprises consequently operate in substandard and/or residential premises; still others resort to variable locations (e.g., operating in open public spaces, using push carts and the like). To the extent they lack direct access, they often resort to "intermediaries" to market their goods and services. Such dependence however could also result from the small scale of operation (and hence uneconomical) and dominance by larger and well established firms operating in this area. Or alternatively, in order to operate in a choice location, the enterprises may have to get the blessings of larger firms for a small fee. The end result of such a dependence, it is argued, is to lower their revenue than otherwise possible.[3]

In addition to capital constraints, shortage of foreign exchange and certain key raw materials would seem to hurt certain types of informal sector activities in selected countries. In some countries imported capital and raw material would seem to play an important role even in the informal sector.[4] Likewise, many informal sector activities rely heavily on traditional raw materials such as leather and metal. The informal sector has no doubt attempted to cope with the shortage of these materials through its own innovative ability and through recycling waste materials. Nevertheless such bottlenecks have either reduced their profitability or even wiped

----

[1] J. Breman: "A dualistic labour system? A critique of the informal sector concept", in Economic and Political Weekly, Vol. 11, Nos. 48, 49 and 50. See also Colin Leys: Underdevelopment in Kenya: The political economy of neo-colonialism (London, 1975).

[2] Chris Gerry: Petty production and capitalist production in Dakar: The crisis of the self-employed, Paper presented at the Institute of British Geographers, March 1977, p. 13.

[3] See for example S.V. Sethuraman: Employment promotion in the informal sector in Ghana (Geneva, ILO, 1979: mimeographed World Employment Programme research working paper; restricted), pp. 36-37; and the case studies therein. See also Bose: Calcutta and rural Bengal ..., op. cit., pp. 98-105.

[4] M.P. Van Dijk: "Enquête sur le secteur non-structuré, Dakar, mars-mai 1977" (Geneva, ILO, 1977), p. 12, according to which 83 per cent of capital goods used by the informal sector in Dakar was imported.

out some enterprises. Besides government policies, such problems also seem to be the consequence of formal sector firms assuming a monopolistic position; or alternatively the formal sector firms bid away the scarce inputs, virtually eliminating the informal sector enterprises using them.[1]

The above arguments, based on varying sources of evidence, suggest that constraints on resources in general and capital in particular have implications far beyond limiting the production potential in the informal sector enterprises. Both the factor and product market imperfections compound the capital constraints and often result in the exploitation of the informal sector. It is not just a matter of exploitation of the informal sector by the formal sector; perhaps it is more accurate to describe this phenomenon as exploitation of the weak by successive layers of stronger ones.

Consequently, one school of thought would argue that the informal sector is caught between higher input and lower output prices. The formal sector, in so far as it is responsible for the situation, appropriates at least a part of the surplus generated in the informal sector.[2] It also follows from this line of argument that making more resources available to the informal sector will not per se contribute to its development unless the mechanisms for channelling inputs and outputs and the underlying relationship between the formal and the informal sectors are also simultaneously modified.[3] In other words, it would be necessary to restructure the socio-economic framework within which the informal sector now operates.

The other school of thought would however argue, as the Kenya employment mission report did, that the informal sector enterprises, with the exception of a few marginal activities, not only provide goods and services demanded by the society but are also economically efficient for otherwise they would not have been able to survive in the absence of protection. Elimination of market imperfections and resource constraints coupled with greater access to market could contribute to an increase in both output and employment.[4] Obviously, the divergence between the two views is basically an empirical question; in so far as the existing socio-economic nexus of relationships hurting the informal sector is primarily a reflection of the underlying resource and market constraints there need not be any conflict between the two. To the extent that this is not true

----

[1] For example in Dakar the multinational BATA was "able to achieve a virtual monopsony in the purchase of fine leather" and thus forced many informal sector enterprises to seek substitutes such as vinyl materials. See Gerry: Petty production and capitalistic production in Dakar ..., op. cit., p. 12.

[2] Bose: Calcutta and rural Bengal ..., op. cit., p. 97.

[3] ibid., p. 105, pp. 121-122; see also "The urban informal sector: critical perspectives", in World Development, Sep.-Oct. 1978; and Leys: Underdevelopment in Kenya ..., op. cit.

[4] Some would even cast doubt on this conclusion: "... it is not at all obvious that active government intervention and assistance would be beneficial". See Chana and Morrison: "Nairobi's informal economic sector", op. cit., p. 122.

it is clear that the focus should be on both. For example, in cases where the formal sector has a monopoly in the use of scarce raw materials that are badly needed by the informal sector owing to the problems of substituting them it may be desirable to "reserve" such materials for the exclusive use by the informal sector on grounds of equity.

The role of public policies

The constraints in terms of access to resources and markets are also often exacerbated by the prevalence of a hostile policy environment. Contrary to the generally favourable policy environment accorded to the formal sector, the informal sector, notably in transport, trade and service activities, have been subject to a variety of constraints either because they cause traffic congestions, health hazards and illegal use of public spaces or simply because they mar the beauty of the city.[1] Needless to say such restrictions, without accompanying positive alternative measures, invariably mean not only a reduction in income opportunities but also induces the enterprises concerned to seek subordinate forms of relationship noted earlier. For example an enterprise with an "illegal" location is often neither "registered" nor is it eligible for credit from formal sources.[2] In contrast the formal sector enterprises not only have free or relatively easy access to resources and markets but also enjoy protection in various forms.[3] But for these restrictive policies, it is argued that the informal sector would have been more efficient.[4]

The informal sector as a source of growth

Much of what is discussed above can be termed as short run measures to assist the informal sector. Considering the number of persons engaged in this sector and the expected additions to it in
----

[1] Among other studies, see also T.G. McGee and Y.M. Yeung: Hawkers in South-East Asian cities: Planning for a bazaar economy (Ottawa, 1977), for a detailed discussion on policies towards the informal trade sector.

[2] See for example Reichmuth: Dualism in Peru: ... An investigation, op. cit., p. 151. In some cases such as Hong Kong the enterprises may prefer to remain "unregistered" in order to escape law enforcement relating to conditions of work and the like. See Victor and Fung Shuen sit: "Factories in domestic premises: A survey of an informal manufacturing sector in Hong Kong", in ASEAN Seminar on Informal Sector, Jakarta, December 1978 (Jakarta, 1978), p. 24.

[3] ILO: Employment, incomes and inequality ..., op. cit., Technical Paper No. 22. See also John Weeks: "Uneven sectoral development and the role of the State", in the informal sector and marginal groups in Bulletin (Institute of Economic Studies), Oct. 1973, pp. 76-82.

[4] In some cases the informal sector enterprises even pay the law enforcement authorities to waive restrictions. See Bromley: "The street traders of Cali ...", op. cit.

the years to come it is doubtful whether the remedial measures
suggested above will per se be adequate to raise the level of
incomes and employment in this sector. It would seem imperative to
incorporate the informal sector explicitly in the development plans
and assign a bigger and positive role to it. This in turn raises
the question of efficiency in the allocation of resources
particularly between the formal and the informal sector. Does it
necessarily imply a conflict between growth and equity objectives?

One of the basic arguments in favour of the informal sector is
its low capital intensity. Second, while the formal sector with
higher capital intensity tends to generate demand more for the
skilled labour, the informal sector tends to generate demand for
semi-skilled and unskilled labour whose supply is increasing both in
absolute and relative magnitudes. Third, in so far as small
enterprises are more likely to adopt appropriate technologies, the
promotion of the informal sector is likely to result in a more
efficient allocation of resources. Fourth, the informal sector in
many developing countries, notably in Africa, is performing an
important role in the formation of human capital by providing access
to training and at a cost substantially lower than that provided by
the formal training institutions. Fifth, the informal sector not
only relies heavily on the use of local resources but also plays a
significant role in recuperating and recycling materials that are
otherwise wasted.[1] And finally, perhaps the most important of all,
recognition of the informal sector explicitly in the development
plans could automatically ensure the distribution of benefits
resulting from development in favour of the disadvantaged groups and
thus depart from the trickle-down philosophy followed hitherto in
many developing countries.

Notwithstanding the above arguments in support of the informal
sector, allocation of more resources to this sector than in the past
both in absolute and relative terms does raise a number of
questions. It was noted in Chapter 1 that in spite of respectable
rates of growth of output the pattern of development in many Third
World countries has been uneven, often benefiting only a fraction of
the population, owing to the emphasis on the formal sector. One of
the reasons favouring the formal sector has been its ability to
generate surplus for investment and hence growth. The emerging
evidence seems to question this proposition.

It was noted earlier that the formal sector, recognising the
constraints within which the informal sector operates, often tends
to exploit the latter by imposing a dominant - subordinate
relationship. In other words, the formal sector is hypothesised to
"appropriate" a part of the surplus generated in the informal
sector. Besides market imperfections, other factors also contribute
to such a phenomenon.

Thus it is argued that the informal sector provides not only
cheap inputs but also cheaper wage goods for the workers in the
formal sector.[2] In other words a significant part of the vitality of
the formal sector and its ability to generate surplus and growth is
attributed to the presence of the informal sector.
----

[1] See for example Bromley and Gerry (eds.): Casual work and
poverty in third world countries, op. cit.

[2] See for example Bose: Calcutta and rural Bengal ..., op. cit.,
p. 98; Martin Godfrey: "Rural-urban migration in a 'Lewis-Model'
context", in The Manchester School of Economic and Social Studies,
Sep. 1979; and Leys: Underdevelopment in Kenya ..., op. cit.

The extent to which (potential) surplus generated in the informal sector is thus appropriated by the formal sector is however a matter for empirical verification depending on the nature and extent of backward and forward linkages between the two. Some studies have shown that the informal sector buys substantial quantities of raw materials from the formal sector and that the latter exercises certain dominant influence in terms of prices and quantities;[1] others deny the existence of any linkage at all.[2] Similar tendencies, it is argued, exist where the formal sector obtains its intermediate inputs through subcontracting from the informal sector.[3] Emerging from the above it is suggested that the terms of trade between the two sectors is generally favourable to the formal sector.[4] To the extent these arguments are valid it is clear that not only the ability of the informal sector to grow is limited by the surplus retained in this sector;[5] but also they cast doubt on the wisdom of promoting this sector by pumping more resources and creating further linkages between the two sectors without restructuring the underlying social and economic relationships for it will only benefit the formal sector. As already implied, such a conclusion is debatable; the extent of linkage cannot per se be an indicator of "exploitation". Much depends on the degree of market imperfection (or perfection).

Yet another argument explaining the ability of the formal sector to generate surplus is based on the favoured treatment accorded to it. For example, it is sometimes argued that the State, in order to induce the international firms to establish and operate, must provide certain political and economic concessions to these enterprises. Consequently "the formal sector develops in a non-competitive environment with privileged access to strategic resources".[6] By implication it follows that the informal sector's ability to generate surplus is limited by the policy environment.

----

[1] Gerry: Petty producers and the urban economy ..., op. cit.; see also Victor E. Tokman: An exploration into the nature of the informal-formal sector of interrelationships, PREALC monograph/2 (Santiago, ILO, 1977) for a detailed discussion; and the articles in Ray Bromley (ed.): "The urban informal sector: Critical perspectives", in: World Development (Special Issue), Sep.-Oct. 1978.

[2] Chana and Morrison: "Nairobi's informal economic sector", op. cit., p. 130.

[3] Tokman: An exploration into the nature of informal or formal sector interrelationships, op. cit., pp. 9-10, for example.

[4] ibid., p. 19.

[5] For some evidence contradicting the above, see Reichmuth: Dualisam in Peru: An investigation ..., op. cit., pp. 128, 140 and 211. See also M.P. van Dijk: Développement du secteur non-structuré au Sénégal: Une étude de son contexte et son potentiel (Dakar, ILO, 1976), p. 17, questioning the inference on exploitation; and House: "Nairobi's informal sector: An exploratory study", op. cit., p. 14.

[6] Weeks: "Uneven sectoral development and the role of the State", op. cit., p. 79.

Notwithstanding the above, scattered evidence suggest that the informal sector enterprises can and do generate surplus, at least in selected activities, even under hostile conditions threatening its survival. In Nairobi for example, the informal sector enterprises seem to have multiplied their initial capital, even though they had been in business for only about five years on the average, by as much as 6 to 10 times, depending on their level of net earnings.[1] In Lomé (Togo), fixed assets in the modern informal sector are estimated to have increased at 5.7 per cent per year and even 8.4 per cent per year in the top decile (i.e., larger enterprises).[2] In Ahmedabad (India), the informal manufacturing sector seems to have increased its productive capital at 21.5 per cent per year (12.3 per cent per year for fixed capital) during the period 1972-76.[3] Even though much depends on the economic environment, the activities and the conditions under which they operate, the fact that almost all these enterprises finance their capital requirements through internal sources suggests they are capable of generating surplus and hence growth. If one takes into account the human capital generated in the informal sector through apprenticeship training and the like, the case for promoting this sector becomes even stronger.[4] It can be argued further that elimination of uncertainty and improvement in the policy environment could, by providing an incentive for savings and investment, further enhance its ability to generate growth.[5]

The case for promoting the formal sector with a relative neglect of the informal sector on the ground that it generates more surplus for investment is thus called into question. The issue however cannot be settled without reference to further empirical evidence. The other factor that casts doubt on the adoption of a new development strategy assigning greater importance to the informal sector is efficiency. Are the informal sector enterprises as efficient as the formal sector enterprises? In other words, can the informal sector generate more employment and output for a given
----

[1] House: "Nairobi's informal sector: An exploratory study", op. cit., p. 17.

[2] Nihan et al.: "The modern informal sector in Lomé", op. cit., p. 634; in Nouakchott half the sample enterprises had an annual rate growth in capital of over 10 per cent. See Georges Nihan and R. Jourdain: "The modern informal sector in Nouakchott", in International Labour Review, Nov.-Dec. 1978, p. 715.

[3] Papola: The informal sector in an urban economy ..., op. cit., p. 43.

[4] The evidence from Ghana in fact casts doubt on the proposition that the formal sector generates more surplus than the informal sector. See Steel: Small-scale employment and production in developing countries (1977), op. cit., Chapter 4.

[5] See for example Carolyn Muench: "Planning for informal sector enterprises", in Informal Sector in Kenya, Institute for Development Studies, University of Nairobi, occasional paper No. 25, 1977, p. 182, suggesting that building codes and regulations could discourage investment in premises. See also Chana and Morrison: "Nairobi's informal economic sector", op. cit., p. 127, showing that the informal sector entrepreneurs are forbidden from improving their business premises.

volume of investment than the formal sector? Many studies have shown that the informal sector requires only a fraction of the capital needed in the formal sector to create a job. In Calcutta, for example, the average amount of fixed capital per worker in the informal manufacturing sector was estimated to be Rs.2,325 or only 16 per cent of that required in the formal sector.[1] In Ahmedabad (India) it was estimated to be around 50 per cent.[2] In fact the Ahmedabad study suggests that the smaller enterprises in the informal manufacturing sector (i.e., those with under Rs.5,000 (or US$625) per establishment) generated both more value-added and employment than the larger ones.[3] The study on Nairobi suggests that even though the informal manufacturing sector requires only K₤182 per worker of capital or 11 per cent of that in the formal sector, it generated output valued at K₤410 per year or 26 per cent of that in the formal sector.[4] In other words an investment of K₤ one million seems to generate K₤2.25 million output and 5,500 jobs in the informal sector as compared to K₤0.774 million and 500 respectively in the formal sector.

The study on Ghana referred to earlier also showed that in the informal manufacturing sector (i.e., enterprises with less than ten wage employees the average capital required per worker was about 2,100 cedis or 11 per cent of that in the formal sector (firms with over 100 workers); the corresponding figure for value added was 1,200 cedis or 19 per cent of that in the formal sector.[5] In other words a given volume of investment appears to generate significantly more employment and value added in the informal than in the formal sector. In Nouakchott, the value of fixed assets like machinery and equipment per worker in the modern informal sector was only 5 per cent of that in the formal sector.[6] The average (median) amount of capital per worker in the informal sector of Bamako (Mali), Kigali (Rwanda), Lomé (Togo) and Nouakchott (Mauritania) has been estimated at US$54,161,187 and 166 respectively - quite small by any standard.

The brief survey of evidence[7] presented above is not only selective but also of varying quality in terms of concepts and coverage. More importantly the question of efficiency cannot be resolved without isolating the consequences of market imperfections
----

[1] Bose: Calcutta and rural Bengal ..., op. cit., p. 96.

[2] Papola: The informal sector in an urban economy ..., op. cit., p. 160.

[3] Derived from data ibid., pp. 47-49.

[4] House: "Nairobi's informal sector ...", op. cit., pp. 7-8.

[5] Steel: Small-scale employment and production in developing countries, op. cit., Chapter 4.

[6] Nihan and Jourdain: "The modern informal sector in Nouakchott", op. cit., p. 715.

[7] In addition to the above see also ILO: Sharing in development: A programme of employment, equity and growth for the Philippines (Geneva, 1974), special paper No. 9; and idem: Mexico: La pequeña industria en la estrategia de empleo productivo, PREALC (Santiago, 1977; mimeographed).

noted earlier on the valuation. Nevertheless, it suggests that the
promotion of the informal sector, at least in the more productive
modern activities, need not pose any conflict between growth and
employment.

Development experience from several Third World countries
suggests that maximising the rate of economic growth has not been
the only objective resulting in the stress on the formal sector.
For example shortage of foreign exchange has often led to the
promotion of import substituting industries which invariably meant
promotion of a capital intensive sector using technologies borrowed
from the developed world. The question then arises whether the
informal sector can provide such import substitutes. Some would
however question the very need to produce import substitutes on the
ground that most of them belong to the class of luxury consumer
goods and that they are produced to satisfy the demand from a
minority of elites who have acquired an international flavour for
consumption.[1] Perhaps a more basic issue is whether the choice of
any product mix can be sustained by a particular pattern of
development stressing the informal sector. It is increasingly
realised now that development is less meaningful unless it also aims
at satisfying the basic needs of masses.[2] In so far as the basic
needs can be produced with local resources using simple technologies
it would seem that a basic needs oriented development strategy would
considerably expand the scope for participation of the informal
sector. On the demand side too, a greater emphasis on the informal
sector could result in higher incomes for the working poor and thus
generate additional demand for basic needs items. Needless to add
these are indeed areas for further research. To the extent these
arguments are valid, such an approach would also lead to an easing
of the burden on foreign exchange, discourage the promotion of
formal sector and the adoption of inappropriate technologies.

Evolutionary or involutionary growth?

Even though increasing dependence on the informal sector for
employment seems not only desirable but also inevitable its
consequences to incomes of the poor are far from clear. One of the
major issues in this context is whether labour absorption in this
sector will be followed by decreasing, constant or increasing
incomes per worker. In other words will the growth of this sector
be involutionary or evolutionary? There are several shades of
opinion on this issue.[3] One view seems to be that the informal
sector can accumulate capital and grow fast enough to absorb the
labour thrust upon it provided the policy environment becomes
favourbale, market imperfections are eliminated and markets for this
sector's output are expanded through greater linkages between this
----

[1] Weeks: "Uneven sectoral development and the role of the
State", op. cit., p. 78.

[2] Louis Emmerij and Dharm Ghai: "The World Employment
Conference: A preliminary assessment", in _International Labour
Review_, Nov.-Dec. 1976.

[3] Tokman: "An exploration into the nature of informal-formal
sector interrelationships", op. cit., for a brief summary of the
controversy.

sector and the rest of the economy. The other view holds that the informal sector is not capable of accumulating capital and hence generate an evolutionary growth since it is subordinated by the formal sector. It is postulated on the premises that the formal sector is linked to multinationals and operates under oligopolistic conditions. It not only retains the surplus generated within itself and creates fewer jobs by choosing capital intensive techniques but it also appropriates the surplus generated in the informal sector by restricting access to modern inputs and product markets on the one hand and by flooding their own products on the informal sector participants on the other. Further it is argued that labour surplus resulting from population growth tends to depress wages even in the formal sector and thus facilitates its capital accumulation.

Obviously the divergent opinions cannot be resolved without resort to empirical evidence and the case in question. It is perhaps true, notably in the case of Latin America, that multinationals play a relatively important role; but the evidence available is far from adequate to prove the contention that the informal sector is in fact prevented by the formal sector from accumulating surplus and generating growth.[1] The evidence quoted earlier, if at all, points to the opposite view, namely, that the informal sector can and does accumulate capital and grow over time although such growth may be limited to relatively more productive activities such as manufacturing. Further the evidence from selected African countries seems to suggest that the older enterprises within the informal sector generally possess substantially larger amounts of capital than those that are relatively younger.[2] Such evidence, if at all, suggests that the rate of capital accumulation is a function of time and that the process of evolution of these enterprises can be accelerated through appropriate policy measures and assistance. And finally, the fact that a significant number of the informal sector participants earn a wage comparable to that of the formal sector (and the legal minimum wage) and that there is some mobility of workers from the formal to the informal sector would seem to contradict the view that growth in the latter is involutionary.[3]

Policies for evolutionary growth

Besides allocation of more resources and elimination of market imperfections, the scope for evolutionary growth depends on the opportunities for productivity gains on the one hand, and the demand opportunities on the other. These opportunities vary with the type of activity. In some activities, the informal sector would seem to
----

[1] See for example Reichmuth: Dualisam in Peru: An investigation ..., op. cit., which contradicts the second view presented above and concludes that the informal sector does generate surplus and that constraints on capital accumulation are the consequence of "lack of access to jobs, credit, education and markets" and not the result of the dominance of the formal sector (p. 214).

[2] Nihan: "Le secteur non-structuré - signification, aire d'extension du concept et application expérimentale", op. cit., p. 23.

[3] See the section below on labour market.

have demonstrated its innovative ability; in others, the opportunities for gains in productivity would appear to be limited. For example personal and household services, in so far as they offer little scope for technological change and productivity gains, clearly growth of demand plays a more important role in determining whether labour absorption will be followed by rising, falling or constant income to workers. The scope for evolutionary growth would seem to vary with the country in question inasmuch as the structure of the sector in particular and the economy in general, institutional rigidities as well as the opportunities mentioned above depend on the level and pattern of development. Finally, it should be noted that the choice of policy instruments could significantly influence the opportunities available to the informal sector as will be seen below.

It is perhaps useful at this point to understand the types of markets from which the informal sector seems to derive its strength for survival or expansion. First, there are certain areas which are exclusively in the domain of the informal sector because the formal sector cannot reach them. For example, the small scale of operation coupled with its labour intensive character often enable the informal sector enterprise to provide goods and services tailored to the individual needs and this could arise from all income groups of households (e.g., repairs, trade, services, tailoring, etc.) and perhaps to some extent even from non-household units (e.g., vehicle repair). Second, the small size of the market does not offer any incentive to the formal sector to enter; as a special case this might include the production and/or services of an import substituting variety (e.g., duplication of imported spare parts on a small scale) based on the innovative ability and recycling of waste materials. Third, certain activities such as collection of waste materials (and garbage in general) are left over to the informal sector either because the local authorities are unable to reach or it is too labour intensive and expensive for the formal sector to reach directly. Fourth, the informal sector may be able to retain certain markets owing to its cost efficiency - cheap labour, economy on overhead costs and the like - or to its locational advantage. Fifth the informal sector may be able to derive its competitive edge from product differentiation. Sixth, the formal sector may be unable to produce certain types of goods and services for the low and middle income groups and thus leaves such markets for the informal sector which, by using substandard materials and simple technologies, is able to develop its own market by emulating the formal sector products. Finally, the formal sector may deliberately seek the co-operation of the informal sector through subcontracting in obtaining intermediate inputs or marketing its output. Not infrequently the informal sector loses out certain markets to the formal sector either because the consumer tastes have changed in such a way or because of cost efficiency. Similarly, certain markets painstakingly developed by the informal sector may be taken over by the formal sector through mass production and cost reduction. Needless to add these are not mutually exclusive categories; neither are they exhaustive.

Many studies seem to confirm that the bulk of what is produced in the informal sector is sold to households, for final consumption. Further, much of this demand seems to originate from among poor and low income households. Given that the income elasticity of demand for informal sector goods and services is positive, it is clear that the rate of growth of income and population play an important role

in determining the demand for this sector's output. To the extent
that the elasticities vary between income groups, changes in income
distribution would seem to be important too.[1] The fact that income
and population in urban areas of developing countries has increased
substantially in recent years would seem to explain the growth of
urban informal sector activities in these countries. Policies aimed
at increasing the incomes of the poor are therefore likely to result
in an expansion of demand for informal sector goods and services.

For at least some of the informal sector goods, notably those
manufactured within the sector, it is quite likely that the demand
is also influenced by the availability of similar products from the
formal sector (e.g. footwear, furniture, etc.). In so far as the
pressure on demand is exerted through prices and quality
differential, policies designed to improve the quality and reduce
the relative price of informal sector products could have a
significant positive impact on demand for the latter. By the same
token, policies designed to diversify the commodity structure of the
informal sector and strengthen its ability to compete effectively
with the formal sector could also result in expanding the demand
opportunities for the informal sector. In an extreme situation it
could take the form of "reserving" certain commodities exclusively
for the informal sector. An extension of this approach would be to
strengthen the capacity of the informal sector to tap demand from
non-household sources as well. Besides promoting linkages with
formal sector firms that are particularly advantageous to the
informal sector, it may be possible for example to involve the
informal sector in other public sector activities, notably in
construction, supply of furnitures and the like to schools,
hospitals, etc.[2] The brief discussion above illustrates the kind of
interventions that can contribute to an expansion of demand
opportunities.

As in the case of demand, it would seem possible to increase
the opportunities for productivity gains particularly through
development and diffusion of appropriate technologies and upgrading
the skills of workers in the informal sector. Several studies show
that the informal sector activities particularly in manufacturing
and repair services are quite innovative, substituting cheaper local
resources. Reorientation of technology institutions specifically to
assist the informal sector, diffusion of better technologies through
appropriate mechanisms, promotion of technological linkages between
the formal and the informal sectors are some possibilities in the
direction of narrowing the productivity gaps between the two
sectors.[3] Likewise innovative measures to upgrade the prevailing
systems of training could contribute to increasing labour

----

[1] See R.K. Wishwakarma: "Urban income distribution and
employment generation", in Nagarlok, Oct.-Dec. 1978, for some
evidence on reduction in income inequality and employment
generation.

[2] ILO: Employment, incomes and equality in Kenya, op. cit.

[3] Susumu Watanabe: Technological linkages between formal and
informal sectors of manufacturing industries (Geneva, ILO, 1978;
mimeographed World Employment Programme research working paper;
restricted), and also the papers cited therein.

productivity as well. More importantly, they will facilitate the participation of the informal sector more widely and effectively in the development process.

The spatial implications

Though the need to develop the informal sector is clear whether it should be encouraged in the large cities or not is a moot question. Accumulating evidence suggests a strong relationship between migration to cities and labour absorption in the informal sector. Several studies suggest that migrants not only have a lower rate of unemployment because of the informal sector but also have a shorter waiting period before finding a job. Also earlier migrants seem to play a catalytic role in transmitting signals, directly or indirectly to potential migrants outside the city. It is therefore argued that any effort to promote income and employment in this sector in large cities could aggravate the urban problem by attracting more migrants.

Needless to add the presence of the informal sector in the cities is not the only factor attracting migrants; a number of other factors noted in Chapter 1 play an important role too.[1] The concern for excessive concentration of population in large cities seems to originate partly from the deterioration in urban environment and partly from the declining standards and inadequacy of basic urban amenities. Some would characterise the latter in terms of an adjustment problem; it simply reflects the failure of urban authorities to respond effectively and adequately and soon enough to cope with the flow of population. In so far as new entrants to the city impose a "cost" on those already living there, particularly the affluent, others are inclined to rationalise the urbanisation process as one of the most effective means of redistributing income and wealth since the bulk of the new entrants are poor and have little capacity to pay for the urban services.[2]

One could go a step further and argue that an appropriate strategy to develop the informal sector in large cities could, by raising the income levels of the poor, increase their ability to pay for housing and other urban services and thereby improve the situation.

Another argument against encouraging the growth of large cities relates to the question of efficiency and the implied diseconomies of scale of large urban agglomerations.[3] Though the search for optimum size of cities has continued, the evidence on
----

[1] See also Peter Peek and Guy Standing: "Rural-urban migration and government policies in low-income countries", in International Labour Review, Nov.-Dec. 1979, pp. 763-776.

[2] In fact the cost imposed on others may even be offset by the provision of cheaper goods and services in the informal sector.

[3] For a detailed discussion of these and other issues pertaining to employment decentralisation discussed below, see P.M. Townroe: "Employment decentralisation: policy instruments for large cities in less developed countries", in Progress in planning (1979), Vol. 10, Part 2, pp. 85-144. See also Paul Bairoch: Emploi et taille des villes, op. cit.

this issue seems to be mixed and inconclusive. It is worth noting, however, that the cost of providing infrastructure in large urban centres seems to be substantially higher than in smaller towns.[1]

The case for restraining the growth of large cities would therefore seem to rest largely on equity grounds besides of course the concern for urban environment noted earlier. Excessive growth of large urban centres could, by increasing the concentration of income and investment opportunities, aggravate regional income disparities.[2] Likewise, within the cities, changing ethnic, religious and/or cultural compositions resulting from migration could have implications for income distribution and hence social and political stability.

The alternatives for promoting the informal sector in large cities include its promotion in smaller towns as well as the development of rural non-farm activities. The available evidence seems to suggest that the rapid growth of the informal sector in cities can be explained largely in terms of the differential rates of growth of income in general between cities, towns and rural areas. Rapid growth of income in large cities, by increasing the demand for a variety of goods and services, seems to have encouraged the growth of the informal sector and perhaps provided an escape from involutionary growth.

Inasmuch as these relationships hold, employment, decentralisation through the promotion of the informal sector in smaller towns cannot be undertaken independently of the over-all development strategy. In other words, informal sector development must form an integral component of the national development plan. It is in this context that the need to study the informal sector in different size groups of urban places deserves attention. Besides income growth, the large cities, by providing greater opportunities for mobility between occupations, may reduce the extent of job and income uncertainty in the informal sector and thus provide an incentive for potential migrants; in contrast, the smaller towns may provide incentives in terms of greater physical access to markets.

The urban informal sector and labour market

One of the crucial questions with regard to the labour market efficiency is whether the development of the informal sector along the lines suggested above will also contribute to a more efficient allocation of labour resources where efficiency can be measured in terms of output or some equivalent measure of social welfare.

----

[1] See for example Townroe: "Employment decentralisation ...", op. cit., Chapter 7.

[2] One must however recognise that regional disparities could reduce in so far as the migrants in urban areas remit a part of their income back to the rural areas where they come from. See Paul Collier and Deepak Lal: Poverty and growth in Kenya, World Bank Working Paper (Washington, 1980; mimeographed), suggesting that rural-urban migration has been beneficial to rural areas (p. 57). See also A.S. Oberai and H.K. Manmohan Singh: "Migration, remittances and rural development", in International Labour Review, Mar.-Apr. 1980.

Labour market performance impinges on a number of factors including the role of minimum wage legislations and unions on the one hand and the structure and efficiency of markets for resources other than labour on the other in so far as they are complementary to the use of labour. In a static sense malfunctioning of the labour market is manifested in such measures as unemployment and wage differentials for comparable units of labour. In the context of a growing economy it could give rise to questions of matching job and skill requirements with particular reference to spatial and sectoral allocations.

Given that the informal sector operates under conditions of market imperfections, policies to remedy the situation and promote this sector will obviously have a significant influence on the labour market leading to higher levels of productivity, wages and employment. Labour market segmentation manifested in the coexistence of high and low wage sectors through rationing of jobs in the former obviously has implications for efficiency: it not only encourages choice of inappropriate technologies and induces socially unproductive investment in education and mismatches between worker skills and job requirements but also contributes to labour shortages and surpluses in different markets.[1] Though there are many difficulties[2] in using wage differentials between the formal and the informal sectors as a means to assess the role of non-market forces on the labour/market performance, they nevertheless provide an indication of the extent of such wage distortions.

Evidence emerging from various studies either compare the earnings of the informal sector entrepreneur with the wage prevailing in the formal sector; or alternatively they shed light on the differential between the average wage paid to informal sector workers and the legal minimum wage that is generally enforced in the formal sector. The main drawback with the former comparison is that it refers to earnings of the entrepreneur which includes not only the return to his labour but also to his entrepreneurial skills and capital owned. In addition to the above, some studies also provide evidence on the extent of labour mobility between sectors or occupations and the factors that constrain such mobility.

According to one study on Nairobi, the regular wage workers in the informal sector received on the average about Ksh.370 per month as compared to the statutory minimum wage of Ksh.350 per month.[3] In contrast the heads of informal sector enterprises earned about Ksh.320 per week (or Ksh.1,280 per month).[4] The averages however mask the variations; the proportion of heads receiving an income

----

[1] A. Berry and R.H. Sabot: Labour market performance in developing countries: A survey (1977; mimeographed). See also Paul Collier and Deepak Lal: Poverty and Growth in Kenya, World Bank working paper (Washington, 1980; mimeographed), questioning the inefficiency of labour markets in Kenya.

[2] ibid., pp. 25-27.

[3] House: "Nairobi's informal sector ...", op. cit., p. 21.

[4] Derived from the weekly earnings which varied between activities substantially: manufacturing, Ksh.295; trade Ksh.401; services Ksh.236; and transport Ksh.174. ibid., p. 5.

below the minimum wage was 45 per cent in manufacturing, 23 per cent
in trade and 53 per cent in services.[1] In the case of Dakar, the
entrepreneurs seem to earn above the wages prevailing in the formal
sector though there are variations between them. The workers in the
informal sector, though earn much less than the heads as compared to
Nairobi, have an average earning comparable to that prevailing in
the formal sector in typical occupations.[2] Similar findings are
reported elsewhere in Africa: among entrepreneurs in the "modern"
informal sector, 82.5 per cent in Nouakchott (Mauritania) received
an income at least equal to the "guaranteed inter-occupational
minimum wage"; corresponding figures for wage earners were
respectively 68.6 per cent and 73 per cent.[3] In Cali, Colombia, the
garbage pickers are estimated to earn on the average about 70 pesos
per day as compared to the legal minimum wage of 62 pesos per day.[4]
The evidence available from Latin America suggests that in general,
between 21 and 50 per cent of those engaged in the informal sector
receive an income below the legal minimum wage.[5] Several studies
also show that there is significant mobility from the formal to the
informal sector; to cite two examples, in Hong Kong, 60 per cent of
the informal sector entrepreneurs were formerly employed in the
formal sector;[6] and in Lomé (Togo), 64 per cent.[7]

Though the brief review of evidence from selected countries
presented above suggests that the labour market is functioning
reasonably well, it would appear that there is considerable scope
for improving the efficiency of labour markets. Besides variations
in the wages of different categories of workers considerable wage
differentials seem to exist within the informal sector.[8] Further
evidence from Latin America for example suggests that such wage
differentials "are only partially explained by differences in human

----

[1] House: "Nairobi's informal sector ...", op. cit., p. 7.

[2] M.P. van Dijk: "Enquête sur le secteur non-structuré: Dakar,
March-May 1977" (Geneva, ILO, 1977; unpublished manuscript).

[3] Georges Nihan et al.: "The modern informal sector in Lomé", in
International Labour Review, Sep.-Oct. 1979, p. 634.

[4] Chris Birkbeck: "Garbage, industry, and the 'vultures' of
Cali, Colombia", in Bromley and Gerry (eds.): Casual work and
poverty in third world cities, op. cit., p. 169.

[5] Victor E. Tokman: Urban poverty and employment in Latin
America: Guidelines for action, PREALC occasional paper No. 1
(Santiago, ILO, 1977), table 1.

[6] Victor and Fung Shuen sit: "Factories in domestic premises: A
survey of an informal manufacturing sector in Hong Kong", in ASEAN
Seminar on Informal Sector, Jakarta, December 1978 (Jakarta, 1978).

[7] Nihan et al.: "The modern informal sector in Lomé", op. cit.,
p. 634.

[8] Papola: The informal sector in an urban economy ..., op. cit.

capital and that for equal skills, sectoral differentials are around 50 per cent."[1]

Persistent wage differentials between the formal and the informal sectors has been explained both in terms of rational behaviour of formal sector firms and in terms of wage legislation and the power of unions.[2] Likewise persistent disequilibrium in the form of open unemployment in urban areas in spite of the presence of the informal sector, where free entry exists and jobs are available albeit at a low wage, has been rationalised in terms of job search models.[3] Notwithstanding the above the extent to which social costs can be minimised through improvements in the functioning of the urban labour markets remains a moot question. Besides other labour market policies such as the elimination of wage distortions, development of the informal sector and policy instruments to promote labour mobility between the two sectors would seem to play an important role. Finally, inasmuch as skill acquisition contributes to labour mobility, appropriate policies to enhance the access to skills and training will result in greater mobility of labour even within the informal sector and hence a better allocation of resources.

The urban informal sector and environment

The urban explosion and the emergence of the informal sector in many developing countries have elevated the concern for environment in a number of ways. First, it relates to a growing imbalance in the distribution of population vis-à-vis land and other resources. Second, arising out of the above, is the concern for deteriorating urban environment owing to increasing population densities within the urban centres. Third, the changes in living styles that accompany urbanisation seem to impose significant costs both in terms of resource use and in terms of environmental quality. Fourth, the prevailing structures and the socio-economic network within which the informal sector must operate seem to aggravate the distribution of population vis-à-vis land and other resources within these urban centres. Fifth, the response on the part of the urban authorities to the emerging imbalances seems to be inadequate in relation to the magnitude of the problem.

To what extent can the development of the urban informal sector offer a solution to the above? Basically it poses a dilemma.
----

[1] Tokman: "An exploration into the nature of informal-formal sector interrelationships", op. cit., p. 7. In Latin America, the average income per person in the formal sector is estimated to be 3.5 times larger than that in the informal sector in Lima; between 2.5 and 2.8 times in Colombia, San Salvador and Asuncion; and 2 times in Santo Domingo. See Tokman: Urban poverty and employment in Latin America: Guidelines for action, op. cit., Paper No. 1

[2] Mazumdar: "The urban informal sector", op. cit., and Berry and Sabot: Labour market performance in developing countries: A survey, op. cit.

[3] D. Mazumdar: "Analysis of the dual labour markets in LDCs", in S. Kannappan (ed.): Studies of urban labour market behaviour in developing areas (Geneva, IILS, 1977).

While it is clear that the informal sector provides an escape for the surplus labour force in the countryside from rural poverty and underemployment, its development in the urban context could aggravate the environmental concerns noted above. Besides rural and regional development in a more dispersed manner already mentioned, one compromise solution has been to avoid any open subsidies and help the urban poor to help themselves e.g. self-help housing schemes and the like. The approach to develop the informal sector presented earlier, by improving the economic environment and conditions under which it now operates, could not only increase the purchasing power of its participants through higher incomes but also reduce the imbalance in distribution of resources and ensure their efficient use. Further, the scope for involving the urban informal sector directly in the improvement of the urban environment as for example, the kampong improvement programmes in Indonesia, needs to be explored. Such efforts could therefore bridge the growing gap between private benefits and social costs. At a global level, a development strategy focused on basic needs and the urban informal sector could alter not only the pattern of consumption but also the pattern of production; as noted earlier, it could facilitate the use of technologies appropriate to the resource endowments in these countries and a greater involvement of the informal sector.

Development of the urban informal sector can have direct consequences too. It calls for a rethinking on the conventional approaches to urban land-use planning. For example it can not only lead to separation of commercial and industrial activities from residential areas and thus contribute to an improvement in urban environment; but it can also facilitate the separation of polluting and non-polluting activities. It could pave the way for improving the conditions of work in the informal sector. Further, informal sector development can arrest the growth of, if not remove, large scale industrial activities that contribute to pollution. Finally, it could provide greater opportunities to collection and recycling of waste materials. These and other possibilities are however discussed in greater detail in Chapter 13.

The urban informal sector and equity

The urban informal sector, almost by definition, is playing an important role in providing income opportunities for the poor. But it would be erroneous to conclude that all the urban poor are in the informal sector. Similarly, not all those engaged in this sector earn an income below the nationally defined poverty line since many studies do suggest that a substantial number of its participants, notably in manufacturing activities, earn a respectable level of income as compared to earnings in the formal sector as already noted. It is nevertheless true that a majority of the informal sector participants receive low incomes, notably in non-manufacturing activities. This is partly due to the fact that they require relatively little skills and capital (as compared to manufacturing) and hence fewer barriers to entry. Further, as the evidence cited earlier shows, a good part of the income variations within the informal sector can be explained in terms of disparities between entrepreneurs and workers. In other words it is argued that there are significant income disparities within the informal sector.[1] By promoting mobility between occupations and between different activities it would seem possible to reduce such income disparities. The evidence on the extent of such mobility and the factors that contribute to it are however inconclusive.

Another aspect of the informal sector problem relates to conditions of work. Even though many in the informal sector, particularly the entrepreneurs in manufacturing, seem to earn an income above the legal minimum as noted earlier, those who do receive an income below that level constitute the major part of the urban workforce who are denied the legal minimum wage. In other words a majority of those working in the urban areas with a wage below the legal minimum belong to the informal sector. For example, in Latin America, this proportion is placed at 73 per cent in main cities of Colombia and Mexico City: 77 per cent in Santo Domingo (Dominican Republic); 80 per cent in San Salvador (El Salvador); and 83 per cent in Asuncion (Paraguay).[2] No doubt these figures are sensitive to the definition of the informal sector; but they do suggest that the conditions of work of the informal sector are far from ideal. Further, many studies suggest that the informal sector workers generally work longer hours than their formal sector counterparts. Low incomes and longer hours of work besides uncertainty of employment and earnings in certain activities would thus seem to call for policies to ameliorate the conditions of work. To the extent such conditions are simply a reflection of the growth of labour force on the one hand and the limited and unequal distribution of opportunities on the other, it is quite likely that the development of the informal sector along the lines discussed will contribute to an improvement.

Conclusion

The challenge posed by the emerging situation in urban areas of developing countries, it is evident, calls for a wide range of measures not excluding a radical departure from the development strategies and policies followed hitherto. However, the elements that constitute a new development strategy are not altogether obvious notwithstanding the wide array of evidence cited thus far. Findings based on a number of studies in Africa, Asia and Latin America presented below, though selective, nevertheless throw additional light on several of the issues raised in this chapter.

----

[1] For the limited evidence available on this, see Mazumdar: "Analysis of the dual labour markets in LDCs", op. cit., table 3, p. 30, where it is shown that 56 per cent of informal sector workers in Asucion earned below legal minimum wage compared to 85 per cent below twice that level; corresponding figures for Santo Domingo were 50 and 81 per cent and for San Salvador, 72 and 84 per cent respectively. See also the Nairobi study cited earlier.

[2] Tokman: Urban poverty and employment in Latin America: Guidelines for action, op. cit., table 2, p. 29.

PART II

<u>Evidence from Africa, Asia and Latin America</u>

CHAPTER 4. THE INFORMAL SECTOR IN FREETOWN: OPPORTUNITIES FOR SELF-EMPLOYMENT

D.A. Fowler

The study on Freetown informal sector, though aimed at a sample of 1,000 enterprises, is actually based on the data collected from 967 enterprises belonging to manufacturing, construction, trade, transport and services. The simple random sampling procedure adopted by the study inevitably led to the selection of a relatively larger number of trade enterprises, about 50 per cent of the sample. Of the remaining, manufacturing was by far the most important activity, with 195 sample enterprises. The detailed distribution of the sample by type of activity is presented in table 1. The informal sector in Freetown thus seems to be dominated by trade, particularly retailing.

The entrepreneur

Nearly a quarter of the heads of sample enterprises were females; their median age was around 35 years. Close to two-thirds of them were in retail trade. Thirty-eight per cent of male entrepreneurs were below 30 years of age as compared to only 23 per cent for females.   Only a small percentage of the informal sector entrepreneurs is typically young, seeking their first job.

Participation of males in different activities, however, showed significant variations with the age of the entrepreneur. Needless to add, such variations have implications for entry into certain activities by different age groups. Males between 10 and 14 years had access only to retail trade or manual labour as head porters. Those between 15 and 19 years were heavily concentrated (80 per cent of them) in retail trading on a very minor scale, requiring low capital investment. Retail trading also accounted for two-thirds of all males in the 20 to 24-year age cohort: the remaining tended to participate in activities requiring relatively more skills and/or capital. Thirteen per cent were tailors, an activity requiring moderate capital investment (i.e. a sewing machine), a strategic spot in one of Freetown's busy streets and about two years' apprenticeship. Another 9 per cent were in repair work relating to retail trade, something which required a period of apprenticeship but little financial investment. The rest of this age group set up business as restaurateurs and local shoemakers. As expected, construction and mechanised transport, with their require-ments of heavy capital investment, did not have any owners under 25 years of age. Yet more diversification is noticed among the 25 to 29-year male group which, in addition to participation in the activities noted above, moved into the motor transport business.

Looking at the data on age distribution within activities the 20 to 29-year group provides 57 per cent of all the footwear manufacturers, 43 per cent of tailors, 48 per cent of all retail trade repairers and 28 per cent of taxicab owners. This last phenomenon is explained by the fact that these owners normally start off as employees of fleet operators and eventually buy their cars second-hand from their former masters. As expected, over 53 per cent of those engaged in manual transport as "omolankey" drivers and head porters are under 30 years of age. Other activities are

Table 1:   Distribution of sample enterprises
           by main activity

Activity	Absolute freq.	Relative freq. (per cent)
Manufacturing		20.1
Food	29	3.0
Tobacco	7	0.7
Textiles	9	0.9
Wearing apparel (except footwear)	72	7.4
Leather products (" ")	7	0.7
Footwear	15	1.6
Wood products	5	0.5
Furnitures	32	3.3
Printing, etc.	1	0.1
Pottery, chinaware, etc.	3	0.3
Metal products	15	1.6
Construction	20	2.1
Trade		65.0
Wholesale	1	0.1
Retail	487	50.4
Hawkers and pedlars	62	6.4
Restaurants, etc.	77	8.0
Hotels, etc.	1	0.1
Transport		3.9
Taxicabs	18	1.9
Cycle rickshaws	18	1.9
Freight transport	1	0.1
Services		8.9
Education	1	0.1
Health services	3	0.3
Other social services	36	3.7
Repair services	47	4.9
Total	967	100.0

apparently closed to males under 30 partly because of the financial prerequisites and partly because of the technical skill requirements. Somewhat similar trends are noticeable for women entrepreneurs as well; with increase in age, a greater proportion of them participate in non-trade activities like food processing and dressmaking. These findings suggest that age of the entrepreneur, acting as a proxy for other variables, seems to be an important factor in promoting mobility between various informal sector activities.

To what extent is education important? The answer is "not very much". Over 70 per cent of the entrepreneurs had no education at all; only about 10 per cent had secondary-level education or more. The educational mix of entrepreneurs showed little variation between activities. Further, contrary to expectation, age and education of entrepreneurs seem to be positively correlated. For example, in the age group 50-54, 38 per cent had primary level or more of schooling as compared to 23 per cent for the sample as a whole, implying that a larger proportion of new entrants (young) have lower than primary level of schooling. The reasons for this phenomenon must be found in the role and pattern of migration discussed below.

Role of migration

Twenty-two per cent of all owners were born in Freetown. The northern province, which is closest to the western area within which Freetown is situated, provided 36 per cent of the total against 3 per cent from the western area excluding Freetown, 2 per cent for the eastern and 4 per cent for the southern provinces. Non-Sierra Leoneans constituted 33 per cent of the total sample (with Guinean nationals accounting for 26 per cent). Twenty-six per cent each of the migrants had been in Freetown for between 10 and 20 years and over 20 years respectively. Twenty-two per cent had spent between 5 and 10 years whilst 14 per cent had lived in Freetown between 2 and 5 years; and 8.6 per cent had been in Freetown between 1 and 2 years. Only 3.5 per cent had recently arrived (i.e. between March 1975 and February 1976).

The pattern of migration is also biased, with a relatively larger proportion of males. Whereas, among entrepreneurs born in Freetown itself, males and females were almost equally represented in the sample (51 per cent to 49 per cent), the situation of those born in other regions is markedly dissimilar. The northern province sub-sample showed that there were 74 per cent men against 26 per cent women, a ratio of almost 3:1. The non-Sierra Leonean sub-sample presented a ratio of males to females of almost 10:1. Even more striking is the absence of any females from the eastern province. The implication here seems to be that the propensity for women to migrate to the capital varies with distance. However, that by itself does not offer a full explanation. Cultural factors are also important in that the non-Sierra Leonean women, mostly Fullahs, are not encouraged to be as adventurous as their male counterparts. They are usually repatriated after a short sojourn in the city and are in addition discouraged by strict measures of tribal social control from participating in trade. Such constraints do not operate in the case of tribes from the northern province.

Further, there are some significant trends in the pattern of migration over time. A greater proportion of recent migrants comes from outside Sierra Leone; for example, 76 per cent of migrant entrepreneurs who arrived in Freetown during the year preceding the survey were non-Sierra Leoneans as compared to 22 per cent among those who arrived more than 20 years ago. Correspondingly, the share of migrants from the northern province has decreased over time. Similarly, with respect to the age composition, less than half of the native entrepreneurs of Freetown were below 39 years of age even though for the sample as a whole over two-thirds of them belonged to this category. In other words, a majority of the migrant entrepreneurs was young.

Turning to the question of education, only 8 per cent of the male entrepreneurs who never attended school were born in Freetown as compared to 48 per cent and 38 per cent respectively for those born in the northern province and non-Sierra Leoneans respectively. The dominance of younger migrants coupled with their relatively lower level of schooling seems to explain the positive relationship between age and education noted earlier.

Migration and job mobility

One of the important hypotheses in the context of research on the informal sector has been whether the sector serves as a stepping stone to move up the socio-economic ladder. In particular, does the sector absorb unemployed and underemployed? Looking at the migrant entrepreneurs, the survey revealed that 45 per cent of them were unemployed or not working before migration. This is quite natural since a relatively larger proportion of them are also young as already noted. But it is also interesting to note that among entrepreneurs between 20 and 24 years of age, 53 per cent had worked before migration. Similar results emerge for the next age group (25-29 years) as well. Among those with previous work experience, less than 1 per cent were in the professional and technical category, mainly primary school teachers and musicians. Two per cent were in the clerical category; 11 per cent were salesworkers, mainly petty traders. Forty-eight per cent were farmers, followed by 26 per cent who were production workers. The majority of the petty traders were once farmers or farmworkers who openly admitted that the drudgery associated with traditional farming for very low returns was responsible for their migration. Those in services and manufacturing migrated, as they put it, to improve their skills and to work in a larger and potentially more lucrative market. They were prepared for the initial hardships and felt on reflection that they are financially better off now than they were before migration. The evidence also suggests that a greater proportion of the younger migrants who had work experience was engaged in agriculture.

When an attempt was made to relate the migrant entrepreneurs' current main activity with the past activity before migration, the following picture emerged. Fifty-eight per cent of migrants now in manufacturing were production workers prior to migration; the great majority among the rest were farmers and farmworkers, with a few from sales services and manual transport. Within the construction sector, 64 per cent had previous experience in construction work but the rest were agricultural workers who had acquired their present skills in the intervening years through apprenticeship. Within the trade sector, only 14 per cent possessed previous trading experience; the majority learnt the appropriate skills in Freetown through on-the-job training. Within the transport sector, 60 per cent of the migrants had engaged in activities unconnected with transport but had developed the requisite skills through a very efficient apprenticeship system. Very few migrants had used technical and vocational institutes to improve their skills and entered the informal sector. Only 3 per cent of migrants with previous job experience were self-taught; those with technical education formed only 1 per cent. The greatest proportion of migrants with previous work experience (56 per cent) underwent a period of on-the-job training for their present careers. This is surprisingly true of those who make the most common switch from agricultural work to petty trading. The remaining 40 per cent indicated that they had learnt the necessary skills prior to migration even though they were in different activities.

The informal sector and opportunities for skill acquisition

The role of the informal sector in skill generation became quite clear when the sample entrepreneurs were asked about the sources of learning skills. Out of 967 heads of enterprises, 383 (mostly in trade) learnt their skills through on-the-job training. A majority of the entrepreneurs, 525 to be precise, acquired their skills through apprenticeship before establishing their business. Only 14 (or 1.4 per cent) of the total went to training institutions to learn the skills. The remaining 45 acquired their skills through self-education.

As expected, entrepreneurs in the professional service with post-secondary qualifications obtained their training from technical institutes. Those who completed secondary school also underwent a period of apprenticeship for most of their activities: this was true in 75 per cent of the cases in tailoring, furniture and metal manufacturing, construction, repair services, restaurant management, taxicab operation and professional services. Only 10 per cent received training in tailoring and construction in a special technical college. In some cases, technical and vocational institute graduates received on-the-job training after entering the business; and in others like printing and glass, construction, repair and professional services (e.g. automobile repairing) prior to actually embarking on business. It is none the less remarkable that over 50 per cent of technical institute graduates did receive training on the job as well. The dominant trend seems to be for secondary school dropouts to undergo a period of apprenticeship for whatever type of activity they entered. Except in petty trading, very few relied on self-tuition.

The situation regarding people who had only completed primary school is remarkably straightforward. Irrespective of the type of activity, 95 per cent of them underwent apprenticeships, the only exception being in retail trading. Primary school leavers were thus able to learn about clothes design and tailoring, leather, wood and cork, and furniture manufacturing, construction and repair. Similar findings hold with respect to people who did not complete their primary schooling or who had only attended Arabic schools. One implication of this trend is the possibility that such extra-mural training could, if properly organised, prove more than a substitute for incomplete primary education.

The enterprise

A majority of the sample enterprises was in fixed locations;
80 per cent had conducted business in the same area for the previous
six months or more prior to the date of the interview. A little
under 5 per cent, mainly hawkers and pedlars, belonged to the
category of both fixed and variable locations. Though only 79 per
cent of all enterprises were one-person ventures to start with,
about 86 per cent of the sample were so at the time of interviewing,
implying a trend towards sole proprietorship. The few who moved in
the direction of joint ventures saw it as a means for escaping
capital constraints, particularly in tailoring, cabinet making and
certain service activities.

Over two-thirds of all businesses are less than five years
old. Indeed over 25 per cent of all enterprises are less than one
year old. The mean age of business is 2.8 years old. This seems to
suggest an increasing awareness of self-employment opportunities as
an alternative to wage employment, especially among those with
little or no formal education. Only one quarter of the sample owned
the premises in which business was conducted. Forty per cent of the
sample were tenants while 14 per cent enjoyed free use of premises.
Tenants included those who paid licences for stalls at market
places. Free use of premises is usually enjoyed by those who
display their wares in front of their dwelling units.

Though the informal sector by definition poses no constraints
to entry in any given activity, a majority of the sample
entrepreneurs in Freetown, 75 per cent, had to cope with one or more
problem(s) in starting their business. When asked about the most
important such constraint, over two-thirds of those responding
stated that raising initial capital was their most difficult
problem. Only 7 per cent referred to lack of premises as the most
difficult obstacle and these were usually relatively large-scale
enterprises wishing to establish business in a strategic location.
Significantly, one quarter of all enterprises reported that they had
no major problems.

In order to overcome their initial problems, 36 per cent of
all enterprises obtained loans to meet their initial capital
requirements. A little over one quarter used their savings in this
direction. Only 16 per cent of the sample were assisted with gifts
from friends or relatives to set up their business. Where official
approval was required for the start of enterprises, proprietors
reported that it was usually granted with the minimum of delay.
Indeed only 14 per cent required official approval. Only 3 per cent
had to train skilled men for starting their business.[1]

Two-thirds of the enterprises worked between eight and 12
hours daily. Twenty-seven per cent worked for over 12 hours a day.
Those who worked less than five hours a day were exclusively women
in the small-scale food manufacturing who had domestic
responsibilities in addition to their business. Taxicab drivers and
tailors usually worked in a shift sytem and were thus able to carry
on business for over 16 hours a day; although they would not
normally admit it, they are never short of apprentices to assist
----

[1] The figures quoted will not add up to 100 per cent since they
do not refer to mutually exclusive categories.

them. These findings, as elsewhere, suggest that there is very little underemployment (in terms of hours worked), if any, in the informal sector.

Employment in the informal sector

Seventy-four per cent of all enterprises had no employees of any sort. The informal sector in Freetown is thus mainly a source of self-employment rather than paid employment. The sample of entrepreneurs argued that the business climate was uncertain and rendered employment of workers a risky proposition. Underlying this was also some fear of unionisation of workers seeking terms and conditions which they as employers would not be able to meet. Turning to the distribution of enterprises by number of workers per enterprise, out of 251 enterprises employing workers, 100 (or about 40 per cent) employed only one person; and 62 (or about 25 per cent) employed two persons. Only about a third of them employed over two workers. The total number of workers employed by 251 enterprises was 835. Thus, including the entrepreneur himself, the sample enterprises provided employment for 1,802 persons, 54 per cent in the form of self-employment and 46 in the form of paid or unpaid employees. The average size of the enterprise in terms of number of persons thus works out to 1.86.

About 84 per cent of the workers were males; very few females were engaged as paid or unpaid employees. Only 57 per cent of those employed were paid regular wages; about half of those not receiving regular wages were in the tailoring, furniture-making and retail trade activity, either as apprentices or as unpaid family workers. Both in paid and unpaid employment males formed an overwhelming majority: 87 per cent and 83 per cent respectively.

How many of the employees are employed on a full-time and part-time basis? Among those reporting, 87 per cent were employed on a full-time basis, while the remaining worked on a part-time basis. Most of the few who are employed on a part-time basis do not receive any regular wages and are mainly employed in retail trade and restaurant activities, and to a lesser extent in tailoring. The data also show that about 60 per cent of regular wage employment is in the trade sector while manufacturing accounts for only 16 per cent. In contrast, 46 per cent of those not having a regular wage employment are in manufacturing activity while the trade sector accounts for only 28 per cent; in other words, manufacturing enterprises take on relatively more non-wage employees, presumably as apprentices.

Wage and non-wage employment is more important in certain activities than in others. For example, 84 per cent of trade enterprises did not have even one employee in contrast to 54 per cent in manufacturing and transport and 30 per cent in construction. Thus, the enterprises engaged in non-trade activities tend to be larger in terms of the number of workers.

Turning to the age structure of the workforce, the study showed that about 85 per cent of the employees were 30 years or above; in other words, the workers were not young starting their working career - contrary to the general expectation. The median age of workers seems to be around 37 years. In terms of education, 80 per cent of the workers had primary-level education or less; in fact, nearly 60 per cent had never attended school. Less than 4 per cent of the workers had completed secondary schooling. These findings raise a question about the workers' mobility: does it mean that the workers are satisfied with their status or that they are unable to become self-employed in their own right? In the absence of data on the number of years with the present enterprise, it is difficult to answer the above satisfactorily.

As in the case of the entrepreneurs, 80 per cent of the workers were born outside Freetown; but only half of them had migrated during the preceding five years. In other words, even though many workers had migrated more than five years earlier they seem to have remained as workers. Since a relatively greater proportion of recent (under five years) migrants is to be found in manufacturing, skill acquisition seems to be an important motive in migration.

A partial answer to the question raised earlier about the workers" mobility emerged when the entrepreneurs were asked about the present career of former employees. Sixty-two per cent of the latter were self-employed in the same line of business and 8 per cent in another line of business; only 8 per cent were paid employees in a similar activity and 3 per cent in another kind of activity. These findings suggest that there is some mobility from worker status to self-employed. The survey data however showed that nearly a fifth of the former employees were reportedly unemployed, due to frictional or other factors.

It was noted earlier that 57 per cent of the employees were on regular wage employment. The sample enterprises paid a total of 4,834 Leones towards the wage bill for paid workers which implies an average wage per person of about 11 Leones (or approximately 11 US dollars) per month. The average wage however showed considerable variations between different activities; it was as little as 5.5 Leones in trade as compared to 13 Leones in manufacturing, and 27 Leones in construction. After making allowance for some part-time wage employment in the sample, the average wage of full-time workers in the informal sector of Freetown seems to have been somewhat higher than 11 Leones per month; but it is still lower than the legal minimum wage.

Turning to workers without regular wages, half of them get regular meals, shelter and training in skills relevant to their job. This applies mainly to workers in manufacturing, transport and some service activities. This pattern applies without exception to foreign workers who usually arrive under the sponsorship of their bosses. Foulahs going into tailoring and transport, and Susu immigrants going into the vehicle repair business arrive from the Republic of Guinea to undergo training with relatives already established in business. In addition to professional training, they assist with domestic chores thus reducing any expenditure that would have occurred in that direction. Those who receive only food and shelter accounted for 26 per cent and were usually in the trade sector where there was little to be taught; 11 per cent received food and training but no shelter; and 13 per cent mainly indigenous workers received training only. The practice of providing training (without wages) is quite common in the fields of radio, television and motor vehicle repairs in the service sector, the justification being that similar training in formal establishments was more expensive and that the masters in the informal sector were training

Table 2: Capital-labour ratio by main activity

Activity	Value of capital* (Leones)	Number of enter-prises	Number of workers	Number of workers (including owner)	Capital* per worker (Leones)
Manufacturing	24 725	195	243	438	56.6
Food, tobacco, etc.	2 664	36	26	62	43.0
Textile	397	9	10	19	20.9
Wearing apparel	12 176	72	89	161	75.6
Leather and footwear	1 945	22	11	33	58.9
Wood, cork and furniture	4 310	37	84	121	35.6
Printing, glass and metal	3 303	19	23	42	78.6
Construction	2 447	20	82	102	24.0
Trade	25 124	628	388	1 016	24.7
Retail trade	13 973	550	236	786	17.8
Restaurants	11 151	78	152	230	48.5
Transport	4 137	37	37	74	55.9
Services	8 773	87	85	172	51.0
Repairs	2 113	47	27	74	28.6
Other	6 660	40	58	98	68.0
All	65 276	967	835	1 802	36.2

* Excludes buildings and working capital.

Table 3: Gross value of output per worker by main activity

	Gross value of output (Leones per month)		
	Total for sample enterprises	Per enterprise	Per worker
Manufacturing	28 121	144	64
Food, tobacco, etc.	6 031	168	97
Textile	1 724	192	91
Wearing apparel	8 808	122	55
Leather and footwear	1 490	68	45
Wood, cork and furniture	6 691	181	55
Printing, glass and metal	3 377	178	80
Construction	7 640	382	75
Trade	82 956	132	82
Retail trade	61 261	111	78
Restaurants	21 695	278	94
Transport	8 465	229	114
Services	11 220	129	65
Repairs	3 654	78	49
Other	7 566	189	77
All	138 402	143	77

potential competitors. Total expenditure on non-wage workers was
3,431 Leones for the sample as a whole which implies an average
compensation per worker of a little under 10 Leones per month.

Capital

Eighty per cent of the sample owned capital equipment as
defined for the purpose of this survey (i.e. machines, tools,
furniture and fixtures, vehicles), 20 per cent did not own any. For
most of the owners such equipment was cheap and locally made by
other small enterprises. Of those owning any equipment, 50 per cent
had equipment costing only up to 25 Leones, and 14 per cent had
equipment valued at between 26 and 50 Leones. These two groups were
mainly traders. Another 12 per cent owned equipment valued between
51 and 100 Leones, mainly non-mechanised transport operators and
some service workers. Twenty-one per cent possessed equipment
costing between 101 and 500 Leones. The remaining 3 per cent owned
a capital equipment worth over 500 Leones; and they were mostly in
the mechanised transport, metal manufacturing and service sectors.

It is generally acknowledged that the informal sector
enterprises use very little capital per worker relative to the
formal sector. Table 2 shows not only the distribution of capital
(other than building) among enterprises in various activities but
also the capital per worker separately for each activity. On the
average, the informal sector in Freetown uses only 36 Leones per
worker; but the capital labour ratio shows considerable variations
between activities, as expected. The most capital-intensive among
the activities is of course manufacturing. Within manufacturing,
manufacture of wearing apparel (tailoring) and manufacture of
printing, glass and metal (which consists mainly of metal-working
enterprises) need relatively more capital per worker - viz. 76 and
79 Leones respectively. The least capital intensive is of course
the retail trading activities; if, however, capital is defined to
include the value of buildings and working capital as well, the
picture might change somewhat. In terms of the net worth, over half
of all enterprises had an estimated value of 100 Leones or less. A
further 23 per cent estimated their business as worth between 100
and 250 Leones. Fourteen per cent were valued at between 250 and
500 Leones. Eight per cent were worth between 500 and 1,000 Leones
and the rest were ranged from over 1,000 to 6,500 Leones in value.

Sales and output

Forty per cent of all enterprises had sales less than 50
Leones per month. About one-quarter had sales worth between 51 and
100 Leones. Another one-fifth had sales between 101 and 200 Leones.
Twelve per cent had a monthly sales of between 201 and 500 Leones,
mostly in the furniture manufacturing category. Four per cent sold
goods and services worth over 500 Leones. The last category
typifies the volume of business conducted in the transport and
construction sectors. The first two categories with a monthly sales
of under 100 Leones were largely concentrated in the trade sector
where they were in competition with many similar enterprises for a
limited number of clients. Mechanised transport is proving to be a
very lucrative undertaking; it has, over the last decade, attracted
a growing number of entrepreneurs. The average value of sales per
enterprise works out to 134 Leones per month.

Prior to the execution of the survey, it was believed that failure to recover debts led to the forced liquidations of enterprises giving credit. It was also hypothesised that offering credit facilities to clients was a means of expanding clientele for businesses. The results of the survey raised some doubts in this regard since they showed that over 60 per cent of enterprises gave no credit, that one-third gave under 50 Leones worth of credit monthly, that only 3 per cent gave between 51 and 100 Leones worth of credit. On further investigation, certain distinct features emerged. Businesses with large capital gave credit to only those whom they considered easily accountable, especially those with steady incomes. Another feature was that credit was given by businesses to those clients who had no choice of getting necessary items from elsewhere. The use or threatened use of socio-ritual sanctions has also reduced the incidence of bad debtor problems.

The sample enterprises had a gross value of output of 138,402 Leones per month or about 143 Leones per month per enterprise. The average gross value of output per person was 77 Leones per month (or 900 Leones per year) though it showed significant variations between activities. Gross value added, obtained as a residual from the gross value of output after deducting the expenses on goods and services used in the business works out to 97,085 Leones per month for the sample as a whole, or 100 Leones per enterprise per month. Gross value added per worker is estimated at 54 Leones per month. A word of caution however is in order in interpreting these figures; since the rental expenses on premises were included under expenses on goods and services only for enterprise renting such premises, the estimate of gross value added is distorted. Nevertheless, these figures do suggest the following: first, the "informal" sector in Freetown seems to contribute substantially to the GNP, assuming that 40 to 50,000 workers in the city are in the informal sector; second, since the capital employed is small relative to value added, the relative share of wages in value added seems to be quite high.

Net revenue to the entrepreneur

It was noted earlier that the sample enterprises paid out 4,834 Leones per month as wages to hired workers; and in addition they also paid a sum of 3,431 Leones per month for non-wage workers. One can therefore estimate the net return to the entrepreneur by deducting these expenses from the gross value added. The net return to all sample entrepreneurs thus works out to 88,820 Leones per month or 92 Leones per entrepreneur per month on the average. Needless to add, this figure represents not only the return to his labour but also the return to his capital invested in the business. Even so, it would appear that the informal sector entrepreneurs in Freetown earn a respectable amount compared to workers with a similar background in the formal sector. The net return to entrepreneurs however shows considerable variations between activities as can be seen from table 4; it varies from as little as 47 Leones per month for those in repair services to as high as 247 Leones per month for those in construction.

Table 4: Net revenue to the entrepreneur by
          main activity (Leones per month)

Activity	Net revenue	
	Total for the sample	Per entrepreneur
Manufacturing	18 333	94
Food, tobacco, etc.	4 471	124
Textile	1 198	133
Wearing apparel	5 607	78
Leather, footwear	1 000	45
Wood, cork and furniture	4 445	120
Printing, glass and metal	1 612	85
Construction	4 949	247
Trade	52 796	84
Retail trade	39 614	72
Restaurants	13 182	169
Transport	4 957	134
Services	7 785	89
Repair services	2 231	47
Other	5 554	139
All	88 820	92

Backward linkages

One of the several themes pertaining to the informal sector is its link with the formal sector. The Freetown study showed that the informal sector enterprises, many of them being in trade, bought their goods mainly from retailers; 38 per cent from foreign retailers, 6 per cent from large local retailers, 24 per cent from small traders within the informal sector as compared to 8 per cent from wholesalers; and most of the remaining depended on a combination of the above.

Turning to specific activities, food and tobacco manufacturing, manual transport, eating houses bought most of the goods and services relating to their business from small indigenous traders; over 50 per cent of the respondents indicated this as the case. At the other extreme, entrepreneurs in textile manufacture, tailoring and dressmaking, footwear manufacturing bought materials for their work mainly from big foreign retailers. Fifty per cent of retail traders, one-third of those engaged in repair services and 50 per cent of the service enterprises bought mainly from big foreign business enterprises. In terms of a duality of formal and non-formal enterprises, only enterprises in food and leather manufacturing and non-mechanised transport escape the grip of the formal sector. The rest of the industrial activities are by their nature closely tied to the formal sector in a distinctly subordinate one-sided relationship.

With regard to the sources of finance for investment, three-quarters of all enterprises reinvest their savings derived from profits back into their business. Mutual credit associations provide loans for 9 per cent of the enterprises while only 2 per cent obtained credit from banks and other financial institutions. About 13 per cent relied on friends and relatives for their credit needs. These findings confirm the difficulty of obtaining loans for investment noted earlier.

About half of these enterprises contemplate expansions on a major scale but cannot obtain the necessary loan facilities. Most entrepreneurs at this level of business activity see banks and other financial institutions as impersonal and hostile structures. They feel a sense of helplessness and inadequacy vis-à-vis the articulateness and self-assurance of the administrators in these institutions. Informal and closer discussions with respondents in this sample revealed the following assessment of their opinion of credit facilities as provided by the financial institutions. Firstly, banks exist for foreign big business and powerful indigenous figures. With their insistence on the production of a surety from people who cannot readily produce it they operate a vicious circle to the advantage of Lebanese and Indians and to the disadvantage of the small businessman. Secondly, entrepreneurs see a perpetuation of this impasse because they, unlike the Asian businessman, lack the necessary financial support of relatives or friends to be able to obtain loans. Through informal contacts already established between the foreign business community and financial institutions, the former enjoy a veritable monopoly in terms of loan facilities. The current Credit Guarantee Scheme launched by the Government through the Central Bank has so far done little by way of supporting small businesses. The definition of small business under the scheme is one whose capital is not in excess of 150,000 Leones. This should qualify all the sample enterprises as eligible for loans; but only 2 per cent have enjoyed such facilities. Most beneficiaries of the schemes are foreign businessmen, because a prerequisite is that candidates be nominated by their commercial banks, who in turn only nominate their current account holders, thus automatically excluding all those who earn under 2,000 Leones per annum and therefore many small businesses in the process. Entrepreneurs born in Freetown seemed to have greater access to bank loans than others. Fifty-five per cent of those receiving bank loans were born in Freetown whereas no non-Sierra Leoneans reported receiving loans from the bank. Northern province was next to Freetown with 20 per cent share of bank loans. Though 70 per cent of those obtaining loans from the banks had above primary level of schooling, it is difficult to conclude that higher education leads to greater access to bank loans since only 17 per cent of entrepreneurs belonged to this educational category.

Finally, with regard to links with training institutions, it was already noted that a vast majority of the informal sector entrepreneurs acquired their skills through on-the-job training or through apprenticeship. Very few, if at all, relied on formal training institutions such as vocational training centres for learning the skills.

Forward linkages

It may be recalled that about two-thirds of the sample enter-prises were engaged in trade and restaurant activities. About two-thirds of all traders dealt in goods consumed daily; and most petty traders and hawkers could be found in this category. About 12 per cent sold household durables, which required a larger capital base and a fixed location. The study sought an explanation for this phenomenon and it was then discovered that trading in everyday consumer goods required very little capital whereas business in the other commercial subsectors required relatively more capital investment. Trading in daily consumer goods would seem to facilitate entry into activities requiring heavy capital investment. Consequently, this subsector also attracted most of the new entrants into the informal sector.

In terms of forward linkages, two factors of significance appear from the data. The first is that most businesses sold almost exclusively to individuals and households (81 per cent of all). Secondly, at the other end of the scale, only 1.1 per cent sold their goods and services to big business, i.e. government agencies, big foreign and Sierra Leonean wholesalers and retailers combined. The rest sold their goods and services to small enterprises and several of the above. It is also interesting to note that a much larger proportion of the younger entrepreneurs (below 34 years of age) sold their goods and services to individuals and households suggesting that most of them are engaged in consumer goods related activities. In relation to the size of the enterprise (i.e. number of workers per enterprise), there is a clear trend suggesting that larger ones have greater forward linkages. Eighty per cent of the one-man enterprises sold their goods and services to individuals and households as compared to 80, 69 and 60 per cent respectively for enterprises having 2, 3 to 5 and over 6 persons.

These findings raise the question of whether the linkages between the small and big business sectors are not unduly one-sided. There are certain services provided by the informal sector which in terms of quality are favourably comparable to those provided by the formal sector and are cheaper. Since some of these services are also required by the formal sector, it would seem possible to promote demand for such services. Besides inherent weaknesses of the informal sector enterprises, the protective measures (e.g. Retail Trades Act) designed to help small businesses in this regard also seem to have worked against their interest.

Competition

Eighty-four per cent of the enterpreneurs responding said that there were too many enterprises similar to their own in Freetown; only 4 per cent felt that there were too few. Those complaining the presence of too many such enterprises were of course greater in tailoring (94 per cent), furniture manufacturing (87 per cent), printing and glass manufacturing (100 per cent), retail trade (87 per cent), restaurant (89 per cent) and taxicab operating (90 per cent) activities. These findings could also be interpreted as a constraint on the market demand for, when asked about competition from larger firms, only about 6 per cent of all enterprises felt that the presence of larger firms in the formal sector had a positive and beneficial influence on them. This constrasted with 94 per cent who felt that the presence of larger firms was detrimental to their survival let alone prosperity. Larger firms, the respondents felt, had an almost exclusive monopoly over access to loans and to debt relief.

Constraints on expansion

Just under one third of all enterprises reported increases in the volume of business conducted, 30 per cent reported no change whilst about 34 per cent reported a decrease in the volume of business. Even allowing for errors in subjective assessment, it is remarkable that about two-thirds of all enterprises were not by their own standards thriving. This has implications for labour absorption in the informal sector. Entrepreneurs are operating in what they consider to be an uncertain business climate and accordingly consider it unprofitable to commit themselves to employing more personnel even if for low wages. A majority of those reporting increase in the volume of business seems to have undertaken some kind of an innovation or diversification in their enterprises leading to an increase in the number of clients. Significantly, one-fifth of all respondents were satisfied with the present situation and saw no need to improve their business. The rest attributed stagnation and decline in volume of business to causes originating from lack of capital or ideas and, in a few cases, to inadequate incentives and domination by big enterprises.

The activities where more than a third of the enterprises reported an increase in the volume of business were: food processing (35 per cent), wood and cork manufacturing (80 per cent), construction (41 per cent), hawkers and pedlars in retail trade (43 per cent), repair services (47 per cent) and taxicab operation (56 per cent). It is also interesting to note that the proportion reporting an increase in volume of business decreases with age of the entrepreneur; and the proportion of those complaining a decrease tends to rise with the age.

When asked about the most difficult obstacle for expansion, 52 per cent reported lack of loan and credit facilities, while 28 per cent (particularly in retail trade) regarded the lack of sufficient numbers of clients as their most difficult obstacle. Surprisingly few (8 per cent) complained of heavy taxes with another 10 per cent stressing the dominant position of large foreign enterprises as an obstacle. The non-repayment of debts did not feature as a major obstacle to expansion as was hypothesised since less than 2 per cent regarded it as such. About 4 per cent of the sample enterprises did not wish to expand; they refused to, or were unable to, imagine the problems of managing an enterprise larger than the present one.

The emphasis on various obstacles to expansion showed variations between activities. Between 60 and 83 per cent of respondents in the following activities reported the lack of loan facilities as their greatest problem: food, textile, leather, wood and cork, and furniture manufacturing and construction. Of those in tailoring, repair services and retail trade about 50 per cent regarded lack of loans as a major problem. For manual transport operators and glass manufacturers lack of clients was a more pressing problem, as was the case with footwear manufacturers, especially since they competed directly with the plastic and rubber footwear manufacturers. The taxicab operators had two different problems: heavy taxation and unfair domination of the larger enterprises, especially in relation to the price of car accessories.

What about the constraints on mobility between different activities? The data on age composition of the enterprises by activity suggest that whereas 82 per cent of the enterprises under one year old were in trade (including repair) activities, only 53 per cent of the enterprises above 20 years of age belonged to this category. Similarly, only 13 per cent of the enterprises under one year of age were in manufacturing as compared to 38 per cent in the classification "above 20 years". These figures seem to imply that the entry point for a large majority of informal sector entrepreneurs is the trade and repair activities and that many of them manage to penetrate into other sectors over time. It is not clear, however, whether this belated entry into other sectors is due to barriers of entry (notably lack of capital and skills) initially. This line of argument, however, assumes that the older enterprises followed the same pattern of entry as the recent ones.

The question of mobility between activities, in so far as it hinges on the time factor, would also seem to have implications for employment in the informal sector. The survey data show that older firms employ more workers. For example, 85 per cent of the enterprises which came into existence during the year preceding the survey did not employ any workers as compared to 62 per cent of the firms which had been in existence for between five and ten years; in other words, a larger proportion of the older enterprises created additional employment. The evidence also suggests that a greater percentage of the older firms is also larger in terms of number of workers; as compared to only 1.6 per cent of recent firms there were 7.5 per cent of older firms (i.e. between ten and 20 years) which employed over six workers.

Another related question is the entrepreneurs' preference for wage employment as opposed to self-employment. It is sometimes argued that the informal sector is a transitory phenomenon in so far as the entrepreneurs are really interested in a formal sector job. The survey data from Freetown seem to negate this view; when respondents were asked to name the type of work they would ideally prefer to do, only one quarter opted to seek wage employment. About 54 per cent elected to continue exclusively in their present activity, showing a considerable amount of commitment to the sector's activity. In addition, 7 per cent, although wishing to operate a business other than their present one, would nevertheless remain in self-employment. Entrepreneurs within the 15-19 age cohorts showed the greatest desire for wage employment only (54 per cent). The desire for wage employment decreased uniformly as participants advanced in age. Indeed, only 21 per cent of the 35-39 age cohort would ideally prefer wage employment only. In contrast, the older age group showed greater commitment to staying in their present occupation than the younger ones. Only 30 per cent within the 15-19 age group would prefer to stay in their present occupation whereas over two-thirds of the 35-39 age set opted for this. However, it is significant that the 20-24 and 25-29 age cohorts showed a stronger commitment to stay in the informal sector than was anticipated; 60 per cent would remain in self-employment at all costs.

It was hypothesised that the higher the level of education the greater would be the tendency to seek wage employment. However, 78 per cent of those who had completed secondary education chose to stay in self-employment against only 22 per cent who desired wage employment. The same pattern was observed among owners who had post-secondary education or technical qualifications; they chose to continue in self-employment in preference to wage employment at a ratio of 2:1. Dropouts from vocational schools and primary schools preferred wage employment because it offered a better financial reward than their present vocation, even allowing for the fact that they were only hoping to get semi-skilled or unskilled jobs.

In relation to migration, 39 and 32 per cent of the entrepreneurs from eastern and northern provinces respectively preferred wage employment as compared to 17 per cent for Freetown-born entrepreneurs. In fact about 60 per cent of the migrants prefered to continue in the informal sector. Women entrepreneurs showed a stronger preference to continue in the informal sector (about 80 per cent). As expected, the proportion willing to continue in this sector increases with the age of the enterprise.

Finally, in response to a hypothetical question on the kinds of government assistance most needed, 64 per cent requested provision of loan facilities for their business. Nineteen per cent felt that the Government, being the largest contractor in many spheres, could give some contracts to them. Only 7 per cent would have the Government abolish taxes altogether; and 8 per cent suggested stricter control over larger enterprise domination. Provision of skills and abolition of licences were major issues for less than 1 per cent of the study sample.

Conclusion

The Freetown study shows that migration is closely linked to the informal sector. A substantial part of the migrants originate from outside the country, notably from Guinea. The migrants are younger and have little education, skills and capital. They nevertheless seem to gain entry into the informal sector by acquiring the necessary skills on the job or through apprenticeship within the informal sector. Many of them manage to acquire the necessary capital through own savings and establish their own business as their duration of stay in Freetown increases. A good number of them seem to enter the tertiary sector owing to its low capital and skill requirements. The evidence seems to suggest that there is some upward mobility in the sense that a greater proportion of the older enterprises is to be found in manufacturing and related activities requiring relatively more capital and skills. Though a substantial number of the migrants were unemployed before, many were previously employed notably in agriculture. Thus the informal sector seems to play a vital role in bringing about the change from agricultural to non-agricultural occupations. Few women seem to participate in the informal sector either as "heads" or as "workers". Most of the enterprises are single person units, concentrated in the tertiary activities. Capital per worker is low; yet the average income of the entrepreneurs is significantly higher than the legal minimum wage or the wage for comparable labour in the formal sector. But the few wage workers, mainly in manufacturing and related activities seem to earn below the legal minimum wage even though the enterprises work long hours.

Though there is a significant dependence on non-indigenous enterprises for inputs and much of the informal sector is starved of capital from the banking system, the major problem confronting these enterprises seems to be one of competition within the informal sector, particularly in trade. This is partly due to the fact that the number of enterprises, mainly in trade, has been growing at an incredibly high rate of about 35 per cent per year. One of the key questions therefore seems to be: how can the emerging enterprises be assisted to move into more lucrative and productive activities and over a shorter period of time?

O.J. Fapohunda[1]

    As in the case of Freetown, the Lagos study focused also on a
wide range of activities including a few enterprises in primary
industries relating to agriculture and mining and utilities; but the
sample size was more than twice as large (about 2,000 enterprises).
A distinguishing feature of the study was that the sample included
a greater proportion of manufacturing and service activities; 40 per
cent of the enterprises from manufacturing and 15 per cent from
services in contrast to 31 per cent from trade including restaurants
(table 1).   The Lagos study is particularly interesting in view of
its emphasis on human resources utilisation and development.

Table 1:   Distribution of enterprises
           by main activity groups

Type of industry or economic activity group	No. of reporting enterprises	Percentage distribution of enterprises
Primary industries	18	0.9
Food and beverages and tobacco	17	0.8
Textiles and leather	549	26.5
Wood and furniture	108	5.2
Paper and paper products	58	2.8
Fabricated metal and machine equipment	51	2.5
Others manufacturing	48	2.3
Utilities	44	2.1
Construction	22	1.1
Wholesale trade	116	5.6
Retail trade	526	25.4
Transport and storage	74	3.6
Communication and social and personal services	320	15.4
Inadequately defined activities	123	5.9
Total	2 074	100.0

The entrepreneurs

    The population of Lagos more than doubled in the ten years
between 1953 and 1963, from 267,000 to 665,000. The population of
Greater Lagos increased by more than twice between 1963 and 1976,

----

    [1] Human Resources Unit (University of Lagos).   The study was
carried out in close collaboration with the Federal Office of
Statistics in Nigeria.

from 1.14 million to 3.55 million. Needless to add, migration played a prominent role in this process. Only 5 per cent of the sample entrepreneurs belonged to Lagos State; as much as 87 per cent came from other States of Nigeria and the remaining 8 per cent from outside Nigeria. Though migrants came from various parts of Nigeria, 57 per cent came from nearby States like Ogun, Oyo and Ondo, within about 350 kilometres from Lagos. Further, 85 per cent of the migrant entrepreneurs came from rural areas.

Though about 70 per cent of the female labour force in Lagos in 1963 was in petty trading and other related occupations, owing to the sampling procedures adopted and the representation of several activities in the sample, only 15 per cent of the heads were females.

In terms of education, 11 per cent of the entrepreneurs had no education at all, while 13 per cent had some informal education. Thus, about three-quarters had at least some formal education. Of these, 75 per cent had six years or less schooling. In other words, about a quarter of those with formal schooling had education beyond the primary level. For entrepreneurs with a formal education, the mean level of schooling is 5.89 years. In this context it is worth noting that Lagos has enjoyed free primary education since 1955 even though the Universal Free Primary Education Scheme came into operation on a countrywide basis from 1976 only.

A vast majority of those with informal education (about 86 per cent) had, however, job-oriented training. Over half of them relied on relatives, friends or neighbours; most of the remaining acquired their skills through on-the-job training in small enterprises or the apprenticeship system. For the entrepreneurs in the sample as a whole, half of them acquired such job-oriented skills from neighbours, friends and relatives (30 per cent) and employers (25 per cent).

The study sought to ascertain whether the informal sector entrepreneurs were better off as compared to their parents by collecting information on the parents' occupation. As it turned out, nearly two-thirds of the fathers of the sample entrepreneurs were engaged as agricultural and related workers; only 11 per cent of them belonged to "production and related workers" and 12 per cent to "sales workers". In contrast, under 1 per cent of the sample entrepreneurs belonged to the "agricultural and related workers" category. It is also interesting to note that a vast majority of the parents engaged in agriculture (87 per cent) owned the land they farmed. These changes would seem to imply a significant shift in job preferences and/or opportunities, from agriculture-oriented rural jobs to non-agriculture-oriented urban informal sector jobs.

How did such a transformation take place? It was already noted that the vast majority of the entrepreneurs migrated to Lagos. Thirty per cent of the entrepreneurs came to Lagos during the five years preceding the date of interview; and 25 per cent had been in Lagos between five and ten years. Thus, about half of the sample entrepreneurs had been in Lagos longer than ten years. The mean duration of residence in Lagos seems to be 9.4 years. And yet these entrepreneurs seem to maintain significant ties with their respective places of origin. Over a quarter of them visited their native place once a year and about 40 per cent several times a year; only about 15 per cent never returned to their native place. The evidence suggests that not only a significant part of the informal sector earnings in Lagos goes to other regions but also such close ties seem to contribute to further flow of migrants to Lagos, through personal contacts of those visiting.

Over 7C per cent of the entrepreneurs did not have a paid employment before coming to Lagos; in fact most of them were unemployed, as compared to 45 per cent in the case of Freetown. Those who did work before worked in a wide range of occupations. Thus, a good many of the entrepreneurs seem to have migrated not only to improve their income and employment opportunities but also to improve their skills. Half of those unemployed before were now engaged in manufacturing and related activities as production workers; only 27 per cent as sales workers in trade activity. These figures suggest that the Lagos informal sector provides significant opportunities for rural unemployed not only in the trade sector requiring little skills but also in the manufacturing sector requiring considerable skills. In other words, the Lagos informal sector provides both opportunities for skill acquisition and self-employment.

Labour market

Very few of the entrepreneurs (20 per cent) knew about the employment offices and tried to seek a job through them; 57 per cent never used them and the remaining did not even know about them. With regard to current employment situations in general, only about 11 per cent cf the sample entrepreneurs felt that they could get another job if they quit the present one. As a matter of fact, 78 per cent of the entrepreneurs felt satisfied with their present jobs; of the remaining, half wanted to change their jobs but in a similar line of activity.

The study sought to assess whether provision of new skills could contribute to better occupational mobility and hence greater income prospects. Though 10 per cent of the entrepreneurs would welcome such opportunities provided there is no loss of income, the majority (about 80 per cent) was not keen in changing their job. As a matter of fact, very few wanted wage employment.

Earnings

Turning to the earnings of entrepreneurs, a total of 1,744 heads of enterprises reported a mean income per month of ₦99, substantially above the legal minimum wage of ₦60 per month. Owing to considerable variations between enterprises, the average quoted above is deceptive; the median income, however, turns out to be only ₦50 per month suggesting that well over half of the entrepreneurs in the Lagos informal sector received an income below the legal minimum. Even though many were satisfied with their current occupation, in terms of real earnings the entrepreneurs do not seem to have improved their positions. Nearly half of the entrepreneurs responding felt that new entrants in a business similar to their own would be earning as much as they do; in fact, over a quarter stated that new entrants in their field would be earning more than themselves.

Wage employment and skill development

The sample of 2,074 enterprises also generated additional employment and provided training opportunities to several workers. Excluding a few cases of non-response, a total of 1,977 enterprises provided employment to a total of 4,161 full-time workers (including the heads). Thus, the informal sector employed on the average a little over two persons (2.10) per enterprise. The size of enterprise, however, showed considerable variations. Half of the sample enterprises had only one person - that is the entrepreneur himself; and 26 per cent of the enterprises had two workers each. Only a quarter of the sample had three or more persons. Though full-time regular workers was the dominant category, some 3.5 per cent of the sample also employed part-time male workers and 0.7 per cent part-time female workers. In addition, a few resorted to hiring casual workers as well. Nearly 90 per cent of the employment in responding enterprises was males.

The average level of schooling of workers appeared to be somewhat lower than that of the entrepreneurs. Though the highest level of education attained by workers varied between the enterprises, the median was around six years of schooling. Little over 10 per cent of the full-time workers had more than primary-level education.

Lack of relevant skills and experience does not seem to affect employment opportunities in the informal sector. Of those enterprises hiring workers, close to 90 per cent indicated that they hire people even if they do not possess the necessary skills and experience; presumably they are trained on the job, as apprentices. Of 1,206 enterprises that employ apprentices, three-quarters of them did not pay any wages; 15 per cent of such enterprises paid reduced wages to the apprentices; the remaining 10 per cent paid full wages to the apprentices.

Since most of the apprentices do not receive any wage, there seems to be considerable labour turnover. Fifty-six per cent of the apprentices left the enterprise that taught the skills, on completion of the training. In addition, a few (8 per cent) left before completion of training, presumably for more remunerative jobs. Further, many of the former apprentices seem to be establishing enterprises of their own. Of the remaining who stay with the enterprises, about half of them leave in three or four years following the training period. The informal sector in Lagos thus serves as a training ground for many ill-educated young workers who wish to become self-employed.

Despite some 6 to 7 per cent unemployment in Lagos, the informal sector enterprises seem to be confronted with shortages in certain types of labour. A third of the enterprises experienced difficulty in recruiting both skilled and unskilled workers and another 13 per cent found it difficult to hire unskilled workers only. Apparently much of this shortage can be explained in terms of poor working conditions including low wages.

Wage and working conditions

Over 60 per cent of establishments employing workers reported that at least some of their workers do not receive any wages, presumably because they are apprentices. Among those who do pay wages, 29 per cent paid in cash only, 30 per cent in both cash and kind, and 41 per cent in kind only. Payment in kind, mainly in the form of food and shelter, generally apply to apprentices. In terms of the frequency of wage payment, about a third of the enterprises paid on a daily basis, a quarter paid on a monthly basis, and most of the remaining paid on an irregular basis. With regard to wage increments, only a sixth of the enterprises gave an automatic annual increment.

What about the wages paid in the informal sector? Based on the response from 619 enterprises, the average minimum monthly wage for males is about ₦35 and the maximum ₦52; corresponding figures for females based on the response from 133 enterprises are ₦26 and ₦40 respectively. These figures are significantly lower than the legal minimum wage of ₦60 per month. And yet less than a quarter of the enterprises reported losing workers during the preceding year; the majority, 73 per cent, did not lose any workers at all. Finally, in terms of hours of work, 92 per cent of the enterprises operated for longer than 9 hours per day.

The informal sector entrepreneur and his household

Having discussed the role of the informal sector in providing employment and training opportunities for the head of the enterprises and the employees, it will be useful to see its implications for the entrepreneurs' household members. A substantial number of the entrepreneurs, 869 out of 2,074, or 42 per cent, did not have any dependants or did not live with their families in Lagos. For the remaining 1,205 entrepreneurs, the average number of dependants works out to 6.52 persons, 81 per cent of them under the age of 14. Given this high dependency ratio, it is clear that most of the entrepreneurs, notwithstanding the reasonable level of income earned in the informal sector, must be living in conditions of poverty. Some of these entrepreneurs however do have a secondary income earner in their respective households; about 659 entrepreneurs (out of 1,205) reported so. A majority of them (463) are regular full-time workers while the remaining are either part-time or casual workers.

What is the source of income for these secondary earners? Interestingly enough, 99 out of 659 entrepreneurs said that the secondary earners are employed in the formal sector (government or large commercial enterprises). A majority of the secondary earners, 352 out of 659, were self-employed in the informal sector; and 87 were wage employees in the informal sector. The remaining 120 entrepreneurs were unable to clearly identify the source of employment for their secondary earners. When asked about their contribution to household income it was discovered that only about a half of the secondary earners were actually making such a contribution, implying that the remaining, even though working, were presumably learning skills or engaged as unpaid family workers. The mean contribution to household income worked out to be ₦38 per month, the corresponding median being ₦25 per month. These contributions, though significant, are considerably lower than the entrepreneurs' own.

What is more disturbing is that 364 entrepreneurs (out of 1,205 with dependants) reported household members who are unemployed and looking for a job. Though the mean duration of unemployment was around six months, nearly 30 per cent of the unemployed had been looking for a job for over one year. Given the close link to the informal sector through the entrepeneur and the ease of entry, one would have expected the unemployed, most of them new entrants to the labour force, to be absorbed in the informal sector itself. But it is difficult to resolve this issue without further evidence on their educational characteristics and motivations.

The enterprise

The evidence presented above suggests the need to ameliorate the employment and income situation of the informal sector participants. Obviously, it cannot be done without further analysis of the data pertaining to the activities themselves. An attempt therefore is made below to throw light on the conditions under which employment and income are generated in the informal sector.

About 93 per cent of these enterprises are owned on an individual basis, the remaining being mostly partnerships. Similarly, 92 per cent were in fixed locations; of these nearly two-thirds are in permanent structures, and the remaining in temporary structures. Further, 61 per cent of them were located as part of a residential unit, while 39 per cent were in non-residential units. Fifty-six per cent of them were in residential locations, while 40 per cent were in areas consisting of mainly commercial buildings. In fact, 24 per cent of the heads of enterprises lived in the premises, 31 per cent lived in the same neighbourhood, and 16 per cent lived within one kilometer from their business premises. Unlike in some other countries, about 81 per cent of the premises are rented and only 8 per cent are fully or partially owned by the entrepreneurs; most of the remaining are neither owned nor rented. Though a majority, about 71 per cent, have remained in the same location since the establishment of business, it is interesting to note that about 30 per cent have changed locations, given that the average age of enterprises is only 5.4 years.

In terms of access to utilities like water and electricity, only a quarter of the enterprises had both and another 50 per cent had electricity only; most of the remaining had neither. Lack of adequate water supply would thus seem to be a major bottleneck. Licence requirement does not pose a threat to the informal sector in Lagos; about three-quarters of the enterprises said that they did not require a licence for operation.

Capital

A large majority, 1,634 out of 2,074 enterprises, possessed at least some capital equipment. Over 90 per cent of them acquired it new, while most of the rest bought them second-hand; a few even constructed their own equipment. The median value of such equipment per enterprise was close to ₦250 even though the mean value was around ₦450; in other words a large majority of the enterprises (about 70 per cent) possessed less than the mean value. Given the median size of enterprise of one person (i.e. the entrepreneur himself), the capital equipment per person works out to approximately ₦250 (or about US$40C).[1] The median value of capital equipment was of course higher in activities like paper and related products, fabricated metals and equipment and transport. Conversely, it was lower in primary industry, trade and food and beverages (table 2). Though the majority of the enterprises owned their capital equipment, some 125 enterprises resorted to renting them. About 60 per cent of them paid a rent of ₦5 or less per week. In a few cases even the workers brought their own tools.

The modest value of capital equipment owned and the general prevalence of renting business premises by the informal sector enterprises are perhaps a reflection of their limited access to capital. About 80 per cent of the enterprises financed the purchase of their capital equipments from their own savings. Given the near-poverty level of living of most of the informal sector entrepreneurs, it is indeed surprising that they were able to spare the necessary amount out of their income for such investment, however modest the amount may be. Another 17 per cent borrowed money from friends and relatives; the formal financial institutions like banks thus played a negligible role in promoting the informal sector.

In fact, 86 per cent of the enterprises found it difficult to raise the capital needed to start their business as compared to 7 per cent who had difficulty in finding suitable premises. Lack of technical know-how and presence of government regulations did not pose much problem except for a very small (2.3 per cent) number of enterprises.

Lack of access to formal channels of credit would also seem to affect the operational efficiency of informal sector enterprises because a good number of them are also confronted with cash-flow problems. Only 63 per cent of the enterprises receive cash payments for sales immediately upon delivery and 3 per cent receive payments prior to delivery. A total of 320 enterprises sold goods on credit. But most of these enterprises had to pay cash for the inputs bought. Most of the working capital requirements were met through personal savings of the entrepreneurs; 91 per cent of the enterprises relied on own savings for working capital needs as compared to 78 per cent for lump-sum investment requirements. Though 82 per cent never made an attempt to seek bank credit, a large majority (88 per cent) of the remaining who did seek failed to get credit. A third of all enterprises did not believe that they could get credit from the formal sector because of the stringent lending requirements; and a quarter felt they could not get credit because of the complicated lending procedures. Interestingly, one-fifth of the enterprises attributed the lack of access to credit to non-recognition of the enterprises by the Government.

Raw materials and services

Turning to raw materials and services, 13 per cent of the enterprises, presumably in service activity, did not buy any raw materials at all. Of the remaining, about 80 per cent bought their raw material requirements mainly from other small enterprises,
----

[1] In terms of simple averages, ₦450 of capital for 2.10 persons or ₦215 per person.

Table 2: Distribution of enterprises by value of capital equipment and by activity

Value of Capital Equipment	Prim-ary Indu-stry	Food+ Beve.+ Tobaccc	Text-tile+ Leath-er	Wood + Furni-ture	Paper+ Paper Prod-ucts	Fab. Metal+ Machin.	Others Manufac-turing	Utili-ties	Cons-truc-tion	Whole-sale Trade	Retail Trade	Trans-port + Storage	Comm.+ Soc.+ Pers.	Inadeq. Defined	Total No.	%
₦50.00 or less	30.0	33.3	12.0	9.7	7.1	4.4	15.2	22.2	36.4	22.7	28.6	15.3	18.5	18.6	283	17.6
₦50.01-₦100.00	0.0	8.3	12.0	18.3	5.4	13.3	15.2	19.4	0.0	13.6	17.8	1.7	15.6	15.1	223	13.9
₦100.01-₦250.00	40.0	16.7	25.2	8.6	8.9	13.3	8.7	19.4	9.1	24.2	23.1	20.3	21.1	20.9	339	21.1
₦250.01-₦500.00	20.0	16.7	27.6	29.0	17.9	20.0	13.0	33.3	18.2	16.7	15.7	25.4	21.5	22.1	360	22.4
₦500.01-₦1000.00	0.0	16.7	16.4	14.0	14.3	22.2	21.7	5.6	18.2	10.6	9.8	16.9	13.3	16.3	227	14.1
₦1000.01-₦2000.00	10.0	0.3	4.1	13.8	33.9	17.8	6.5	0.0	0.0	4.5	2.5	6.8	6.3	3.5	96	6.0
₦2000.01-₦5000.00	0.0	0.0	2.6	6.5	8.9	8.9	10.9	0.0	18.2	6.1	2.2	8.5	3.0	3.5	62	3.9
₦5000.01-₦9500.00	0.0	8.3	0.2	3.2	3.6	0.0	8.7	0.0	0.0	1.5	0.3	5.1	0.7	0.0	18	1.1
Total	10	12	493	93	56	45	46	36	11	66	325	59	270	86	1 608	100.0
%	0.6	0.7	30.7	5.8	3.5	2.8	2.9	2.2	0.7	4.1	20.2	3.7	16.8	5.3		

though few also depended on households. Most of the rest obtained their raw materials either from large enterprises or from the Government. However, there seems to be a small element of market imperfection in so far as 15 per cent of the enterprises depended on a single enterprise for their raw materials. Nearly 80 per cent of the firms buying raw materials spent less than ₦75 per week on the mean and median values respectively were around ₦125 and ₦25 per week.

As regards the purchase of services, about half of the enterprises did not require them; most of the remaining bought them from small enterprises and households. Thus, the Lagos informal sector seems to have stronger backward linkages within the informal sector itslef. In terms of expenditure, close to three-quarters buying services spent ₦10 or less per week; the mean and median values of expenditures on services were ₦20 and under ₦10 per week respectively.

Revenue

When asked about their sales revenues, only 71 per cent were able to respond; it is not clear whether the remaining were unable to recall their sales or were deliberately avoiding the question. Eighty-three per cent of those who did respond had a sales revenue of ₦75 or less per week, the mean and median values being about ₦101 and ₦25 per week respectively.

Value added

Varying degrees of response with regard to revenue and expenses on inputs make it difficult to arrive at a figure of value added. However, one can derive some rough order of magnitude of the value added per enterprise on the basis of the data on entrepreneurs' income (which includes returns to his own labour and capital owned) and the wage bill. It was stated earlier that the average value of the master's income was around ₦100 per month. Since the average number of workers (excluding the head) per enterprise was 1.10 and the average wage per worker was around ₦40 per month, the total value of income generated would seem to be around ₦144 per month per enterprise (about ₦1,700 per year); value added per worker is thus estimated at ₦69 per month. Needless to add, the above estimate excludes rent paid on business premises and capital equipment if any. It is therefore likely that the value added figure of ₦1,700 per year per enterprise is an underestimate. Further, considering the variations in income and employment between enterprises, it is reasonable to expect that a majority of the enterprises has a value-added figure below ₦1,700 per year.

Forward linkages

Turning to other aspects of the enterprise, to whom do they sell what they produce? As in many other countries, 87 per cent of the enterprises sell mainly to households and 9 per cent mainly to other informal sector enterprises. Thus, forward linkage with the formal sector seems to be negligible. Since a majority of the enterprises is located in residential areas, it is quite logical to expect that about 55 per cent of the enterprises rely on customers

within 20 minutes walking distance from the enterprise. In other
words, a substantial part of the informal sector activity is
location specific, which in turn has significant policy implications
for relocation of these enterprises.

Constraints on growth and expansion

Since a large majority of the enterprises have rented
premises, very few had any incentive to effect improvement in them.
Only 15 per cent of the enterprises had undertaken any major
improvement in the premises though over half had undertaken minor
improvements. When asked about their desire to expand and improve
their method of production, about 95 per cent expressed an interest
in doing so. About 80 per cent of the enterprises cited lack of
access to credit as the main obstacle to expansion; this percentage
was however higher for certain activities like wood and furniture
manufacturing, textile and leather manufacturing, fabricated metal,
machinery and equipment manufacturing and paper and paper products
manufacturing. In an attempt to improve their business prospects,
some 18 per cent of the enterprises even tried to diversify their
products. Also about 21 per cent of the enterprises seem to have
effected substantial improvements in their method of production.

To what extent is the Lagos informal sector threatened by
competition? The evidence suggests that about half the enterprises
felt there were too many enterprises similar to their own while the
rest were apparently not so much worried about this problem. About
40 per cent of the enterprises felt that competition from large
enterprises led to a reduction in their sales while for the rest it
was not a problem.

Presence of competition could be interpreted as a limitation
on the market for informal sector goods and services and hence the
demand potential. To clarify this, the study also asked questions
about the changes in demand. Three-quarters of the enterprises
reported an increase in demand for their products since their
establishment, though only 11 per cent reported a substantial
increase. Only a small fraction, about 4 per cent, complained of a
decrease in demand. Activities like food, beverages and tobacco
manufacturing, textile and leather manufacturing, fabricated metal
products and equipment, other manufacturing and wholesale trade had
a greater percentage of firms reporting a substantial increase in
demand. Likewise, 80 per cent of all the enterprises increased the
quantity of goods and services sold and only 4 per cent complained
of a decrease. It would therefore seem that the Lagos informal
sector is doing reasonably well; policies designed to improve their
market share by improving their competitive edge over the formal
sector could further accelerate this process.

In spite of the increase in demand and production in a
majority of the enterprises, only 21 per cent of the sample firms
reported increasing the number of workers. A majority maintained
their level of employment. It is not clear how far lack of capital
(fixed and working) played a role in explaining the apparently
inelastic demand for labour with respect to output. Poor employment
response could also be due to lags in adjustment. In any case this
is a matter that requires further investigation.

Another dimension of the growth problem pertains to the growth
of the number of enterprises. Obviously it is difficult to assess

the rate of growth through a one-shot survey like the present one. Nevertheless, one can draw some conclusions based on the age structure of the sample enterprises. About 18 per cent of the enterprises were under one year old, 19 per cent between one and 2 years, 30 per cent between 2 and 5 years old, 16 per cent between 5 and 10 years old, and the remaining 17 per cent over 10 years old. These figures could be interpreted as suggesting a crude birth rate of 21 per cent per year of informal sector enterprises at least during 1975-76, as compared to about 35 per cent for Freetown (Sierra Leone). It is also interesting to note that a greater proportion of the enterprises in food, beverages and tobacco manufacturing and trade is of more recent origin (over 75 per cent below 5 years old).

Even though there is a fairly well organised apprentice system in the informal sector, 62 per cent of the entrepreneurs expressed a need for one type of skill or another. About half of the entrepreneurs felt that the Government could help the enterprises in upgrading the skills. Twenty-four per cent said that the Government could organise short-term courses for workers while another 16 per cent wanted regular schools, operated during convenient hours of the day; and some 16 per cent wanted on-the-job training. It is also interesting to note that 20 per cent of the enterprises were even willing to share the cost of training, if small; and a few were even willing to let their workers participate in training during working hours, in spite of the fact that many entrepreneurs expected their workers to leave after training.

It is sometimes argued that the Government has an unfavourable influence on the informal sector, through negative policies restricting their growth. In the case of Lagos, it was noted earlier that most of the enterprises operate without any licence from the Government. Further, only one-seventh of the enterprises were subjected to any kind of inspection or regulations, and only a quarter of them paid any taxes to the Government. Among the few who had any link with the Government, a little over half felt that the Government played a helpful role. Of the several kinds of government assistance, only three received support from a majority of the enterprises: credit facilities, market facilities and policies designed to increase the demand for informal sector goods and services from the formal sector and the Government, in that order of importance.

Besides favourable credit policies, provision of infrastructure including premises and utilities in suitable market locations emerges as a key area for assistance. It is particularly attractive because most of these entrepreneurs are already operating in rented residential locations. Thus, public investment in such facilities can be a self-paying and viable proposition, which incidentally could also make a valuable contribution to better urban environment. In fact, two-thirds of the enterprises were even ready to move out of Lagos if appropriate incentives were provided. Even the rest who were, unwilling to move out, were favourably disposed to the idea of alternative locations in Lagos. In response to a hypothetical question of how they would use a windfall assistance of ₦500, a large majority replied in favour of improving the premises and/or equipment in business.

Conclusion

The findings based on the Lagos study are in many respects similar to those of Freetown. Migration plays an important role in informal sector employment; unlike in Freetown only a small proportion of the migrants originate from outside the country. The study also confirms the role played by the informal sector in generating skills and in facilitating a smooth transition from agricultural to non-agricultural occupations. Irrespective of the level of education, training on the job and apprenticeship in the informal sector seem vital to employment generation. A majority of the entrepreneurs in this sector seem to have been unemployed before migration to Lagos.

Though some 60 per cent of the enterprises had apprentices, few of them were paid. Consequently, a majority of the apprentices tend to quit their masters once the skills are acquired and establish their own enterprises rather than seek wage employment. This is not surprising because studies elsewhere in Nigeria show a substantial rate of return to investment in skills. For example, it is estimated that the private rate of return to investment in skills related to furniture craft in Western Nigeria is around 30 per cent; for autorepair, 12 per cent.[1] Further, the Lagos study shows that wage workers earn less compared to the heads of enterprises.

With regard to the functioning of the labour market, 80 per cent of the entrepreneurs seem to be satisfied with their current job and were not interested in changing their job. This is partly explained by their current level of income (including return to capital owned) - 60 per cent higher than the revised legal minimum wage of ₦60 (or about US$100) per month. It is true, however, that there are substantial variations between entrepreneurs, notably between activities and different size groups. Most of the entrepreneurs were not even aware of employment offices, perhaps due to their preference for self-employment. For wage workers, on the other hand, the conditions of work seem to be far from satisfactory as in the case of Freetown. Wages were significantly lower than the legal minimum wage; hours of work were longer; and yet only a quarter of the enterprises reported losing workers. In other words, conditions of work are closely related to job mobility and opportunities for employment. Finally, women participation, both as entrepreneurs and as workers, seemed to be quite small.

Though some 40 per cent of the entrepreneurs did not have any dependants, the average size of the household for the remaining was over six persons. About half of these households seem to have additional earners though their contribution to household income was estimated to be only 38 per cent of the masters'. Notwithstanding the respectable level of income of the entrepreneurs, many of them thus seem to fall below the poverty line.

And yet the Lagos study shows that the average amount of capital per enterprise, mostly acquired through own savings, was
----

[1] Adewale F. Mabawonku: "An economic evaluation of apprenticeship training in Western Nigerian small-scale industries", in African Rural Economy Paper No. 17, Department of Agricultural Economics, Michigan State University (East Lansing, 1979), table 4.6.

around ₦450 (or ₦215 per worker). No doubt there are substantial variations; the median value per enterprise was only ₦250. Even though these figures are only a fraction of the capital labour ratio prevailing in the formal sector, it is remarkable that the informal sector generates respectable levels of income to the entrepreneurs. It is even more interesting to note that three-quarters of the enterprises witnessed an increase in demand for their output. It is this feature that probably explains the significant growth in number of enterprises - 18 per cent of them came into existence during the year preceding the survey. One explanation for this growth could be that the GDP in the industrial sector (mainly the formal sector for which statistics are collected) in Nigeria grew at 12.6 per cent per year during 1970-76.[1] In other words, the growth of the formal sector seems to have a significant impact on the growth of the informal sector. Since much of the Lagos informal sector output was sold to households, the link between the two sectors seems to be indirect, via consumer income and expenditures.

Finally, what about the informal sector's contributions to GNP? If one takes a rough estimate of the Lagos city population at 2.0 millions[2] and applies an activity rate of 45 per cent[3] then the working population in 1978 works out to about 900,000 persons. Since half of this figure is estimated to belong to the informal sector (Appendix table 4), an average value-added figure of ₦840 per worker per year[4] would imply a total value added by the informal sector in Lagos of about ₦380 million (or about US$650 million), which is indeed not an insignificant amount. Considering the fact that the informal sector generates substantial investment in human capital, the above estimate is clearly biased downwards. It is therefore heartening to note that the Third National Development Plan of Nigeria has accorded an important place for the informal sector in employment promotion.

----

[1] World Bank: World Development Report, 1978 (Washington, 1978), p. 78.

[2] O.J. Fapohunda et al.: Lagos: Urban development and employment (Geneva, ILO, 1978), p. 12.

[3] ibid., p. 38. Figure based on 1963 census for Lagos Federal Territory.

[4] Based on the figure of ₦69 per month per worker reported in the text.

CHAPTER 6. THE INFORMAL SECTOR IN A SMALL CITY: THE CASE OF KANO (NIGERIA)

A.L. Mabogunje and M.O. Filani

Kano is the third largest city in Nigeria with an estimated population of about 420,000 in 1972. Though it is a medium-sized city far away from Lagos, the city has grown at a rapid rate of 6.2 per cent per year in terms of population since 1952. Only 8 per cent of the population is over 44 years of age, and consequently more than half of the population is actively participating in the labour force. The main reason underlying this feature is of course migration, as will be shown later. The city's population is dominated by two ethnic groups, Hausa and Fulani, which account for about 80 per cent. Kano city had two-thirds of the total urban population in Kano province in 1967.

Rough estimates for 1972 placed the share of migrants in total population of the city at 25 to 30 per cent. Kano, being a primate city surrounded by a heavily populated rural zone, seems to be the major pole of attraction for rural population inadequately served with relevant infrastructure facilities. The importance of Kano as a major commercial centre in the region would also seem to have played a role in attracting migrants. For example, urban Kano is estimated to account for 95 per cent of both industrial output and employment in the province in 1964/65. Over two-thirds of the formal sector industrial establishments with more than ten workers in former Northern Nigeria were in textile, furniture and sawmilling, printing and stationery, oil milling and chemicals, and vehicle repairs during the mid-1960s. It is also true that poor working conditions and low earnings in agriculture have induced a few to migrate to Kano city.

One of the interesting features of this study, unlike that of Freetown and Lagos, is that it attempted a complete listing of all informal sector enterprises employing ten or less persons in Kano city before drawing a sample. A total of 6,665 enterprises was thus enumerated in 52 types of activities. As expected, about 4,000 of them were in trade activity. The sample of 505 enterprises used for an in-depth inquiry, however, focused more on the non-trade activities. Thus, only 14 per cent of the sample belonged to trade as compared to over 70 per cent in manufacturing and repair services. Over 80 per cent of the sample enterprises were concentrated in three of the eight wards in Kano city, the largest concentration being inside the old city, which incidentally had two-thirds of the Kano metropolitan population in 1962.

The informal sector participants

The sample of 505 enterprises provided employment and income opportunities to a total of 903 persons, including entrepreneurs, workers and apprentices. Of this total 63 per cent were heads, 21 per cent were journeymen and the rest apprentices. Nearly three quarters of all participants were in the age bracket of 15 to 44 years, the average age being only 26.5 years, much lower when compared to Freetown. Further, more than 15 per cent were below the age of 14 years. Young people below 14 were particularly important in trade, and other services like painting, mechanics, welding, electrical repair, panel beating, etc. where they are engaged as apprentices. Agricultural services including livestock keeping and fishing were the only activities which had nearly 40 per cent of the participants above the age of 45.

Another feature of the participants is that 89 per cent were males. The low participation of women in the informal sector is attributed to the dominance of the moslem religion in this part of Nigeria. In certain activities like sewing, milling and hairdressing, women account for more than 60 per cent of the participants. Turning to education, 46 per cent of the participants had only Arabic training, unlike in Lagos. And 12 per cent had no education at all. Of the remaining, almost three-quarters had primary-level or more schooling, most of whom are also young (below 35 years).

About 57 per cent of the Kano informal sector participants were married, the average number of dependants being 4.7 per married participant, which is significantly lower than the corresponding figure of 6.6 for Lagos.

Lastly, the Kano study suggests, as did the study on Lagos, that 59 per cent of the participants found the present job through their own efforts, after a brief period of search. Most of the remaining were introduced into their current occupation by friends and relatives: virtually none depended on the employment offices.

Role of Migration

Compared to Lagos and Freetown, a smaller proportion of Kano informal sector participants, only about 35 per cent, were born outside Kano city. This is of course consistent with the figure of 25 to 30 per cent migrants in city population mentioned earlier. Nearly 90 per cent of the migrants came from other States of Nigeria. Further, about 60 per cent of the latter came from southern States, more than 1,000 kilometres away. The average age of migrants was slightly lower (24.8 years) than the over-all average of 26.5 years for all participants noted above. Also, 85 per cent of them were males. But the migrants in general had more education; unlike in Freetown, 59 per cent of them had primary level or more schooling. There also seems to be a significant relationship between the origin of the migrants on the one hand and their location in the city on the other. This should be expected given the importance of interpersonal contacts in inducing migration.

One of the striking features of migration in Kano is that even though only about a third of the participants were born outside, most of them arrived in recent years. Two-thirds of the migrants came to Kano during the five years preceding the survey (i.e. 1972 to 1976) as compared to under 30 per cent in Freetown and 30 per cent in Lagos during the same period. In fact, 34 per cent had migrated during the two years preceding the date of interview; 33 per cent between two and five years; 21 per cent between five and ten years; and the rest had been in Kano for over ten years.

Two major reasons might have accounted for the large percentage of recent migrants in Kano. First, it is possible that certain generation of migrants (especially of northern origin) who have lived in the city for very long periods – more than 50 years or so - now regard themselves as Kano indigenes since most of them were born here and have had subsequent generations after them. The other reason might be the effect of the civil war. Many migrants left the city during the war. Some of those who have returned since the cessation of hostilities might refer to the duration of their second trip rather than their pre-war residency in answering questions on their length of stay. Also there must have been some new arrivals since the war ended.

What is even more remarkable is that over two-thirds of the migrants – as compared to 60 per cent for the natives - owned their enterprises even though a majority of them had arrived in Kano recently. Nineteen per cent of the migrants were apprentices in contrast to 16 per cent of the natives. Consequently, the proportion of wage workers among migrants was relatively smaller. Another interesting finding was that, unlike in Freetown, the migrnats seem to have penetrated in all activities, not just the trade and services. These findings imply that the migrants, though young, had managed to overcome the barriers in terms of skills and capital in a relatively short period of time.

Looking at their work status before migration, the study showed that 59 per cent of them had worked before, half of them as farmers or traders. The remaining 41 per cent were unemployed. Since their arrival in Kano, 75 per cent of the migrants had not changed their jobs. Some 60 per cent of the migrants were satisfied with their current job; but 55 per cent of all were willing to change their occupation provided skills are taught and incomes increased. In terms of links with their place of origin, over 60 per cent of the migrants visit their home only once a year and 14 per cent never visit; the rest visit several times a year.

Income variations

Table 1 below shows the distribution of participants in the informal sector by level of income per month.

Table 1. Distribution of informal sector participants by level of income

Ħ per month per person	All participants			Migrants
	Males	Females	Total	
0	32 (-)	40 (-)	36 (-)	30 (-)
1-60	26 (38)	36 (60)	27 (42)	37 (53)
60-100	42 (62)	24 (40)	17 (27)	17 (24)
100+			20 (31)	16 (23)
All	100 (100)	100 (100)	100 (100)	100 (100)

Notes: Figures in parentheses exclude participants with zero incomes

First, 36 per cent of all participants did not receive any income at all presumably because they were either apprentices or unpaid family workers. Second, of those who did receive income, a majority (58 per cent) earned above ₦60 per month or the legal minimum wage. Third, even though few women (11 per cent) participated in Kano informal sector, a majority (60 per cent) of those receiving incomes fell below the legal minimum wage. Thus, there seems to be unequal earning opportunities between men and women; perhaps this can be explained in terms of the activities in which women tend to participate. Fourth, since the data refer to both owners and other categories of workers, it is quite likely that much of the income variations can be explained in terms of the participants' work status. Finally, 70 per cent of the migrants did receive income; but only 47 per cent of them had an income above ₦ 60 per month as compared to 58 per cent among all participants.

These findings seem to suggest that among the income receivers, the median level of income for females was under ₦50 per month; for migrants about ₦60 per month; and for all participants, well above ₦60 per month. Thus, even though the migrants received a lower level of income as compared to the natives of Kano, it is remarkable that about half of them receiving incomes manage to get the equivalent of the legal minimum wage. Clearly, the informal sector participants in Kano are significantly better off than those in Lagos. These figures also compare favourably with the average earnings of workers in the Kano formal sector: ₦800 per year in government and ₦520 per year in large-scale industries in 1972, before the legal minimum wage of ₦60 per month was introduced. It is not therefore surprising that many migrants come from places as far away as 1,000 kilometres; nearly three quarters of them reported that their income increased significantly.

Given the relatively smaller household size and larger average income per person in Kano as compared to Lagos for example it is clear that the per capita income of Kano informal sector participants is relatively high. It is not therefore surprising that only a quarter of the participants, mainly young, were not satisfied with their present job (due to low income, job insecurity, no future prospects, etc.) and many of them were actually seeking a change. These findings seem to suggest that there is scope for promoting the informal sector in secondary urban centres.

The enterprise

Seventy-six per cent of the sample enterprises in Kano operated in fixed locations and the remaining, mostly traders, in variable locations. Two-thirds of those in fixed locations operated in residential structures, 21 per cent in commercial buildings and the remaining few in open sheds and the like. Being located in residential areas, some of these activities like processing, panel beating and mechanics workshops seem to have a detrimental effect on health and environment. In terms of access to utilities like electricity and water, Kano enterprises seem to be better off compared to Lagos. Thirty-seven per cent had access to both while another 40 per cent had either of the two; only a quarter or less had neither of the facilities, presumably those without fixed locations.

Forty-two per cent of all enterprises (or 55 per cent of those in fixed locations) were on rented premises. A majority of the remaining 45 per cent presumably owned their premises - results comparable to that of Freetown. A greater proportion of those located outside the city, mostly migrants, pay rent on their premises. In other words, a majority of the natives of Kano, generally located within the city, seem to own their premises. On an average the enterprises in rented premises paid about ₦15 per month; but the median value was only around ₦11 per month.

Regarding legal status, a large majority of the enterprises felt that they did not require any licence from the Government, as in the case of Lagos. Only 20 per cent of the sample enterprises had a licence. It is also interesting to note that some 8 per cent of the enterprises were affiliated to one form of "association" or another.

The average number of persons per enterprise (including the head) is only 1.8, as noted earlier. In fact over two-thirds of the sample enterprises did not have any worker other than the entrepreneur himself. Thus self-employment is a major characteristic of the Kano informal sector. In some activities, however, the enterprises are larger: bakery, 5.3 persons; construction, 4 persons; leather manufacturing, 3.8 persons; welding, 3.4 persons; and roadside mechanics and electrical works, 3 persons. As indicated earlier, 505 enterprises provided employment to 565 heads, 187 journeymen and 151 apprentices. Thus, the few who do employ additional workers seem to have on the average one apprentice and one journeyman each.

Given the reasonable levels of income generated in the Kano informal sector, the average initial capital outlay in these enterprises is surprisingly small, particularly when compared to Lagos. The median value of capital per enterprise was only ₦50 (or about US$80); the corresponding mean, ₦282 suggesting enormous variations in capital between firms.[1] Roughly a quarter each of the sample had an investment of under ₦10, ₦11-50, ₦50-200 and ₦200 or more. As should be expected, agricultural, personal and repair services had a lower capital than the rest of the activities. The average capital-labour ratio was thus ₦157, which is only a fraction of the capital investment required per worker in certain formal sector activities in Kano: tanning, ₦2,000; groundnut processing, ₦2,000 to 4,000; weaving, ₦1,200; steel fittings, ₦1,200; and soap manufacturing, ₦200.

As in the case of informal sector surveys elsewhere, 70 per cent of the enterprises relied on personal savings for their investment expenditures. Borrowings from friends and relatives was the source for most of the remaining; only 1.4 per cent of the enterprises had access to bank credit.

The Kano study also confirmed the pattern of forward and backward linkages found elsewhere. For example, 87 per cent of all sales were directed to households and 10.5 per cent to small enterprises. In terms of backward linkages, though much of the raw materials and inputs originate from the formal sector, the informal sector does not have a direct link with it because retail traders play an intermediary role.
----

[1] The corresponding figures for Lagos were ₦250 and ₦450. See Chapter 5.

With regard to expansion of business, 77 per cent of the
enterprises expressed their willingness; however, 83 per cent of
those willing cited lack of capital as a major constraint.
Consequently, about 80 per cent of the enterprises reported credit
as the major field of government assistance desirable. With regard
to training as a means for job mobility, 59 per cent of the
participants were interested in changing their job if additional
skills are provided. About a third of those willing to do so were
even prepared to pay for such training. Forty-one per cent,
however, did not wish to change their job under any circumstances.
Quite naturally, most of those willing to change their job belonged
to the age groups 15-24 years and to a lesser extent 25-44 years.
Only a few of those willing to change their job, however, desired a
wage employment in the formal sector.

When the migrants were asked about their willingness to move
out of Kano city, 57 per cent were ready to consider such a move
provided it is beneficial to them. The proportion of migrants so
inclined was, however, much higher in certain low-income activities
like personal services and agriculture-related activities.

Implications for urban environment

One of the important implications emerging from the Kano study
pertains to urban environment. As noted earlier, the migrants to
Kano tend to be concentrated in certain geographical locations in
and near the city. Consequently, most of their activities are also
located there. The study also found that the room occupancy rate in
these localities was higher than elsewhere; and a majority of them
live in rented accommodation, paying an average monthly rent of ₦8.
Of course the rental would be higher were it not for the fact that
several migrants from the same place share a common room. With
regard to the types of houses inhabited by the migrants, the
majority live in modern tin-roofed houses built with concrete
blocks, as found in Southern Nigeria where many migrants originate.
These, however, are not particularly suited to the climatic
conditions prevailing in the northern part. Only a quarter of such
housing is provided with both water and electricity. Though two-
thirds of the city population is well served with electricity, water
supply is poor in general. The cost of getting water through
private carriers ranges from ₦2 in the city to ₦3 per 1,000 gallons
in localities inhabited by migrants. Likewise, sanitary conditions
in the above localities are also relatively poor. Thus, though
migration is beneficial to those involved, it has also caused
certain environmental problems. One of the ways to tackle the
situation seems to be to remove any uncertainty associated with the
migrants' employment opportunities in the informal sector and
thereby encourage the migrants to invest in housing. It is also
necessary to find ways of improving migrants' adjustment to city
life and of encouraging them to develop a sense of belonging in
order to improve their own conditions of living and urban
environment.

Conclusions

The Kano study plays an important role in generating
employment and incomes particularly for the young, unlike in
Freetown. As elsewhere, trade accounts for 60 per cent of all

informal sector enterprises in Kano city, followed by tailoring - 17 per cent. This structure is partly accounted for by the importance of Kano as a commercial centre in the region. Migration seems to have been a relatively less important factor in Kano as compared to Freetown or Lagos for only a third of the informal sector participants were found to be migrants. Perhaps this is due to the choice of sampling procedure giving greater weight to the numerically less important activities. Though trade and tailoring accounted for over three-quarters of the Kano informal sector enterprises, only 10 per cent of the sample belonged to these activities. This difference must be borne in mind while comparing the findings from Kano with those elsewhere.

As elsewhere, very few women participate in the informal sector. The average level of education of participants is only around six years. Most of them rely on informal sources of training and set up their business with their own savings. Though the bulk of the sample enterprises is engaged in secondary activities the average capital per worker seems to be only ₦160 (or US$260), a fraction of that in the formal sector. Yet the average level of income of participants is comparable to those in the formal sector. The evidence suggests that there is scope to promote employment in the informal formal sector even in smaller cities.

Perhaps the striking feature of the study is its finding with regard to income opportunities for the migrants. Though the bulk of the migrants in Kano had arrived only recently (i.e. during the five years preceding the survey), a majority of them had accumulated sufficient capital and skills to set up their own business in a wide range of activities. And half of them were earning at least ₦60 per month - the legal minimum wage. This is an impressive achievement given the fact that some 40 per cent of them were unemployed and most of the remaining were engaged in farming, trading and similar activities before coming to Kano.

The study also throws light on the consequences of migration to environment. A major part of the informal sector activities is being carried out in residential premises and some of them would seem to pose a threat to health and environment. Poor infrastructural facilities and inadequate access to urban services notably in the areas where migrants tend to settle have contributed to a deterioration in living and working conditions. One of the ways to improve the situation seems to be to encourage migrants to invest in housing and premises by eliminating uncertainties associated with their job and stay in Kano. Since informal sector activities are largely consumer oriented, the study emphasises the need to integrate urban development policies with employment promotion.

CHAPTER 7. THE INFORMAL MANUFACTURING SECTOR IN KUMASI

George Aryee

Kumasi, located in the Ashanti region, is the second largest city in Ghana after Accra, though it is somewhat smaller than Kano in Nigeria, with a population of about 350,000 and a labour force of 139,000 in 1970. The rate of population growth in Kumasi was, however, substantially lower than in Kano - only 3.75 per cent per year between 1960 and 1970 as compared to 6.2 per cent in Kano. A part of the explanation for the above may be attributed to the fact that the share of manufacturing employment in total in Kumasi remained stagnant during the sixties even though, for the country as a whole, employment in large-scale manufacturing increased at 8.4 per cent per annum.

About 10 per cent of the labour force was unemployed in 1970. As in the case of Kano, two-thirds of employment was in the tertiary sector including trade and services, reflecting the importance of Kumasi as a commercial centre in the Ashanti region. The study nevertheless focused on manufacturing and related repair services. Of about 30,000 persons engaged in manufacturing and motor repair activities in 1970, only a third was estimated to be in the formal sector. Broadly speaking, manufacturing employment in Kumasi is distributed as follows: 40 per cent in textile and leather, 23 per cent in food processing, 14 per cent in wood and related activities and 15 per cent in vehicle repair and maintenance.

Partly because of the small size of the city and partly because the informal manufacturing activities were visibly concentrated in selected geographic locations, the study was able to list the relevant enterprises before drawing a sample. The sample, consisting of 298 enterprises, was distributed among all manufacturing activities other than food processing (since they were carried out as household industry) and a majority of the sample enterprises was in three subsectors: fitting (74), tailoring (71) and leather manufacturing (69).

The entrepreneurs[1]

As in Kano, 86 per cent of the labour force in Kumasi was between 15 and 44 years old; the main difference between the two is, however, the importance of youngsters (15-24 years) in Kumasi, who accounted for over 40 per cent of the labour force. But among the head of the enterprises in the sample, only 25 per cent were below 25 years of age and 64 per cent between 25 and 44 years. More importantly, the median age of entrepreneurs was only around 28 years but those engaged in carpentry, blacksmithing and fitting were somewhat older. Almost all these heads were sole proprietors.

One of the unique features of the Kumasi informal sector is the relatively high level of education of entrepreneurs compared to many other countries. Though 28 per cent of the entrepreneurs did not have any formal schooling, 60 per cent had middle-level

----

[1] Though data were collected from 330 enterprises, the results presented below refer to 298 enterprises only, headed by males.

education (ten years' schooling) or more. The proportion of
entrepreneurs with more education is of course higher among younger
ones. For example, 67 per cent, 80 per cent and 69 per cent of
those in the age groups "below 20", 20-25 and 25-30 years had
middle-level education compared to under 40 per cent in age groups
36 and above.

A third of the entrepreneurs were migrants from outside the
Ashanti region. Of the remaining, only 3 per cent were born in
Kumasi and the rest had come from other parts of the Ashanti region
itself. A small proportion, about 5 per cent, came from outside
Ghana. Thus, there is a strong link between migration and informal
sector activities in Kumasi. Unlike in Kano, migrants from outside
the Ashanti region had relatively fewer years of schooling, 40 per
cent had no education as compared to 22 per cent for those belonging
to the region.

All entrepreneurs seem to have undergone one form of training
or another before setting up their business. Over 90 per cent of
them had training through the apprenticeship system of the informal
sector; only 3.4 per cent relied on training institutions and 5 per
cent on apprenticeship in the formal sector. Most of those trained
in the institutions - about 90 per cent - possessed middle or
technical education. Training through apprenticeship in the
informal sector, on the other hand, was not confined to those with
little education; 58 per cent of entrepreneurs thus trained
possessed middle-level education. Thus, the informal sector plays
a key role in skill acquisition. The median number of years spent
in apprenticeship was a little over three years; some 20 per cent of
the entrepreneurs had spent five years or longer. Some 10 per cent
of the entrepreneurs had apparently acquired some skills in the
formal sector too since they were wage employees in that sector
before setting up their own business.[1]

The enterprise

By virtue of the sample design adopted, the selected
enterprises were clustered in specific locations within the city.
Each such location tended to be homogenous with regard to the type
of activity carried on. For example, in Suame Magazine, most of the
enterprises were engaged in fitting, auto repair and related
activities. Likewise, in Angloga, the dominant activity was
carpentry. Even though the Kumasi City Council took a positive view
of the informal sector activities and allowed their operation in
specific locations within the city, many of these enterprises were
housed in temporary structures and most of them lacked the minimum
support facilities. Nearly 80 per cent of the enterprises had
access to neither water nor electricity. In some locations, such as
the Magazine, though the city council owns the land and allows
informal sector enterprises to continue on a token rent, building
permanent structures is forbidden since the council plans to build
----

[1] See also Ali N. Hakam: Technology diffusion from the formal
to the informal sector: The case of the auto-repair industry in
Ghana (Geneva, ILO, 1978; mimeographed World Employment Programme
research working paper; restricted), p. 43, where it is stated that
15 per cent of the masters had their training in foreign
subsidiaries or state-run factories.

permanent workshops eventually. In Angloga, for example, the enterprises are viewed by the council as occupying the land illegally and hence are not considered eligible for any support facilities.

The Kumasi informal sector is not very different from those in other cities discussed earlier in other aspects. About half the enterprises do not observe fixed hours; a majority of those who do work for over eight hours a day. Only a fifth of these enterprises were registered with the Government, though in woodcarving nearly 90 per cent belonged to this category to take advantage of the marketing assistance provided by government agencies. With regard to the age structure of these enterprises, about half of them were under 5 years old. In fact, 11 per cent were under 2 years old; 16 per cent between 2 and 3 years; 13 per cent between 3 and 4 and 12 per cent between 4 and 5 years; and the rest were above 5 years old.

Employment

The sample enterprises (298) provided employment to a total of 1,329 persons including 315 working proprietors. Of those working with the masters (i.e. 1,014 persons), 86 per cent were apprentices, mainly in fitting, tailoring and leather manufacturing. Very few were journeymen - only 7.3 per cent. Most of the remaining few were unpaid family workers. Needless to add, the overwhelming importance of apprentices has significant implications. First, the informal sector provides training to a substantial number of youngsters. Second, since the apprentices are not paid full wages, the entrepreneurs benefit from cheap labour and thus enjoy a comparative edge over the formal sector by keeping their costs down. Third, the enterprises are able to overcome their working capital needs in the form of wage bills since the apprentices generally receive only a small amount of pocket money plus food and sometimes shelter (i.e. between 2 and 2.5 cedis per week). Fourth, apprentices seem to be a source of finance for investment since they pay a fee to the masters.[1]

Turning to the size distribution, only 15 per cent of the enterprises did not have any employees or apprentices as compared to a large majority in Freetown, Kano and Lagos (table 1). Nearly half the sample had between two and four workers and the remainder had over five workers. A majority of those in the middle range (64 per cent) were textile and leather manufacturing enterprises, while half of the larger ones were in fitting. Thus, activities with a greater scope for training employed more persons, mainly as apprentices. If apprentices are excluded, only 17 per cent of the sample had more than one person (i.e. the entrepreneur himself). Unpaid workers were common only in about 10 per cent of the enterprises.

The evidence on the structure of employment presented above indicates that the average size of an informal sector enterprise in Kumasi is close to 4.5 persons. Though this figure is well above the over-all average observed for other cities discussed earlier,
----

[1] Ali N. Hakam, op. cit., where it is shown that apprentices in auto-repair activities contributed a substantial part of the investment by masters.

the difference is mainly due to the exclusion of mon-manufacturing activities in Kumasi. Another major difference is with regard to the proportion of wage workers; in Kumasi reliance on apprentice labour is much greater, as already noted.

Table 1. Size distribution of enterprises by activity
(per cent)

ISIC code	Activity	Number of persons engaged per enterprise					No. of enterprises
		1	2-4	5-9	10 +	total	
9513	Motor repair and mainten-ance	2.7	18.9	60.8	17.6	100.0	74
3813, 3819	Metalworking	15.0	40.0	35.0	10.0	100.0	20
3811	Blacksmithing	11.1	77.8	11.1	0.0	100.0	9
3311	Carpentry	14.7	38.2	35.3	11.8	100.0	34
3220	Tailoring/ seamstressing	16.9	64.8	16.9	1.4	100.0	71
3319	Woodcarving	14.3	42.9	42.9	0.0	100.0	7
3320	Cane weaving	33.3	44.4	22.7	0.0	100.0	9
3214	Carpets/ doormats	0.0	40.0	60.0	0.0	100.0	5
3233, 3240	Footwear/ leatherware	24.6	63.8	10.1	1.4	100.0	69
All activities		14.8	47.3	30.9	7.0	100.0	298

Capital

Turning to the use of capital, table 2 shows the distribution of sample enterprises by level of fixed capital. Though the capital measure excludes working capital and fixed capital in the form of premises (which seems to be minimal since most enterprises are located in simple temporary structures), the distribution suggests that the median value of investment at original cost was only around 400 cedis per enterprise (or US$330); the corresponding average is, however, larger - around 780 cedis (or US$680). The table also shows significant variations in capital between enterprises.

Table 3 shows the average size of the enterprise, the amount of capital, gross output and value added per enterprise and per worker in selected activities. It is clear that the average capital labour ratio shows considerable variations between different activities. Further, the average amount of capital required per worker in the informal sector is only a small fraction of that prevailing in the formal sector. The average capital per worker (at original cost) in selected formal sector manufacturing in 1970 was as follows: food manufacturing, 13,800 cedis; textiles, 8,900 cedis; chemicals, 6,200 cedis; paper products, 3,900 cedis; wood products, 1,000 cedis and furniture and printing, 1,500 cedis.

Output and value added

Table 3 also shows that the average value of output in sample enterprises was around 193 cedis per week; the amount varied between 102 cedis in tailoring to 260 cedis per week in metal working. The average value added per enterprise was a little under half the corresponding value of output - about 87 cedis per week. The average value added per worker per year is estimated at 1,014 cedis or about 85 cedis per month. Though the value added per worker seems to be correlated to the capital per worker, it is interesting to note that in leather manufacturing it takes only 58 cedis of capital per worker to generate a value added of over 2,000 cedis per worker per year; it seems to be not only least capital intensive but also most productive.

Earnings of masters and apprentices

Defining gross earnings as a difference between value added and wage bill (including remuneration to apprentices), the average earnings of a master work out to 78 cedis per week in contrast to the legal minimum wage of 2 cedis per day applicable to the formal sector. The median value, however, was only around 40 cedis per week. It varied not only between activities but also with the size of the enterprise. In enterprises with a single person (i.e. the master alone), it was 68 cedis per week; in the size group 2 to 4 persons, 79 cedis per week; in 5-9 persons, 76 cedis per week; and in the size group 10 and above, 104 cedis per week. In other words, the greater the number of apprentices, the greater the earnings of the master. The fact that masters without any apprentices also earn 68 cedis per week suggests that the informal sector generates substantial incomes even if it does not rely on cheap labour in the form of apprentices. In other words, the average earnings of the entrepreneurs in the Kumasi informal manufacturing sector is considerably higher than the wages of tradesmen grade II (to which most of these entrepreneurs would belong had they been employed in the modern sector) - about 80 cedis _per_ _month_ before taxes. No doubt the earnings of entrepreneurs represent not only return to his own labour but also to his managerial input and own capital; even if allowance is made for them, they seem to be significantly better off than the wage employees in the formal sector.[1]

The Kumasi study also showed that entrepreneurs with more education tended to have higher gross earnings. Whereas those with no education at all had only 60 cedis per week, entrepreneurs with primary and middle-level education earned respectively 75 cedis and

---

[1] In addition to the above, some 14 per cent of the heads had income from other sources as well.

Table 2. Distribution of enterprises by capital (per cent)

ISIC code	Activity	Fixed capital in cedis[a] (original purchase value)						
		1-50	51-100	101-250	251-600	601-1000	1000	Total
9513	Motor repair and maintenance	0.0	0.0	6.8	28.4	23.0	41.9	100.0
3813, 3819	Metalworking	0.0	0.0	10.0	10.0	30.0	50.0	100.0
3811	Blacksmithing	0.0	0.0	11.1	22.2	11.1	55.5	100.0
3311	Carpentry	0.0	5.9	50.0	32.4	5.9	5.9	1C0.0
3220	Tailoring/seamstressing	2.8	2.8	19.6	42.3	21.1	11.4	100.0
3319	Woodcarving	0.0	14.3	14.3	14.3	14.3	42.9	100.0
3320	Cane weaving	44.4	0.0	44.4	11.3	0.0	0.0	1C0.0
3214	Carpets/doormats	100.0	0.0	0.0	0.0	0.0	0.0	100.0
3233, 3240	Footwear/leatherware	30.4	29.0	24.5	8.6	4.3	2.9	100.0
	All activities	10.7	8.4	20.5	24.8	15.1	20.5	100.0

[a] 1 cedi = US$0.87.

Table 3. Capital output and value added per enterprise and per worker in selected activities

Selected activities	No. of enterprises	No. of persons	Per enterprise			Per worker		
			Fixed capital	Weekly gross output	Weekly value added	Fixed capital	Annual gross output	Annual value added
Fitting	74	5.35	1 479	251	90	276	2 440	874
Metalworking	20	4.40	1 575	260	132	358	3 073	1 560
Blacksmithing	9	3.44	1 362	144	78	396	2 179	1 180
Carpentry	34	4.26	347	122	49	81	1 487	598
Tailoring	71	3.14	646	102	58	206	1 690	962
Footwear and leather manufacturing	69	2.86	165	250	112	58	4 545	2 038
All activities (including others not shown)	298	4.46	778	193	87	174	2 250	1 014

Note: All values in cedis. One cedi is valued at approximately US$0.87.

86 cedis per week, the over-all average being 78 cedis per week.
Likewise, those who had moved from the formal to the informal sector
earned 85 cedis per week as compared to 77 cedis per week for the
rest. Thus, education and training do seem to have a significant
positive impact on the earnings of informal sector entrepreneurs in
Kumasi.

In contrast to the earnings of masters discussed above, the
apprentices received, on the average, only 2.4 cedis per week which
includes token pocket money plus food provided by the master. Since
the median value was around 2.2 cedis per week, it is clear that
half the apprentices received very little compensation. Since most
apprentices pay a lump-sum fee to the master, this implies that the
apprentices not only contribute to investment by masters but also
relieve them from the burden of working capital needed to pay wages.

Size of the enterprise and efficiency

Table 4 shows how output, value added and capital per worker
varies with the size of establishment. As expected, smaller firms
use more capital per worker but also generate more output and value
added per worker. Assuming that the enterprises operate for 50
weeks per year on the average, then a million cedis of investment in
various size groups of enterprises would seem to generate employment
and value added as shown in table 5.

Table 4. Output, value added and capital per worker by size

Size group (no. of persons per enterprise)	Per worker (cedis)		
	Output per week	Value added per week	Capital
1	118	68	318
2-4	61	29	218
5-9	33	14	152
10 +	28	9	136
All	43	19	174

Table 5. Value added and employment per unit of capital, by size of enterprise for an investment of 1 million cedis

Size group (no. of persons per enterprise)	Value added per year (millions)	Employment (persons)
1	10.69	3 145
2-4	6.65	4 587
5-9	4.60	6 579
10 +	3.31	7 353
All groups	5.46	5 747

The above figures are no doubt overestimates because the capital measure is only partial. It is nevertheless interesting to note the systematic inverse relationship between the amount of value added and employment as the firm size increases. This seems to suggest a trade-off between value added and employment but such a conclusion will be hazardous. In so far as smaller enterprises are engaged in activities distinctly different from the larger ones, what the data above indicate are the differences in product-mix rather than production technologies. More importantly, since the larger firms employ more apprentices, one of their major outputs, namely the production of skills, is not reflected in the value added figure. If the value of skills generated are included in the value added, it seems more likely that the relatively larger enterprises are more efficient in the sense they generate both higher value added _and_ employment. However, one cannot stretch this conclusion too far owing to the difficulties of measuring capital and labour (particularly apprentice labour) in comparable terms across the enterprises. Nevertheless, it seems quite clear that the informal sector in Kumasi is significantly more efficient than the larger, formal sector firms.

Linkages between the formal and the informal sectors

Nearly 90 per cent of the sample enterprises bought their raw materials and services requirements mainly from retailers, including individuals and small shops. Some 2 per cent obtained them mainly from discarded materials, and 7 per cent from both the above sources. Thus, only a negligible proportion had direct backward linkage with the formal sector. Since Ghana depends heavily on imported raw materials and inputs even in informal sector manufacturing, the above findings imply that the link with the formal sector (which imports) is indirect. Perhaps it is more illuminating to look at the linkage in terms of input expenses. Of 298 enterprises, 30 obtained more than half their inputs (in value terms) from the modern sector. For the sample as a whole, only 9.4 per cent of total expenditure on intermediate inputs was on purchases from the modern sector. Lastly, larger enterprises within the informal sector seem to have stronger backward linkage with the formal sector. Turning to the question of forward linkages, over 72 per cent of the enterprises sold their output mainly to households and individuals; virtually none directly to the formal sector. Also, the linkage with the households was greater among smaller enterprises. In terms of value of output, only 5 per cent was sold to the formal sector. These findings are similar to those in other cities discussed earlier.

Though the direct linkages with the formal sector are weak, a significant amount of indirect linkages through middlemen or intermediaries seem to exist. For example, in one location, Angloga, merchants buy wood in bulk quantities from sawmills and sell them to carpenters at much more than twice the ex-factory price in the formal sector. Similarly, traders secure bulk orders for furniture from schools and other similar formal institutions and obtain their furniture requirements from the informal sector at low prices. These examples suggest that at least some of the informal sector enterprises are exploited by the middlemen. Finally, in terms of access to credit from banks, only 3 per cent of the Kumasi enterprises had ever obtained a loan from the bank. With regard to skills, only a few relied on formal training institutions, as already noted.

Involutionary or evolutionary growth?

The Kumasi study differs from other studies reported earlier in that it sheds some light on the informal sector's ability to accumulate capital and absorb more labour over time. First, looking at the cross-tabulation of enterprises by activity and by age of business, a greater proportion of capital-intensive activities, like metalworking and carpentry, are older; in other words, a relatively larger proportion of recent enterprises seems to be entering activities with lower capital requirement. It is not clear how far this is due to constraint on capital availability and how far due to changes in market conditions. Also, most of the new enterprises are smaller than the older and well-established ones. For example, 36 per cent of the enterprises under 2 years old had only 1 person (the master himself) as compared to 11 per cent for those over 5 years old. In fact, the differences in size structure seem to disappear once the enterprises are established for at least three years. For example, the average size of firms under three years was only 3.26 as compared to 4.92 for older ones. In other words, the new enterprises seem to approach the size structure of the older firms once they become 3 years old; this interpretation no doubt hinges on the assumption that the old enterprises went through a similar process. Perhaps three years is the minimum time required to accumulate the necessary capital and engage more apprentices as the older firms do.

That the informal sector enterprises tend to accumulate more capital as their duration in business increases seems to be supported by the evidence. If one ranks the sample enterprises by size of capital, the average age of enterprises in the bottom decile turns out to be 4 years as compared to 4.9 years in the top decile. The corresponding figures for manufacturing activities in the informal sector of Freetown are 2.8 years and 3.9 years; and for Lagos, 2.8 and 3.3 years. In other words, the older enterprises had both more fixed capital and more employment than the younger ones. In fact, in metalworking and carpentry, fixed capital seems to have grown faster than employment by some 30 to 40 per cent. In footwear, leather manufacturing and tailoring, though both the volume of capital and employment increased with the age of business, employment seems to have increased faster than capital. For the sample as a whole, the capital-labour ratio seems to increase with the age of business: 147 cedis for enterprises under 2 years; 161 cedis for those between 2 and 3 years; and 177 for those above 3 years. These data are not particularly suited to test the hypothesis of involutionary (or evolutionary) growth since the capital and employment data do not refer to the same enterprises over time. They nevertheless suggest the enterprises do grow as their duration in business increases.

Conclusion

Migration plays an important role in the Kumasi informal sector as elsewhere. The Kumasi entrepreneurs have a significantly higher level of education than in other cities discussed earlier. They are also relatively young, as in Kano (Nigeria). The informal sector plays a key role in providing skills to migrants and in generating self-employment. Perhaps the distinguishing feature of the Kumasi informal sector is its ability to absorb substantial quantities of labour, particularly youth, in the form of apprentices. The latter benefit from the apprenticeship system in terms of opportunities for skill acquisition at little cost. The masters, on the other hand, are able to command a larger amount of labour resources without any additional burden on their working capital needs. The apprentices in fact seem to facilitate their capital accumulation by paying apprenticeship fees. Consequently, the masters are able to utilise a larger amount of both labour and capital and earn incomes substantially higher than those prevailing for comparable skills in the formal sector. The available evidence also suggests that the informal sector in Kumasi uses very little capital per worker as compared to the formal sector. In other words, the sector uses relatively little capital, generates higher levels of income and employment than the formal sector and contributes to capital formation in the form of skills.

The sector has virtually no direct linkage with the formal sector. But in selected activities the linkage seems to be indirect, through intermediaries who in turn take advantage of the market imperfections. Thus, it would seem possible to improve the profitability of at least some of the enterprises through appropriate remedial measures. There does not seem to be any evidence of subordination to the formal sector. Further constraints on capital accumulation would seem to be indirect, through market imperfections. Even though only a handful of enterprises managed to get credit from formal sector institutions, the establishments with a longer duration in business generally possessed more capital and labour and, in many activities, capital-labour ratio appears to have been higher for older enterprises. These findings suggest that the informal sector enterprises in Kumasi have been generally successful in overcoming the barriers to expansion.

What is perhaps amazing is that the Kumasi informal sector is able to absorb labour, generate income and skills for many poor and youth and grow over time, notwithstanding the fact that they are located in a poor physical environment. Most of them are in temporary structures without access to adequate urban services and many are forbidden from investing in their physical premises. High density of activities coupled with poor physical environment and supporting services raise questions with regard to occupational safety, pollution and conditions of work in general. It would therefore seem necessary to review the prevailing public policies that discourage investment in premises and infrastructural facilities, on the one hand, and introduce appropriate measures to improve the conditions of work and the conditions under which training is imparted. In view of the proximity of Kumasi to most rural areas in Ghana, the informal sector could also make a positive contribution to rural development by providing goods and services to the agricultural and other sectors of activity.

Marga Institute, Colombo

Unlike the African countries, the city of Colombo in Sri Lanka
is unusual in that it had virtually no migration in recent years.
The city population increased at an annual rate of only 1.9 per cent
from 426,000 in 1958 to 512,000 in 1963; between 1963 and 1971 the
annual rate of increase was still lower, only 1.2 per cent. Several
reasons have been offered for this phenomenon: a planned programme
of population resettlement from densely populated wet zone of the
country (western, southern and central regions) to the sparsely
populated dry zone (north central, north eastern and eastern
regions); effective social welfare policies improving the living
standard of rural population; extensive road and transport network
linking rural and urban areas, eliminating the need for permanent
migration; and diffusion of major industrial projects in various
parts of the country. Perhaps the most important reason was the
absence of spectacular growth in employment and income opportunities
in the Colombo region.

Though the city population itself showed only modest
increases, one should however remember that the city itself is a
part of the larger complex including outer areas where the
population has increased somewhat faster (3.7 per cent per year
during 1963-71) but still at a rate far below that of many African
cities. Most of the informal sector activities are, however,
concentrated in the city, particularly the Municipality of Colombo
itself. The study on Colombo is thus an interesting case analysing
the role of the informal sector in the absence of migration.

A recent sample survey[1] estimated 69,600 dwelling units in the
Colombo municipal area (Colombo M.C.) of which 44 per cent were
tenements (mainly for lower middle income groups) and 18 per cent
were in shanties (temporary living quarters for low income groups).
It is also worth noting that 30 per cent of the labour force in 1977
in the same area were unemployed, nearly three-quarters of them in
the age group 15-24 years.[2] More importantly, the number of casual
workers, defined to include employed persons who are not reasonably
assured of their employment for 30 days following the date of
interview, was estimated at 23,500 persons or about 20 per cent of
those already employed. The extent of unemployment and
underemployment quoted above already raises a number of questions
about the role of the informal sector in Colombo with regard to
labour absorption.

The 1977 household survey cited above also showed that 82 per
cent of those employed in Colombo M.C. were employees; only 11 per
cent were own-account workers; and 7 per cent were employers. The
informal sector survey in Colombo on the other hand estimated some
34,400 persons as employed in the informal sector amounting to about
----

[1] Ministry of Plan Implementation, Department of Census and
Statistics: Report on the Urban Family Budget Survey, 1977 (Colombo,
1978), table 10.2.

[2] ibid., table 4.

20 per cent of the labour force. One is therefore tempted to conclude that absence of migration implies a relatively smaller size of the informal sector. In so far as migration itself is caused by the growth of employment and income opportunities, the relatively smaller size of the informal sector in Colombo can be attributed to lack of growth in urban regional income.[1]

The structure of the informal sector

The number of informal sector units in Colombo was estimated at 30,000 in 1976. Though the study covered a range of activities including agriculture and fishing, manufacturing, construction, trade, transport and services, the informal sector in Colombo is dominated by trade (including restaurants and the like), as elsewhere. About 63 per cent were in trade (including sale of prepared food) and 20 per cent in services; manufacturing accounted for an incredibly low figure of under 5 per cent, transport 8 per cent, construction little over 1 per cent, and agriculture and fishing 3 per cent. Over 60 per cent of those in trade dealt with such perishable commodities like vegetables, fruits and fish; within the services category 43 per cent were self-employed unskilled labour mainly engaged in loading and unloading goods and 50 per cent in repair services (cars, cycles, radio, watches, locks, etc.). The few that were engaged in manufacturing included tailoring, shoe manufacturing, metalworking and jewellery. In transport, a majority of the units were engaged in non-mechanised transport like pushcarts and baskets. It follows from the above that the Colombo informal sector has little capital investment to speak of.

In terms of size, 85 per cent of the units were one-person enterprises without anyone except the owner himself. The average number of persons engaged per enterprise is only 1.14. A majority of those employing additional labour employed one or two persons besides the owner himself. As elsewhere, 93 per cent of the units were operated on a sole proprietorship basis.

Two-thirds of the units had a fixed location for carrying on their business. Among those without a fixed location, some 40 per cent had a hand-operated or animal-driven cart. Even among those in fixed location, 46 per cent were conducting their business in open pavements without any structures at all; one-third were housed in temporary or semi-permanent structures on pavements or public land and the rest on private land. Further, a majority of the informal sector units (62 per cent) operated in residential areas. And two-thirds of the participants in this sector lived close to their workplace, usually within a radius of some 3 kilometres.

Of those in permanent or temporary structures only a few operated in their own premises. For example, 11 per cent in trade, 10 per cent in manufacturing and about 22 per cent in services owned their premises. The proportion of enterprises renting their premises in the three activities was respectively 54, 64 and 51 per cent. Thus about a third or so operated in rent-free premises.

----

[1] The GDP originating from the industrial sector seems to have increased at a slower rate in recent years: only 3 per cent per year during 1970-76 as compared to 6.7 per cent per annum during 1960-70 period. See World Bank: World Development Report, 1978, op. cit., p. 78.

What about the age structure of these units? The results based on a sample of 1,200 enterprises showed that nearly 10 per cent of them had been established during the year preceding the date of interview; 8 per cent between one and two years and 20 per cent between two and five years. But over 60 per cent of the units had been in operation for longer than five years as compared to 48 per cent in Kumasi (manufacturing), 34 per cent in Lagos and 31 per cent in Freetown. And the age structure showed little variations between activities. Unlike in other studies presented earlier, the average age of business in manufacturing is not higher than that in trade and services.

The informal sector participants

As already, observed, there were few employees in the Colombo informal sector; consequently, the discussion below on the participants essentially refers to the entrepreneurs themselves. Eighty-eight per cent of the participants were males. Thus, as in the case of Africa, only a small number of women participated in the Colombo informal sector. The Colombo informal sector had fewer Sinhalese but more Tamils and other ethnic groups. Further, the evidence suggests that certain ethnic groups tend to dominate certain types of activities.

The median age of participants was around 35 years; the proportion of females in the total was under 12 per cent and their median age was significantly higher, around 45 years. Thus, males dominated the informal sector. One of the interesting features of the age distribution is that only a quarter of the participants were under the age of 24 years even though, as already referred to, 75 per cent of the unemployed in Colombo Municipal Council area were in this age group. It would therefore seem that, unlike in Africa, the Colombo informal sector absorbs few young unemployed persons. Besides the social value placed on informal sector occupations, the maze of socio-economic inter-relationships within which the sector operates would also seem to have played a role in restricting entry. The Colombo informal sector in this respect is distinctly different from those elsewhere.

In terms of education: illiterate, 10 per cent; literate with no formal education, 8 per cent; 30 per cent with under 4 years of schooling; 40 per cent with between 5 and 9 years of schooling; and the remaining 12 per cent had over 10 years' schooling. The median level of schooling in the Colombo (about four years) informal sector is thus comparable to the evidence from Africa. But when compared to the average level of schooling of unemployed (around 10 years), the informal sector participants have very little education, partly because they are relatively older. It is doubtful if such segmentation of the labour market can be attributed solely to socio-economic factors restricting entry into the informal sector; individual preferences favouring white-collar jobs coupled with the traditional nature of the informal sector would seem to play an important role too.

Migration

It was mentioned at the outset that migration to Colombo played an insignificant role in the city's population growth. The

informal sector study showed that only 14 per cent of the
participants were migrants and most of them (79 per cent) had
migrated over ten years ago. Over 80 per cent of them came from the
adjacent western and southern regions. Thus, there seems to be
little link between migration and the informal sector. In fact one
could argue that the relatively small size of the informal sector
(about 20 per cent of the employed labour force) in Colombo can be
attributed to the above. Another interesting feature of the Colombo
informal sector is that not all the non-migrants (or the natives)
reside in Colombo city; of the 86 per cent belonging to this
category a third (or 28 per cent of the total) resided outside the
city and commuted frequently.[1] Since most of the migrants had been
in the city for longer than ten years, quite naturally two-thirds of
them never visited their place of origin.

Conditions of work

Forty-six per cent of the units operated on all days In terms
of operation, 46 per cent of the units operated on all days during
the week; only some 16 per cent worked for less than five days a
week. Virtually all the units do not observe fixed hours of work.
Another aspect of the working conditions originated from the
government regulation. The units operating in certain central
locations are subjected to constant threat of eviction by police
arising from a concern for traffic congestion and/or illegal
occupation of public pavements. The informal sector's response to
such law enforcement has been to organise themselves and let their
views be known; a pavement hawkers' union with a membership of
18,000 even tried to agitate, demanding more considerate treatment
and relaxation of the municipal by-laws affecting their fortunes.
Such harassments, besides hurting their income opportunities, would
also seem to have discouraged the small enterprises from saving and
investment in business following increased uncertainties.

Notwithstanding the concentration of informal sector
activities in trade and services and the small capital investment in
the form of premises, the participants of this sector seem to have
done reasonably well in terms of the net earnings. The median daily
income was around Rs.19 - about the same as the average daily
earnings in the large-scale manufacturing sector of Sri Lanka in
1977.[2] The bottom 25 per cent had an income below Rs.10 per day and
the top 10 per cent had at least Rs.100 per day. Thus, the earnings
within the informal sector are subject to considerable variations.
The bulk of the wage employees seems to fall below the median level
of daily earnings. Likewise many of the entrepreneurs with a larger
workforce belong to higher income brackets. Whether the earnings
quoted above are adequate or not is a different matter and it can be
answered only after taking into account other sources of income if
any and the household size, which are discussed later.
----

[1] Heavily subsidised transport facilities would seem to explain
this phenomenon. See A.S. Owerai: An overview of state policies and
internal migration in Asia, Paper presented at the ILO Workshop on
State Policies and Internal Migration, Bangkok, 28 April-1 May 1980,
p. 33.

[2] ILO: Year Book of Labour Statistics, 1979 (Geneva, 1979), p.
404.

Linkages

Though the study was unable to collect reliable data on capital and value added owing to a high degree of non-response, it did try to assess the question of availability of capital. The Colombo study confirmed the findings of studies elsewhere; about 70 per cent of the entrepreneurs relied on own sources such as personal savings for their capital requirements; only 6.2 per cent sought help from formal credit institutions. Over three-quarters of those who borrowed relied on friends and relatives.

With regard to forward linkages, it is already clear from the nature of activities pursued that a large majority of them are engaged in the production of final consumer goods and services. About three-quarters of the enterprises sold their goods and services to households, mostly to middle and lower income groups (table 1). A significant proportion of sample enterprises, however, seem to sell their goods and services to the formal sector as well.

Table 1: Distribution of enterprises by type of clientele and by activity

Activity	Households (per cent)			Enterprises and institutions	
	Low income	Middle income	Higher income	Informal sector	Formal sector
1. Trade	34	32	13	10	11
2. Manufacturing	19	23	15	9	34
3. Services	37	26	14	10	13
4. Transport	23	29	17	12	19
5. Construction	14	39	16	12	19
6. Agriculture	37	26	20	12	5

Socio-economic structure and the informal sector

Perhaps the merit of the Colombo study lies in its focus on the socio-economic framework within which the informal sector operates. In so far as earning opportunities are location-specific, choice locations within the city are not easily accessible to new entrants because of the dominance of other well-established informal sector enterprises. Not infrequently the new entrant to the sector has to pay kappang, or a protection fee, to those who thus control the location in question. In other words, capital is not the only barrier to entry.

Inadequate access to skills, both technical and managerial, also forces new entrants to seek the help of well-established informal sector enterprises; it could take the form of a wage employee or an apprentice. Again it is not easy to gain such entry unless the well-established entrepreneurs have full confidence in the new entrant. In this respect the Colombo informal sector entrepreneurs would seem to be less liberal in their attitude when compared to their counterparts in African cities; in other words, some kind of a patron-client relationship is required in order to gain entry. To complicate the matter, ethnicity and regional origin also seem to play an important role in this process. In the vegetable and fish trade, for example, the Sinhalese from the southern region dominate while in the non-mechanised transport activity the Tamils dominate.

What is perhaps more interesting is that some of the informal sector enterprises are unable to extricate themselves from the above inter-relationships even if certain forms of assistance were extended to them. For example, when a programme was developed to assist hand-trolley operators to acquire their own vehicles through liberal credit it turned out to be a failure. In the process of severing the link between the trolley operator and the fleet owner on whom he depends, the former also lost his clientele partly because he was unable to provide a guarantee for the safety of the goods to be transported and partly because he could not wean the customers away from the fleet owner.

The urban informal sector, living conditions and environment

About one-third of the participants in the Colombo informal sector were not married. Nevertheless, only 9 per cent of the participants belonged to single-person households. As many as 46 per cent of the participants' households had six or more persons per household. The median household size was thus close to six. In relation to the household size, the earnings of informal sector participants reported earlier seem to be quite modest or even inadequate for a decent living. Taking the average income per participant at Rs.500 per month, the per capita income per month works out at less than Rs.100 (or approximately 8 US dollars). These figures imply that the informal sector does not generate income adequate to meet the basic needs of households dependent on this sector.

But a tabulation of households by earning members revealed that many of them had other earning members besides the participant. For every three persons engaged in the informal sector there were two employed in the formal sector; and 70 per cent of those employed in the formal sector were in the public sector. Additional earners were particularly important in households depending on informal trade and services. In addition to contribution from other earners, many of the participants also seem to derive income from farming. Per capita income per month in these households from all income sources would thus appear to be well above the per capita figure implied by the average observed in 1977 for the whole of Colombo M.C. area, namely Rs.741 per month per household.[1]

The implication of the above is of course that a majority of the informal sector particpants' households have a respectable level
----

[1] Department of Census and Statistics, Government of Sri Lanka: Report on the Urban Family Budget Survey 1977 (Colombo, 1978), table 16.

of income. This is also reflected in the fact that about 50 per
cent of the participants live in well-constructed houses with
masonry and tiled roof. Some 30 per cent live in houses with
plastered walls and thatched roof and 10 per cent in houses with
masonry and thatched or asbestos roof. This is indeed in quite a
contrast with the living conditions of informal sector participants
elsewhere. In terms of ownership, a third of the permanent type of
dwelling units were owned, half rented and most of the remaining
shared. Of the few with temporary structures, 62 per cent were
owned, 20 per cent rented and 12 per cent shared. Further, a
majority of the permanent type of housing was served with
electricity and had private watertaps. As for the rest of the
permanent type of housing, they had electricity, common water supply
and common toilet facilities. In other words, the living conditions
of the informal sector participants were significantly better than
the working conditions, thanks to the contribution of secondary
earners.

Evolutionary or involutionary growth?

The respectable levels of income generated in the informal
sector should lead one to believe that there is a significant amount
of savings and hence the capacity to grow. A number of case studies
undertaken concurrently with the sample survey suggested that in the
overwhelming majority of cases the successful entrepreneur utilises
his savings either to start a different activity in the same
locality and diversify his business or alternatively uses it for
investment in children's education or in land. In other words, very
little vertical expansion would appear to take place in the informal
sector of Colombo; much of the growth results from horizontal
expansion. This is also consistent with the ownership status of
business premises noted earlier. Even though a majority of the
informal sector units had been in operation for several years only
about a third of the sample units had any kind of structure at all
and very few among them were owned. Given the negligible amount of
capital used in these enterprises, it is clear that the bulk of the
income generated in this sector accrues to labour. Absence of
capital growth also seems to explain the dominance of single-person
units (85 per cent of the sample) even though the median age of
business was close to ten years. Notwithstanding the low level of
capital requirement and the prevalence of substantial unemployment,
the growth of informal sector units has been modest - only 10 per
cent of the enterprises emerged during the year preceding the survey
as compared to 26 per cent in Freetown and 18 per cent in Lagos for
example. These findings seem to suggest that growth, if any, in the
Colombo informal sector has been neither evolutionary nor
involutionary. Two factors seem to explain this phenomenon: first,
a decrease in the rate of growth of the formal sector in recent
years noted earlier probably led to a poor growth in demand for
informal sector goods and services; and second, the bulk of the
unemployed being young and more educated either do not find it
attractive to enter the informal sector or are unable to break the
socio-economic barriers to entry discussed earlier.

Conclusion

Though various social welfare measures, particularly in the countryside, seem to have played an important role in preventing rural-urban migration flows, poor economic performance in the Colombo region would appear to be equally, if not more, important in explaining the absence of pull factors. Unfortunately no regional income data are available to prove this contention. The only indirect indicator of this trend is based on the household survey data for the periods 1969/70 and 1977. Between these two periods the average proportion of household income spent on food and drink in the urban sector increased from 48.3 per cent to 55 per cent, suggesting a substantial decline in average real incomes. Another piece of evidence suggests that the average real income in the urban areas of Sri Lanka declined at the rate of 1.8 per cent per year during 1963-73.[1]

In the absence of an adequate real economic growth in the Colombo region it is quite natural to expect little or no migration. It is also quite logical that the well-established informal sector enterprises seek to preserve their market share in the face of a stagnant, or even declining, aggregate demand for their goods and services through a variety of socio-economic relationships. The Colombo study would thus appear to suggest a positive relationship between the growth of the informal and the formal sectors. If this is true then it follows that the scope for labour absorption in the informal sector cannot be influenced in a significant way through various kinds of assistance to the enterprises; the major focus would have to be on the process of economic development itself.

Many of the participants in the Colombo informal sector seem to have additional earners in their households, notably in the formal sector. Consequently only a small proportion of them, perhaps a quarter or so, seem to fall below the poverty line. It also follows that a large majority of the participants have decent housing and greater access to urban services as compared to other cities even though the conditions of work are less than satisfactory. Perhaps the major implication for environment emerges from the poor infrastructural facilities since only a few enterprises have temporary or permanent structures. An integrated approach to land-use planning, making provision for the location of informal sector enterprises without alienating them from the market opportunities could remove uncertainties associated with investment in premises and thus facilitate the growth of this sector.

----

[1] Oberai: An overview of state policies and internal migration in Asia, op. cit., p. 33.

CHAPTER 9. OCCUPATIONAL MOBILITY AND THE INFORMAL SECTOR IN JAKARTA

Hazel Moir[1]

Even though Jakarta regional income increased at a respectable rate of some 6 to 7 per cent per year since the mid-1960s, the rate of unemployment in the city jumped from 7.4 per cent in 1961 to 12.8 per cent in 1971.[2] Jakarta is one of the fastest-growing cities in south-east Asia; from about half a million in 1930 the population increased to over 4 1/2 million in 1971. The annual rate of increase in population during the 1960s was 5.6 per cent, double the natural rate of increase. Needless to add, migration has played an important role in the process. Consequently, the labour force increased at an annual rate of 3 per cent. As in other developing countries, the formal sector was unable to absorb the increases in the labour force and thus almost half of the employed population of over 1 million is estimated to be engaged in the informal sector. Both the absolute and relative size of the informal sector in Jakarta makes it an interesting case study.

The study on Jakarta covered manufacturing construction, transport, trade and services activities; and the sample, as already noted, was representative of all parts of the city. Also the Jakarta study differed from the studies cited thus far in that it sought to identify the informal sector activities through the households rather than directly. As a result, the study was able to collect information not only about the enterprises from the respective heads but also about other informal sector participants in the selected households and about the households themselves. The evidence emerging from the above is disclosed below but in the reverse order.

Households with informal sector participants

Data collected from 4,364 heads of households suggest that the population in them is evenly divided between males and females. The median household size was between five and six. Surprisingly, the proportion of single-member households was only 2 per cent. As much as 14 per cent of the households had ten or more members.

----

[1] The author is currently at the Bureau of Industry Economics in Australia. The study was carried out by the National Institute of Economic and Social Research (LEKNAS), Indonesian Institute of Sciences, Jakarta. The author is grateful to Dr. Suharso and Mr. Soetjipto Wirosardjono (of PPMPL and BPS) who were instrumental in carrying out the study. A shorter version of the study on which the chapter is based appeared in 1977: Hazel Moir and Soetjipto Wirosardjono, "Sektor Informil di Jakarta", in Widyapura, Nos. 9-10, 1977, pp. 49-70. The full-length version of the study appeared as Jakarta Informal Sector, LEKNAS Monograph Series, Jakarta: LEKNAS-LIPI, 1978 (163 pages). The author prepared the study while at LEKNAS as a Demographic Consultant.

[2] S.V. Sethuraman: Jakarta: Urban development and employment (Geneva, ILO, 1976).

Less than a third of the households lived in permanent structures, of which some 84 per cent had water facilities and 38 per cent electricity; and 16 per cent had neither of the two. What is more interesting is that 14 per cent of these households, though living in permanent structures, were actually homeless; they neither owned nor rented nor shared the premises. The proportions of households owning, renting and sharing accommodation were respectively 61, 19 and 6 per cent. Eleven per cent of such housing was claimed to be illegal.

Among those in temporary housing (about 70 per cent of the sample households), a majority did not have either water or electricity. Only 4 per cent had electricity. Over a quarter of these households claimed that they were homeless. Some 46 per cent owned their premises while 22 per cent rented, and the remaining few shared the accommodation. Again, as expected, 70 per cent of the temporary housing was illegal.

The housing situation for these households in Jakarta is thus in sharp contrast to that in Colombo; over 40 per cent of the total illegal and without either water or electricity. More than a quarter of the total were actually homeless or nearly so. The poor living conditions for a substantial proportion of these households raise several issues concerning the role of the urban informal sector in Jakarta in ameliorating the urban environment. In particular, the relationship between self-help housing schemes in the Kampongs (or slums) and the informal sector activities needs to be explored further.

Informal sector participants

The number of participants in the informal sector, as a head operating his own enterprise or as a paid or unpaid worker, in the sample households was 5,359; they were identified as belonging to the informal sector through a screening process, viz. by addressing a few questions to all those above 10 years and working, in the selected households. Thus, at least some of these households had earning members outside the informal sector, viz. formal sector including the Government. Of the 5,359 participants, 4,367 or 81 per cent were heads, running their own business. In other words, one out of five participants was a paid or unpaid worker in the informal sector. In view of the dominance[1] of the heads of enterprise among the participants much of the evidence below can be interpreted as applying to the entrepreneurs.

As elsewhere, only a minority of the participants, about a quarter, were women. The median age, for men and women, was between 35 and 39 years - significantly higher than 28 years observed for migrants, discussed later. Less than 18 per cent of the participants were young, below 24 years; nearly a quarter of them were above 44 years. Turning to education, significant differences were found between males and females. Among males, 20 per cent had no schooling and 60 per cent had primary level of education or less; the corresponding figures for females were 50 per cent and 38 per cent. Though the average education of men was higher than women,

----

[1] Dominance of heads of informal sector enterprises in the sample was due to the sample design.

the median number of years of schooling for both combined was around three years of schooling, much lower than is found elsewhere. It is also interesting to note that the informal sector participants in Jakarta had fewer years of schooling on the average as compared to that of total employed population in the city in 1971, which should be expected.

Role of migration

It was mentioned at the outset that migration played an important role in Jakarta's population growth. Sixty per cent of the participants (59 per cent of males and 63 per cent of females) were born outside Jakarta but only a few of them were recent migrants. Of those born outside Jakarta, 61 per cent had migrated more than ten years preceding the date of interview and 19 per cent between five and ten years. Thus, 20 per cent may be called as recent migrants who came to Jakarta during the preceding five years; the corresponding figures for Freetown and Lagos were respectively 26 and 30 per cent. But when compared with the 1971 population census, the above figure appears to be substantially lower. As much as 38 per cent were reported to have migrated to Jakarta during the five years preceding the census.[1] Though one could argue that the sample did not cover adequately the areas where recent migrants tend to settle, the difference is at least partly attributable to the dominance of enterprise heads in the sample. The median age of recent migrants, as mentioned earlier, is substantially lower (27 years) than for all the participants. But still it is significantly above that recorded in the population census (about 22 years); the difference could partly be attributed to the dominance of heads of enterprises in the sample who generally tend to be older than the workers.

Migrants in the informal sector of Jakarta did not differ substantially from the natives in terms of education. For example, among males 17 per cent of the migrants had no schooling as compared to 22 per cent for natives of Jakarta. A greater proportion of the recent male migrants had between one and six years of schooling as compared to the natives (67 per cent versus 59 per cent).

One of the interesting findings of the Jakarta study pertains to rural-urban origin of the migrants. Of 85 per cent who migrated from within Java to Jakarta, over two-thirds originated from rural areas. But if one looks at the recent migrants only, of 86 per cent from within Java, over three-quarters come from rural areas. These findings suggest that: (a) migration from within Java is more important than that from outer islands; (b) rural-urban migration is more important than urban-urban migration; and (c) rural-urban migration seems to be gaining more importance. As elsewhere, the region adjacent to Jakarta, West Java, accounted for 44 per cent of the total number of migrants in the informal sector; but among recent migrants Central Java, slightly farther from West Java, is more important (45 versus 36 per cent).

Unlike in Lagos where 85 per cent of the migrant entrepreneurs visited their place of origin at least once a year, only half of the

----

Sethuraman, Jakarta: Urban development and employment, op. cit., p. 95.

migrant participants in Jakarta visited their place of origin at
least once during the year. Thus, the link between the urban
informal sector and the migrants' place of origin is relatively
weak. Of course, such links tend to be weaker the longer the
duration of residence in Jakarta.[1]

Occupational mobility and labour market

Ninety per cent of the informal sector participants were in
two occupational categories: 63 per cent as sales workers and 28 per
cent as production workers. Relatively more sales workers and fewer
production workers were present among migrants. To what extent have
the migrants improved their position by entering the informal sector
in Jakarta? In the absence of relevant income data, the structure
of previous and current occupation of migrants would seem to throw
some light on this issue. First, 64 per cent of the migrants never
had a job before they migrated to Jakarta. In other words, they
were unemployed or outside the labour force. This percentage was
slightly smaller, 61 per cent, for recent migrants. Second, of
those who were employed before migration, half were in agriculture.
These findings suggest that migration was indeed beneficial to these
persons though the exent to which they benefited is not known. Only
about 6 per cent of the participants, both migrants and natives, had
unstable (or variable) occupations throughout the year.

One of the interesting aspects of the Jakarta study is its
focus on occupational mobility within the informal sector. Does
this sector provide opportunities to its participants to improve
their occupational, and hence income, status? First it should be
noted that for nearly two-thirds of the participants their current
job is their first job; that is, they were unemployed or outside the
labour force before. Among those who did change their occupations
(i.e. 1,860 participants), a third changed to other jobs within the
same occupational category. Other significant changes in
occupational distribution (only for those who changed) were as
follows: 61 per cent were in sales worker category at the time of
the survey as compared to only 34 per cent before; 28 per cent were
in production worker category at the time of the survey as compared
to 15 per cent before; none were in agriculture during the survey
period as compared to 28 per cent before; and 9 per cent were
currently employed as service workers as compared to 13 per cent
before. Thus there seems to be a tendency for informal sector
participants to concentrate in two specific occupational groups:
sales workers and production workers.

One of the hypotheses examined by the Jakarta study in this
context was that learning new skills contributed to greater
occupational mobility. The survey results indicate that of the 35
per cent who did change their occupation 46 per cent did so after
learning new skills. Further, it appears that the more educated
persons resorted to learning skills before changing occupations to
a greater extent than those with little education. For example,
----

For some evidence contradicting the above, emphasising the
importance of circular migration, see L. Jellinek: "Circular
migration and the pondok dwelling system: A case study of ice cream
traders", in P.J. Rimmer et al. (eds.): Food, shelter and transport
in south-east Asia and the Pacific (Canberra, 1978).

only 40 per cent of the illiterates and 42 per cent of primary school dropouts who changed their occupation learnt new skills before doing so; in contrast, the corresponding percentages for junior and senior high school graduates and university graduates were respectively 55 and 58 per cent.

It is also clear from the evidence that the less-educated participants rely more on friends for learning such skills than the better-educated ones who acquire their skills from training centres, employers and other sources. For example, 83 per cent of illiterates who learnt new skills before changing their job relied on friends as a source as compared to 38 per cent for high school and 28 per cent for university graduates from the same source. The incidence of job mobility, however, showed little variation between different educational categories; the proportion of participants reporting a change of occupation was: illiterates, 36 per cent; literates with no schooling, 38 per cent; incomplete primary, 37 per cent; completed primary, 34 per cent; junior high school, 30 per cent; senior high school, 28 per cent; and university graduates, 38 per cent as compared to the over-all figure of 35 per cent.

When asked about job satisfaction, two-thirds of the participants were satisfied; of the remaining, a majority was looking for a better job in a similar occupation while the rest in a different occupation. But the greater the level of education, the greater the proportion dissatisfied with their current job. These findings would seem to suggest that there is some positive relation-ship between the level of education and occupational mobility.

The survey data showed that 38 per cent of the participants secured their current job without much effort while 46 per cent had to do some search and 16 per cent after a great deal of search. Participants with few years of education (i.e. between one and six years) had to undertake more search than others; but those with junior high school education or more had to put in considerable effort, presumably because they have stronger preferences for certain types of jobs. To assess the current labour market situation, the participants were asked whether they could find another job similar to the one they were holding if they quit. Interestingly enough only 11 per cent of the sample participants replied in the affirmative; over half, particularly among the uneducated or less educated ones, admitted that they would have great difficulty in finding another job.

Though the extent of occupational mobility was limited among the participants as a whole, the data for wage earners show a different picture. First, 18 per cent of the male wage earnrers had held their current job for less than a year and 40 per cent for between one and two years. It could either mean that there is considerable labour turnover in the sector or that most of the wage earners are new entrants to the labour force. For women wage earners, 47 per cent had held their current job for less than a year and 37 per cent for between one and two years. These findings suggest that there is a considerable amount of labour turnover among the wage employees in the informal sector.

One of the policy instruments for improving the incomes of informal sector participants is to use training as a means for greater job mobility. But the Jakarta study showed that surprisingly more than 75 per cent of the participants did not want to change their job at all. In fact the less-educated ones were more reluctant to do so. Of those who were willing to change, 37 per cent would accept free training without any reduction in their current wages; and most of the remaining were willing to be trained with reduced wages or even without wages. Thus, training would seem to play only a limited role in bringing about job mobility. In other words, most of the participants seem to anticipate little benefit from training per se; credit and other kinds of assistance would seem to be much more important to them.

It is also sometimes hypothesised that the informal sector participants have a general preference for wage employment rather than self-employment. But an overwhelming majority of the Jakarta sample, 86 per cent, preferred self-employment which may be partly due to the stress on self-employment in the sample design; and two-thirds of them wanted assistance in the form of capital and/or legal recognition and 26 per cent, particularly those with more education and those in production activity, in management skills.

Conditions of work

The Jakarta survey found, as in the case of Colombo, that nearly a quarter of the participants had no fixed place of work; presumably most of these were hawkers and vendors and to some extent transport workers. Among those who did have a fixed place of work, 46 per cent operated in their own residence which, as already noted, was generally poor in terms of urban facilities; and another 43 per cent worked in the same neighbourhood, within a kilometre radius from the residence. Thus, they are strongly linked to the neighbourhood in which they also live. It also implies that their working conditions cannot be improved significantly without improving the living conditions themselves unless the place of work is separated from residence.

Over half of the male and two-fifths of the female participants worked for over eight hours a day; there seems to be some underemployment in terms of hours of work per day. Since the question of wage payments is applicable to wage earners only, only a small fraction of the participants responded to this question. A third of the male wage earners received their wages on a daily basis; 29 per cent on a weekly and 18 per cent on a monthly basis. Eighty per cent of them received wages in cash. For most of the wage earners, the wages received did not vary (or varied very little) between different wage periods.

The enterprise

It was noted in the last section on informal sector participants that a quarter of them did not have a fixed location for work. In the sample enterprises however a slightly larger proportion, about a third, did not have a fixed location. Half of those in variable location were in trade (as hawkers) and a quarter in transport. Surprisingly, some 6 per cent of them were also in manufacturing. Most of the transport enterprises, quite naturally, did not have a fixed location since they operated vehicles, half power operated (three-wheelers) and half manually operated (cycle rickshaws or becaks). Even in other activities, some 20 per cent or so had some kind of a vehicle for business purposes. As expected, larger enterprises without fixed location tended to use power-operated vehicles more frequently while the smaller ones relied on manually-operated vehicles.

In terms of other operational characteristics, only 13 per cent of the enterprises were subjected to seasonal fluctuations in hours of operation. Seventy-four per cent had fixed hours of work and the average number of hours worked per day was nine.

Virtually all the 4,367 enterprises were run on a sole proprietorship basis. Age distribution of the enterprises shows that 10.6 per cent of them came into existence during the year preceding the survey which seems to suggest that the gross annual birth rate of enterprises in the informal sector has been around 12 per cent. The corresponding rate for trade and services sectors was higher and for manufacturing and construction sectors substantially lower. In other words, as in the case of Africa, a greater proportion of the recently emerging enterprises was in trade and service activities which require relatively little capital as compared to manufacturing and construction. The age distribution also shows that 21 per cent, 30 per cent, 19 per cent and 20 per cent of the enterprises were in the age groups 1 to 2 years, 2 to 5 years, 5 to 10 years and over 10 years respectively. Unlike in Colombo, where a majority of the enterprises were over 5 years of age, only 39 per cent of the Jakarta enterprises belonged to this category. In this respect, Jakarta is closer to Lagos and Freetown where two-thirds or more of the enterprises were under 5 years old. Thus there seems to be a positive relationship between migration flows and the growth of the informal sector in terms of number of enterprises.

Size distribution of enterprises and employment

Only 10 per cent of the informal sector enterprises in Jakarta had workers in addition to the head of the enterprise. Three-quarters of them had between one and three workers besides the entrepreneurs. The sample of 4,367 enterprises had a total workforce of 5,802 persons including the head; thus, the average size per enterprise was only 1.33. As elsewhere, a greater proportion of those engaged in manufacturing hired workers; while 58 per cent were one-person enterprises, 17 per cent employed five or more persons including the head.

As in the case of the participants discusssed earlier, the bulk of the 1,435 employees in the informal sector (5,802 minus 4,367 heads) was males (79 per cent). Most of them were employed on a full-time basis. A majority of the enterprises having employees paid wages, mostly on a regular basis (daily, weekly, monthly or annually). Thus, only a few enterprises in the informal sector had unpaid workers.

When the enterprises were asked about the origin of their workers, it was discovered that only 12 per cent of them obtained their workers from other enterprises. Over half of the enterprises said that their workers were unemployed before. Only a quarter of the enterprises reported that their workers were migrants, mostly from rural areas.

Wages and value added

Though many enterprises did not respond to questions on wages the evidence emerging from the study is nevertheless worth noting. Based on the response from some 200 enterprises, the average daily wage paid to workers varied between a minimum of Rp.468 and a maximum of Rp.611 suggesting that the actual average might have been around Rp.500 per day. Both the minimum and the maximum were somewhat higher in manufacturing. In fact the distribution of enterprises by average daily wage shows that 19 per cent paid a wage of under Rp.200 (or roughly US$0.50) per day; 26 per cent between Rp.200 and Rp.400; 8 per cent between Rp.400 and Rp.500; 14 per cent between Rp.500 and Rp.600; and 32 per cent above Rp.600. The median daily wage seems to be around Rp.500 (or US$1.25). Taking 25 working days per month the above implies an average monthly wage of Rp.12,500. How does it compare with the incomes elsewhere in Jakarta? The minimum wage for the government worker in the lowest grade with about six years of schooling during the early 1970s was about Rp.6,000 per month. The minimum wage in the foreign private sector seems to have been around Rp.8,800 per month during the early 1970s.[1] Making allowance for an average rate of inflation of about 23 per cent per year during the 1970-76 period, the average income of informal sector workers in Jakarta estimated above would seem to be substantially lower than that in the formal sector. Thus, only a few wage workers seem to earn incomes comparable to the minimum in the formal sector.

Gross value added showed considerable variations among the enterprises. Though 28 per cent of the enterprises had a gross value added per worker per week of over Rp.15,000 (or US$36), the median value was around Rp.7,000 (or US$17) per week. In terms of per annum it works out to about US$850 per worker, which is not a small sum considering the little capital employed and the conditions under which it is generated. It is more than thrice the estimated annual per capita income of US$240 in 1976. For enterprises without any employees besides the head - i.e. single-person establishments - the median value added is also around Rp.7,000 per week since 90 per cent of the Jakarta sample belonged to this category. This implies that the median value of earnings of heads is about Rp.7,000 per week - i.e. net return after meeting all production expenses. In other words, the median earnings of entrepreneurs in this sector seems to be more than twice the median wage of workers noted above. It also suggests that the average income of entrepreneurs compares favourably with the minimum prevailing in the formal sector.

Since the value added shows considerable variations ranging from negative values for some 5 per cent of the enterprises to over Rp.15,000 per week for some 28 per cent of the enterprises, perhaps it is more appropriate to use the weighted average value rather than the median. Excluding the few with a negative value added and taking Rp.15,000 per week as the average value for the top 28 per cent (i.e. underestimating the latter's contribution), the average value added per enterprise works out to Rp.8,448 (or approximately US$21) per week. (The corresponding figure for single-person enterprises is also about the same in view of their overwhelming importance in the sample.) These findings thus seem to support the evidence from other studies that there are significant disparities in income even within the informal sector.

----

[1] Sethuraman, Jakarta: Urban development and employment, op. cit., p. 118.

Contribution to GDP

The evidence above suggests that the average value added per enterprise was about US$21 per week or about US$15.8 per person per week. Taking 50 work weeks per year, the average value added per worker per year was around US$800. Given that at least half a million persons were employed in the informal sector in the mid-1970s,[1] it would seem that this sector generated a total gross value added of at least US$400 million. The regional gross domestic product of Jakarta in 1971 was Rp.252 billion[2] (or US$611 million) which however excludes much of the income generated in the informal sector. Taking an annual rate of growth of 9 per cent observed for the late 1960s, the regional gross domestic product originating from sectors other than the informal sector in 1976 might be estimated at US$940 million. In other words, the informal sector in Jakarta would seem to contribute about 30 per cent of the total income generated in the region (i.e. US$400 million as a per cent of US$1,340 million).

Linkages and competition

It was already stated that the bulk of those in fixed location operated within their own residential neighbourhood. Most of those without fixed locations seem to operate in commercial areas. This is also consistent with the finding that a third of the sample enterprises reported that they approach their customers, presumably in hawking, vending and transport activities.

Eighty-seven per cent of the enterprises sold their goods and services to households exclusively. Most of the remaining few sold to other small enterprises and/or households. Linkage with the formal or the government sector was thus virtually absent. Given the strong orientation toward the final consumers, it is quite natural that over 80 per cent of the enterprises saw little scope in increasing the demand for their products through the formal sector.

There are, however, other forms of linkage with the Government. Though only a quarter of the enterprises were registered and had a licence, in transport activities more than half reported so. About two-fifths of the sample enterprises said that they were recognised by the Government. Similarly, only a minority reported paying taxes; only a quarter of the sample claimed that they were legal; and 21 per cent were subject to some kind of an inspection. Most of such linkages were confined to transport enterprises.

What about backward linkages? Only a few of the sample enterprises bought services, and that too mostly from other individuals. But, in terms of raw materials purchase, half of them relied on small enterprises and 22 per cent relied on other sources in addition to small enterprises. Most of the remaining, particularly in trade, depended on households.

----

[1] Based on the assumption that 41 per cent of total employment in Jakarta is in the informal sector; and that the labour force has been growing at 2.9 per cent per year in Jakarta. See Sethuraman: Jakarta: Urban development and employment, op. cit.

[2] ibid., p. 11.

With regard to competition, about half the enterprises, particularly in transport activity, felt there was too much competition. Some 12 per cent of the enterprises felt that other enterprises produce goods and services similar to their own and cheaper. The results suggest that demand constraint is more important than competition based on lower costs and better quality of goods and services produced.

Growth and expansion

One of the important dimensions of growth within the informal sector is the number of enterprises. It was observed earlier that the number of such enterprises seems to be growing at a gross annual rate of some 12 per cent. Breakdown of the data by size of enterprise also suggests that the new enterprises that are emerging are smaller in terms of employment. For example, 91 per cent of the enterprises under one year old were single-person enterprises as compared to 87 per cent among those ten years and older. The implication of this is of course that the rate of growth of employment is somewhat smaller than the rate of growth of number of enterprise in the informal sector. Further, as already noted, a somewhat larger proportion of the older enterprises seemed to be in more productive activities such as manufacturing. For example, 54 per cent of manufacturing units were five years old or older as compared to 37 per cent in trade.

With regard to vertical expansion, nearly three-quarters of the sample enterprises seem to be faced with one constraint or another. For 30 per cent it was lack of demand, and for 35 per cent it was lack of capital. Though the remaining mentioned other constraints, government policies and lack of premises were cited as constraints only by a few. As expected, for those engaged in transport activity, government policies were a more important constraint than either capital or demand; this is understandable because the Government of Jakarta has been gradually restricting the areas in which the cycle rickshaws (or becaks) are allowed to operate.

But when the enterprises were asked about the kinds of assistance they would like to receive, over three-quarters mentioned about cheaper credit facilities. Unlike in other studies, over two-thirds also wanted suitable business premises. Elimination of taxes and licence requirement, provision of training facilities and technical know-how, etc. were important only to a third or so of the sample enterprises. Preference for different kinds of assistance, however, showed some variations between activities. Though credit facilities and provision of premises were mentioned by all, for those in manufacturing and construction, assistance in the form of technical know-how and training facilities, incentives to produce and measures to increase formal sector demand for their products were important too. When the enterprises were asked to rank the different forms of assistance, provision of credit facilities and premises, in that order, turned out to be the most important; 44 per cent voted for credit and 26 per cent for premises.

Environmental policies

The Jakarta study, as noted earlier, showed that many participants in the informal sector live in poor housing conditions;

further, a substantial proportion of them are also migrants. Notwithstanding the respectable levels of employment and income generated in the informal sector, much of the population dependent on this sector is living under poor housing conditions with inadequate urban infrastructural facilities. The study therefore wanted to ascertain the extent to which the present concentration of informal sector activity in Jakarta can be decentralised. The informal sector participants in general and the entrepreneurs in particular were therefore asked about their willingness to move out of Jakarta and, if yes, under what conditions.

Of the 5,359 participants, only 14 per cent were willing to move out of Jakarta. The reasons for not moving out were: travel cost (9.8 per cent); children's education (10.3 per cent); employment for other family members (16.6 per cent); other reasons (38.4 per cent); and the remaining cited a combination of the first three reasons.

Among the 4,367 heads, only 11 per cent were ready to move out of Jakarta; 23 per cent were ready to move out, but unwillingly; and the remaining two-thirds were not willing to leave at all. Interestingly enough, 53 per cent of the heads were not even willing to move within Jakarta to another location; 27 per cent said that they will move unwillingly and 2) per cent will move readily.

The above findings would seem to suggest that any policy designed to improve the urban environment through population redistribution could only have a limited success.

Though the flow of migrants into Jakarta in recent years seems to be significantly smaller than for example in Africa, the findings suggest that a large majority of the informal sector participants live and work in poor physical conditions. Further, work opportunities seem to be highly location-specific. Also many enterprises operate in residential premises or areas. In so far as these enterprises are engaged in certain types of manufacturing and repair activities and catering prepared food that contribute to pollution and/or deterioration in urban environment, clearly there is a need to improve the physical conditions and infrastructural facilities. The Jakarta Government's current efforts to relocate certain activities in a better environment without necessarily hurting the employment opportunities are of course steps in the right direction. Similarly the Kampong improvement programmes based on the self-help approach that are unique in Indonesia already seem to have made a significant impact on the environment in slums. The scope for involving the informal sector enterprises in this task however requires further exploration.

Conclusion

Though only about 60 per cent of the informal sector participants in Jakarta had migrated mainly from rural areas as compared to 80 per cent or more in Freetown, Lagos and Kumasi, perhaps half the total employment in the city is generated in the informal sector. The informal sector probably contributes about 30 per cent of the total income generated in the Jakarta region. Most of the participants were men and less than a third were below 30 years old, though a greater proportion of the migrants were younger. The median level of education seems to have been only three years or so. In terms of occupation, most of them belonged to either sales worker or production worker categories. For nearly two-thirds of the migrants, the informal sector seems to have provided their first job, emphasising the employment-generation aspect of this sector. For many others, the sector facilitated their switch from agricultural to non-agricultural employment. Further, within the informal sector, a third seem to have moved to different jobs though generally within the same occupational groups. -Thus the sector seems to offer some job mobility. The trends in mobility also suggest a tendency for concentration in sales and production worker categories. To some half of those who experienced job mobility, particularly the better-educated ones, acquisition of new skills seems to have facilitated their move. As elsewhere, informal sector sources of training played a dominant role.

Some two-thirds of the participants were satisfied with their current job; and the level of dissatisfaction seems to be greater for better-educated ones. Also the less-educated ones experienced less difficulty in finding a job. Though only a small fraction of the informal sector participants were wage workers, the latter seem to have greater job mobility; nearly 60 per cent had held their job for under two years. This is partly explained by the poor working conditions reflected in low wages, long working hours and job instability. But an overwhelming majority of the participants in general preferred self-employment.

Signficant income inequalities within the informal sector seem to exist, partly due to differences in earnings between the heads and the workers. Since only a tenth of the enterprises engaged wage workers, much of the inequality seems to be the result of variations in capital and in the type of activity. The median daily wage of workers seems to have been around Rp.500 per day or Rp.3,000 per week, which is substantially lower than the minimum wage prevailing in the formal sector. In comparison with the median earnings of heads (about Rp.7,000 per week), it is less than half.

Notwithstanding the sizeable number of persons engaged in this sector (perhaps half a million), most of the participants (over two-thirds) lived in temporary structures with poor urban services and many operate their business in their own premises or in the same neighbourhood. These findings raise serious questions: to what extent can improvements in the physical environment contribute to better working conditions and higher productivity and incomes in this sector? And to what extent can the development of this sector contribute to improved living and working environment? These are indeed the major issues for initiating action-oriented programmes in this field.

CHAPTER 10. THE MANILA INFORMAL SECTOR: IN TRANSITION?

Gonzalo M. Jurado et al.[1]

Occupying only a little more than one-tenth of 1 per cent of the country's land area, Greater Manila had about 8.9 per cent (3.7 million) of the national population (41.8 million) in 1975. The unemployment rate in Manila ranged from 7.1 to 14.2 per cent of the labour force during the period 1967-74 as compared to 4.4 to 9.8 per cent for the country as a whole. That internal migration continues to play an important role in the process is evident from the regional income disparities: 5,059 pesos per capita per year in Greater Manila as compared with 2,160 pesos for the nation, in 1975. It is in this context that the study on the urban informal sector in Manila assumes considerable significance. For example, what has been the role of the informal sector in absorbing labour and bridging the income gap between the city and the countryside?

The Manila informal sector survey carried out during March-May 1976, unlike other informal sector studies, relied on an existing sampling frame of small enterprises with fewer than ten workers per enterprise. This approach, while facilitating the sampling procedures, might have led to the exclusion of very small enterprises without a fixed and/or permanent location. Though an effort was made to include new enterprises which came into existence in recent years, the bulk of the sample units had been in operation for at least four years. Further, the adoption of a stratified simple random sampling procedure led to a heavy concentration of the sample enterprises in trade activity. Though the survey sought to cover manufacturing, construction, transport, trade and service activities, 71 per cent of the sample belonged to trade alone; 15 per cent were in services and 12 per cent in manufacturing; thus, only a negligible proportion of the sample units were engaged in construction or transport activities. However, the number of manufacturing units covered was around 400 since the sample size was larger (3,500 units). The distribution of sample units by activity already suggests the overwhelming importance of trade activity in the Manila informal sector as in the case of Jakarta and elsewhere. Unlike other studies, evidence emerging from the survey is presented below separately for each of the major sub-sectors.

THE INFORMAL MANUFACTURING SECTOR

Nearly two-thirds of the sample enterprises were engaged in the manufacture of textiles, wearing apparel and leather products (other than footwear); food processing accounted for about 11 per cent; wood and related manufacturing, 6 per cent; and metal-related manufacturing, 8 per cent. Thus, manufacture of consumer goods plays a dominant role.

----

[1] Associates in this work were: Ruperto P. Alonzo for the informal transport sector; Dante B. Canlas for the manufacturing sector; Ricardo D. Ferrer for the trade sector; Rosa Linda P. Tidalgo for the services sector; and Armando A. Armas and Judy S. Castro for the overview.

Partly as a result of the sampling procedures adopted, virtually all the enterprises had a fixed location, mostly (95 per cent) in permanent structures; 91 per cent of them had access to water and electricity - unlike in other cities cited earlier. Also 96 per cent of the enterprises were accessible through paved roads. Furthermore, most of them were legally recognised and many (81 per cent) were even subject to government regulations or inspections. In this sense they are similar to their formal sector counterparts.

Employment, labour market and earnings

The average size of these enterprises in Manila in terms of employment was somewhat smaller than 4.46 persons for the informal manufacturing sector in Kumasi. It was close to four persons including the head; the 402 sample units provided employment to 1,566 persons. Over 90 per cent of the workers were employed on a full-time basis; about a third of them were females. Nearly half the sample enterprises did not have any employees at all.

Unlike in other studies, the Manila study showed that almost all the informal manufacturing enterprises (96 per cent) hiring workers had difficulty in recruiting skilled labour; provision of skills could thus play a singificant role in employment promotion in this sector. It is also encouraging to note that 57 per cent of the entrepreneurs showed interest in availing government training facilities for the benefit of their workers provided the cost of doing so is small.

Turning to wages, table 1 below shows the range of wage paid to males and females.

Table 1: Distribution of enterprises with full-time wage workers by minimum and maximum daily wage paid to males and females

(per cent)

Daily wage (pesos)	Males		Females	
	Maximum	Minimum	Maximum	Minimum
Under 5	0.9	30.7	14.3	47.6
5-10	27.1	42.7	33.3	35.7
10-15	36.9	20.9	36.9	14.9
15-20	20.0	3.6	8.9	1.8
20-25	9.3	1.3	6.0	-
25+	5.8	0.9	0.6	-
Total	100.0	100.0	100.0	100.0
Average daily wage (pesos)	13.7	8.5	10.9	7.2

First, it should be noted that the study sought to collect wage data from the head of the enterprises. Second, since some enterprises had several workers the study, instead of collecting data on wages paid to each worker, simply obtained the minimum and the maximum paid to males and females separately. The evidence suggests that in the case of males, 37 per cent of the enterprises engaging male workers paid a __maximum__ daily wage of under 10 pesos - the legal minimum wage; only about a quarter of these enterprises paid a __minimum__ of 10 pesos per day. It is thus clear that a large majority of these enterprises paid wages to male workers below the legal minimum. What about females? The situation seems to be worse. Nearly half the enterprises engaging female workers paid a maximum daily wage below the legal minimum - suggesting that women are worse off. It is more striking to note that only 16 per cent of the enterprises paid at least the equivalent of the legal minimum wage. Perhaps it is more illuminating to look at the average minimum and maximum daily wage. For males, the minimum daily wage was around 8.5 pesos and the maximum 14 pesos; and for females the corresponding figures were respectively 7.2 and 10.9. These findings are similar to evidence cited in other studies; though the average wage of workers was around the legal minimum, a majority was below that level. Further, women receive lower wages than men. These findings are somewhat surprising given that most of these enterprises are subject to government inspection/regulation.

How do the earnings noted above compare with the formal sector? Taking 250 working days per year, the above findings imply an annual wage of between 2,125 and 3,500 pesos for males and between 1,800 and 2,725 pesos for females. Based on the 1972 census of establishments, the average wage per worker in small manu-facturing units in Manila was estimated at 1,893 pesos per year; taking an average annual rate of inflation of 15 per cent, it is equivalent to about 3,300 pesos per year in 1976. But according to the same source of data, the average wage in large establishments was around 7,917 pesos per year (or about 14,000 pesos per year in 1976). It follows that many workers in the informal manufacturing sector not only receive below the legal minimum wage but also less than a quarter of what their counterparts earn in the formal sector.

Capital

One of the virtues of the informal sector is its low capital requirement per worker. The Manila study showed that capital in the form of fixed assets (excluding land and buildings) varied enormously between the enterprises from under 50 pesos to 150,000 pesos, the average, however, was around 8,000 pesos per enterprise or about 2,000 pesos [approximately US$300] per worker - substantially higher than elsewhere. That the distribution of enterprises by fixed assets employed is highly skewed is clear from the fact that the median value of such assets was only 3,000 pesos per enterprise. Since most of the enterprises were renting the premises the survey did not attempt to capitalise the value of such assets. Capital being a major constraint, as will be shown below, only 62 per cent of the enterprises obtained their capital goods new; most of the remaining bought them as second hand. Thus, recycling of capital goods seems to be an important feature in this sector.

Value added

Table 2 presents the distribution of enterprises by gross
value added per week separately for manufacturing and other sectors.
The median and mean gross value added per week per enterprise seem
to be around 260 and 425 pesos respectively. Taking the average of
four workers per enterprise these figures imply a weekly gross value
added figure of 65 and 106 pesos per worker respectively (or 11 and
18 pesos per day, assuming a six-day working week). The average
labour productivity would thus seem to exceed the legal minimum
daily wage of 10 pesos.

Table 2: Distribution of enterprises by gross
value added per week

(per cent)

Gross value added (in pesos)	Manufacturing	Trade	Transportation	Services
Total	100.0	100.0	100.0	100.0
Under 50	17.9	27.8	20.9	20.9
51 - 99	10.0	6.6	9.0	10.1
100 - 149	9.0	6.9	9.0	9.0
150 - 199	9.0	6.3	5.8	6.7
200 - 299	10.1	8.3	7.5	9.7
300 - 399	8.0	5.7	9.0	7.3
400 - 599	11.9	9.2	7.5	8.4
600 - 799	6.2	5.1	4.5	4.7
800 - 999	3.0	3.4	3.0	5.0
1 000 - 1 499	5.7	6.2	4.5	6.4
1 500 and above	9.2	14.4	19.4	11.8

Is the informal sector efficient?

One of the arguments for promoting the informal sector is
based on efficiency considerations. The informal sector is
hypothesised to generate not only more employment but also more
output for a given amount of capital in comparison with the formal
sector. Table 3 compares employment and value added per unit of
investment in the Manila informal sector with those in organised
manufacturing in the Philippines. First, the data for the organised
sector in the country as a whole suggest a trade-off between
employment and value added as the size of the firm is increased:
while the smaller ones generate more employment, the larger ones
contribute more value added. Second, the data based on small and
medium industries survey in Manila suggest that employment and value
added per unit of investment are comparable to the figures quoted
for the Philippines as a whole. Third, and most important, the
evidence from the informal sector survey in Manila suggests not only
more employment but also more value added, for the same amount of
investment, than the organised sector. Needless to add the two sets
of data are not, strictly speaking, comparable because (a) the years
to which the data refer are different; (b) the value added figure

from the informal sector survey includes depreciation on fixed assets: and more importantly, (c) the informal sector survey data on fixed assets excludes investment in land and buildings. The last two factors tend to overestimate the employment and output effects of a given volume of investment and thus exaggerates the efficiency of the informal sector. However, the conclusion that the informal sector in Manila is more efficient than the formal sector in using capital seems inescapable even if one makes a drastic assumption that the value of land and buildings is of the same order as that of other fixed assets implying a halving of the figures (in table 3) for the informal sector.

Table 3: Value added and employment per unit of
          capital, by size of enterprise

Size of enterprise	Investment of 1 million pesos	
	Employment (persons)	Value added (million pesos)
(a) Manila informal manufacturing sector (<10 persons)[1] survey 1976	491	2.68
(b) Organised manufacturing in the Philippines, 1970[2]		
5 - 19	225	0.96
20 - 49	112	0.98
50 - 99	95	1.24
100 - 199	65	1.25
200 - 499	47	1.18
500+	59	1.11
5+	70	1.13
(c) Greater Manila small-scale and medium industry survey, 1972[3]	190	1.01

[1] Based on the Manila Informal Sector Survey, 1976. Employment and value added resulting from an investment of 1 million pesos in fixed capital excluding land and buildings. Value added includes depreciation.

[2] Source: Derived from ILO: Sharing in development: a programme of employment, equity and growth for the Philippines (Geneva, 1974), Table 128, p. 533.

[3] Source: ibid., p. 544.

Linkages

Proximity to buyers seems to be a major consideration in the actual location of these enterprises; close to two-thirds of the enterprises reported so. Some 20 per cent reported that they had no choice. Availability of transportation facilities was important to 9 per cent of the enterprises. Any move to relocate them must therefore pay due attention to these findings.

The informal manufacturing sector in Manila is also fairly well integrated with the rest of the urban economy. As table 4 shows, a majority of them depend on other small enterprises exclusively or partially for their input requirements. A few (12 per cent) depend on the formal sector. Households as a source of supply of inputs seems to be relatively less important. With regard to services, 55 per cent did not buy any; three-quarters of those who did buy relied on small enterprises and/or households.

With regard to forward linkages (table 5), most of what is produced in this sector is sold to households rather than to enterprises. It therefore seems unlikely that these enterprises are confronted with market imperfections resulting from the presence of one or few buyers.

The Manila study confirmed, as did studies elsewhere, that access to credit and capital is indeed a major problem. Over 90 per cent of the enterprises relied on their own savings for meeting major expenditures; only 2.5 per cent resorted to banks or other equivalent agencies. For working capital, 97 per cent of the enterprises relied on their own savings.

Table 4: Backward linkages: Distribution of sample enterprises
          by sources of inputs and by sectors
                           (per cent)

From whom goods and services are bought	Manufac-turing	Trade	Transpor-tation	Services
1. SOURCES OF GOODS				
Households only	8.7	9.5	9.0	6.9
Small enterprises only	45.3	41.3	43.3	43.0
Household and small enterprises	20.4	21.5	16.4	13.1
Large commercial and government enter-prises	12.2	16.2	16.4	18.7
All of the above	9.0	6.2	6.0	5.4
Does not buy goods	3.5	3.4	6.0	10.1
No answer	1.0	1.9	3.0	2.8
All	100.0	100.0	100.0	100.0
2. SOURCES OF SERVICES				
Households only	8.2	11.1	10.4	9.0
Small enterprises only	26.9	20.1	34.3	20.9
Household and small enterprises	7.2	5.8	11.9	6.7
Large commercial and government enter-prises	1.5	2.0	9.0	3.0
All of the above	0.7	1.3	3.0	0.6
Does not buy services	54.7	57.7	28.4	57.2
No answer	0.7	1.9	3.0	2.6
All	100.0	100.0	100.0	100.0

Table 5: Forward linkages: Distribution of enterprises by sectors
                           (per cent)

To whom goods and services are sold	Manufacturing	Trade	Transpor-tation	Services
Households and individuals	95.3	96.2	85.1	96.1
Other small enter-prises	1.2	2.6	2.6	1.9
Big commercial/govern-ment enterprises	0.0	0.4	0.4	1.3
All of the above	0.0	0.0	0.0	0.0
No answer	3.5	0.1	0.1	0.7
All	100.0	100.0	100.0	100.0

Constraints on expansion

It is sometimes argued that besides capital, factors like demand also play a crucial role in the promotion of the informal sector. The Manila survey revealed that nearly half of the manufacturing enterprises experienced a slight or substantial increase in the quantity of goods and services produced in recent years, only some 12 per cent of the enterprises reported a contraction. But the increase in employment does not seem to be commensurate with the increase in output; only 17 per cent of the enterprises hired more workers. Over two-thirds of the enterprises did not change the level of employment. Thus, employment seems to be inelastic with respect to output, at least in the short run. It is also interesting to note that a quarter of the enterprises produced and sold new goods and services in recent years and 36 per cent had introduced some change for the better in the methods of production and operation.

The findings above are also reflected in the constraints identified by the entrepreneurs themselves: lack of access to credit at moderate interest rates is an important factor for 27 per cent of the enterprises preventing business expansion. Only 8.5 per cent of the sample units complained of inadequate demand as an important factor preventing expansion. It is also worth noting that for 22 per cent the question of expansion was "not applicable" in their view. But if credit were made available on easy and favourable terms three-quarters of the enterprises said that they would expand. When asked about their belief in getting credit from the banks, 71 per cent answered in the affirmative; most of the remaining felt that the lending procedures are either complicated or stringent.

Finally, with regard to attitudes and preferences of entrepreneurs, over 80 per cent of them thought that the Government was helpful. Ninety per cent felt that the Government can help in the field of training for workers; in fact, 40 per cent of the entrepreneurs were willing to release their workers for such training. When asked about their willingness to move out of Manila, only 23 per cent replied in the affirmative.

THE INFORMAL TRANSPORT SECTOR

The sample in this case included 20 Jeepneys (vehicle to carry up to 15 passengers or so) operators, 15 motorised tricycles, 8 calesa operators and 10 freight truck operators, or a total of 53 units.[1] As modes of public service, almost all forms of public transport are required by law to have a Certificate of Public Convenience (CPC) or an equivalent permit for operation, the exception being pedicabs (pedal operated rickshaws) and calesas (horse driven vehicles to carry 2 or 3 persons). To give some idea about the importance of these vehicles in Metro Manila, there were 10,479 authorised Jeepneys even though the number of operators (or owners) was estimated to be only 2,577, in 1976. But the number of
---

[1] Though 67 enterprises were selected, comparable data on value added and fixed assets were obtained from 53 only.

Jeepneys registered in 1975 was already 14,287. These figures
clearly indicate that many of the vehicles in operation are
unauthorised. The number of other vehicles in Manila is
comparatively few; for example, there were only 3,979 freight
trucks registered in 1975. The freight trucks cost between 100,000
to 150,000 pesos as compared to 20,000 to 25,000 pesos for Jeepneys
and 6,500 pesos for motorised tricyles.

One of the interesting features in this subsector of
activities is the prevalence of what is known as the "boundary
system" whereby the vehicle is essentially leased on a daily basis
by the operators to the drivers for a fixed sum, depending on the
actual use of the vehicle. Much has been written in newspapers and
magazines about the "evils and excesses" of the illegal boundary
system. Drivers are said to be forced to work longer hours in order
to meet the daily boundary requirements; and they are subject to
job insecurity.[1] This is a good example of how capital or other
constraints lead individuals to seek dependent relationships in
order to make a living even though the working conditions are far
from satisfactory.

The study defined enterprise in terms of the operator (and
owner if he operates) of vehicles since in many cases the latter
performs an entrepreneurial function. The median age of these
enterprises varied between three and eight years depending on the
type of vehicle, or five years for all types combined. Though hours
of operation varied between enterprises, most of the vehicles were
utilised for nine hours or longer per day. Excluding owners, most
of whom do not participate in the activity, the sample enterprises
provided employment for 127 persons, 90 per cent of them being
males. Most of the workers (83 per cent) were employed on a full-
time basis (40-50 hours per week). The mean age of workers was 30
years as compared to 40 for the owners. The number of workers in
freight truck operations was larger (5.2 persons per enterprise)
than for the sample as a whole (2.4) owing to the use of helpers in
loading and unloading.

The mean and median weekly earnings of workers in these
activities were respectively 100 and 70 pesos, implying that the
daily earnings of at least half the workers was below the legal
minimum daily wage of 10 pesos. These figures are somewhat similar
to those for manufacturing workers noted earlier. Nearly a third of
the enterprises paid a maximum daily wage of under 10 pesos for
males. Likewise only 16 per cent paid a minimum daily wage of 10
pesos to all its male workers. In other words, only a small
fraction of workers received the legal minimum daily wage even
though many work longer hours and face job insecurity.

What about the earnings of the entrepreneurs or the owners of
vehicles? The average net return per week per enterprise after
meeting the operating costs (including the payment to workers) and,
maintenance expenses, was 301 pesos for Jeepneys, 145 pesos for
tricycles and 126 pesos for calesas. Since most of these
entrepreneurs did not themselves participate in the activity the
figures above would seem to indicate return on their capital.
Assuming that the vehicles were operated all through the year, the
----

[1] Similar situations prevail in Indonesia too, notably in the
case of becaks, or the cycle rickshaws.

above figures employ an annual gross return on capital of 15,650, 7,540 and 6,550 pesos respectively for Jeepneys, tricycles and calesas. Since the average value of capital investment per enterprise was 28,000, 10,200 and 4,000 pesos respectively in the above three types of vehicles, the evidence suggests an incredibly high gross rate of return on capital. It is likely that the implied rate of return on capital is somewhat exaggerated owing to the exclusion of assets in the form of buildings and the like at least for some enterprises and the assumptions regarding capital utilisation. Nevertheless the findings do raise a question: in spite of the fairly high rate of return on investment why is it that the workers in this sector do not themselves own the vehicle? Perhaps a part of the answer to this lies in the access to credit; almost all the owners relied on their own savings for investment and a few tried unsuccessfully to get credit from formal financing institutions. It is probably also true that workers are unable to develop their clientele, as in the case of Colombo.

Finally, with regard to capital intensity, the average capital-labour ratio in these activities works out to: 13,000 pesos for Jeepneys, 6,600 pesos for tricycles, 3,600 pesos for calesas and 24,500 pesos for freight trucks. The over-all average is estimated at about 16,000 pesos - twice that of manufacturing. If however freight trucks are excluded then the average capital requirements per worker turns out to be close to 10,000 pesos. Even though calesas require relatively little capital and generate decent levels of income for those involved, they are apparently on the decline not only because of competition from other more efficient means of transport but also because of the public policies restricting their areas of operation within the city, owing to problems of traffic congestion and public hygiene. This is a good example of the kind of dilemmas posed by the promotion of such informal sector activities.

THE INFORMAL TRADE SECTOR[1]

By far the largest proportion of the sample was devoted to the trade sector which included 2,492 enterprises. Seventy two per cent of them dealt with daily consumer goods and another 16 per cent in clothing, footwear and other household durables. It is not therefore surprising that 97 per cent of the enterprises sell their goods mostly to households and individuals as will be seen later. Virtually all the enterprises were in fixed location, as a result of the sampling procedures adopted. Eighty-eight per cent were in permanent structures; over two-thirds of the enterprises had both water and electricity and most of the remaining had electricity only. Also 95 per cent of these structures were constructed with government approval. It is interesting to note that half the enterprises used their premises for residential purposes as well when they are not used for business. Further nearly three-quarters of the enterprises rented their premises and almost all the
----

[1] For some complementing evidence on the informal trade sector see McGee and Yeung: Hawkers in south-east Asian cities ..., op. cit., and Simeon G. Silverio Jr.: The neighbourhood sari-sari store (Manila, 1975).

remaining were owned by them. These findings are in contrast to
those emerging from other cities discussed earlier. Ninety-seven
per cent of the sample enterprises indicated that a government
permit was necessary to conduct business and almost all of them
possessed such a permit. As in the case of manufacturing, 90 per
cent of the units were subjected to government regulation or
inspection. In terms of hours worked, only 15 per cent of the
enterprises operated eight hours or less per day. Over 60 per cent
were open for business between 11 and 16 hours per day. Also only
15 per cent observed Sundays and other public holidays and closed
their business; most of the remaining closed at will.

Employment and earnings

The sample units (2,492) seem to support about 7,600 workers
including the owner, suggesting an average size of enterprise of
about three persons - substantially higher than in the studies cited
earlier. Perhaps the employment figure is exaggerated since about
60 per cent of the total were participating owners. If one looks at
wage employment alone, 58 per cent of the enterprises did not have
any wage workers; and 12 per cent each had one and two workers.
These figures imply that on the average an enterprise had only one
wage worker. About 90 per cent of paid workers were on a full-time
basis, and about half the wage employees were females — indicating
that female participation in wage employment in Manila is higher
than elsewhere. The overwhelming importance of unpaid workers,
almost all family members of the owners, suggests significant
underemployment; not all of them are fully occupied for the whole
duration of the working hours. It also explains the unusually long
hours of business noted above.

In terms of wages, about half the enterprises paid a _maximum_
daily wage of 10 pesos or less for males (full time), suggesting
that the median _maximum_ wage was about the same as the legal minimum
wage. But only 16 per cent of the enterprises paid the _minimum_
daily wage of 10 pesos for males (full time) implying that a large
majority of the enterprises hiring such workers do not pay the legal
minimum. As in the case of manufacturing the situation is worse for
females. Notwithstanding the wage variations between enterprises,
the average wage for males seems to be around 8 pesos per day; and,
for females, somewhat lower. These findings point out that workers
in the informal trade sector tend to earn somewhat less compared to
their counterparts in manufacturing noted earlier.

What about the earnings of owners of the enterprises? Table
6 shows the distribution of enterprises by weekly earnings of
owners. It is obvious that the earnings vary enormously between
enterprises, partly due to the number of unpaid family workers and
partly due to the amount of capital. The mean and median level of
weekly earnings were 262 and 125 pesos or 44 and 21 pesos per day
respectively. Needless to add, these figures include compensation
for family workers as well as for the capital invested by them.
Even if an allowance is made for the latter, many entrepreneurs in
the trade sector would seem to receive an income significantly above
the legal minimum wage. It is not therefore surprising that 81 per
cent of the heads were satisfied with their current occupation and
were unwilling to change their occupation even if new skills were
imparted.

- 132 -

Table 6: Distribution of enterprises by weekly earnings
          of entrepreneurs in trade

Earnings per week (pesos)	Number of enterprises	Per cent distribution
Under 50	571	22.9
50 - 99	470	18.9
100 - 149	457	18.3
150 - 299	363	14.6
300 - 599	326	13.0
600 - 1 499	217	8.7
1 500+	88	3.5
All	2 492	100.0

Turning to the question of labour market, 43 per cent of the heads of enterprises found their current job or occupation without much effort; 44 per cent with considerable search and delay; and the rest, after a great deal of search and delay. But when asked about finding a similar job now, only 28 per cent felt they will succeed without much effort; 49 per cent with some difficulty. Interestingly enough, 82 per cent were not inclined to change their job even if new skills are taught. Similarly, only 23 per cent were willing to leave the Greater Manila area if a similar or better job were provided. Thus it would seem there are limitations to a policy of relocating informal trade enterprises.

Capital and value added

Though working capital is of greater relative importance for trade enterprises, the survey collected data on fixed capital only. Further, data on capital exclude investment in premises operated in their own residential premises and only a quarter actually owned them. It is clear from table 7 that a quarter of the sample enterprises did not even possess any capital. The amount of fixed capital possessed by these enterprises varied from virtually nothing to over 15,000 pesos (table 7). The median value seems to be around 700 pesos per enterprise; but the mean is substantially higher - about 3,000 pesos per enterprise. These figures compare with the median and mean values of 3,000 and 8,000 pesos per enterprise in manufacturing noted earlier. The evidence confirms the findings elsewhere - that trade requires relatively little capital compared to manufacturing.

Notwithstanding the low amount of fixed capital in these enterprises, the value added per enterprise is significant and comparable to that in manufacturing (table 2). The mean and median value added per week per enterprise were respectively 473 and 275 pesos. Given the average size of the enterprise of three workers (including the heads) the above figures imply a value added per worker of 158 and 92 pesos per week or 26 and 15 pesos per day respectively. In other words the average value added per worker in trade seems to be significantly higher than in manufacturing noted earlier even though the former uses less capital per worker.

Table 7: <u>Distribution of enterprises by size of
fixed capital owned</u>

Fixed capital owned per enterprise (pesos)	Number of enterprises	Per cent
None	622	25.3
Less than 500	509	20.4
500 - 999	299	12.0
1 000 - 1 999	200	9.0
2 000 - 4 999	344	13.8
5 000 - 9 999	225	9.0
10 000 - 14 999	75	3.0
15 000 and above	139	7.5
All	2 492	100.0

Linkages and competition

It was noted at the outset that over 70 per cent of the trade enterprises dealt in daily consumer goods. It is not therefore surprising that 97 per cent of the sample units sold their goods directly to households and individuals. Further, a large majority (80 per cent) of the households belonged to the middle income group; only 5 per cent sold to rich and the rest to poor households. These findings cast doubt on the proposition that the urban informal sector mainly serves the poor; a part of the explanation, however, seems to lie in the fact that many of the sample enterprises in Manila are fairly well established (as will be seen later), in permanent locations and structures and possess a relatively large amount of capital than, say, in Freetown or Jakarta. In other words, the nature of linkages seems to depend on the definition of the informal sector.

With regard to backward linkage, over two-fifths of the sample obtained their goods for sale from other small enterprises while another fifth depended on both small enterprises and households. Linkages within the informal sector would therefore seem quite significant. Only one-sixth of the sample enterprises buy their requirements from large establishments and government agencies or the formal sector. Further, since 16 per cent of the trade enterprises obtained their goods for sale exclusively from a single enterprise (or individual) it is quite likely that there are some elements of market imperfection. The dominant influence of the formal sector on at least some of the informal sector enterprises cannot therefore be ruled out. And lastly, in terms of access to capital, 94 per cent financed their capital formation through own savings.

The strong forward linkage with medium income households noted earlier leads one to expect that the informal sector in Manila is to some extent exposed to competition from the formal sector, which generally attracts rich and midile income groups. This seems to be

borne out by the evidence. Eighty per cent of the enterprises felt
that the presence of larger enterprises (in the formal sector)
affects their revenue; in fact 45 per cent reported that the effect
is quite substantial. It is also interesting to note that nearly 50
per cent attributed this effect to the formal sector's ability to
sell cheaper; 19 per cent attributed it to better quality (and
lower price). Most of the remaining rationalised formal sector's
strength to its easy and convenient location in the city.

Constraints on and policies for expansion

The age structure of the informal trade enterprises shows,
partly as a result of the sampling procedures adopted, that two-
thirds of them are over 5 years old - as compared to 63 per cent in
Colombo and 39 per cent in Jakarta. Twenty-six per cent had emerged
between two and five years preceding the survey date and 7 per cent
between one and two years; none during the preceding year. Thus a
majority of them had been in business for a significant length of
time - the average being 9.1 years.

Notwithstanding the competition from the formal sector noted
earlier, half the sample establishments reported having increased
the quantity of goods sold in recent years; only a fifth of them
however experienced a substantial increase. Ten per cent reported
a decrease in the volume of sales. But, as elsewhere, 84 per cent
of the enterprises remained stagnant in terms of employment; 10 per
cent increased and 6 per cent decreased their levels of employment.
These findings cast doubt on the hypothesis that the informal sector
is involuntionary. A third of the enterprises seem to have changed
their method of operation; for 64 per cent there was no change and
for the remaining 3 per cent it was a change for the worse.
Likewise, a third had expanded the range of goods sold in recent
years.

What about the constraints on expansion? Nearly 80 per cent
showed a desire to expand, which is quite natural since only a small
fraction experienced a decrease in sales. When asked about the
constraints on expansion, surprisingly 30 per cent of those desiring
expansion cited government regulations, permits, etc., as a
constraint even though most of them were already operating within
the legal framework. Over one-third referred to lack of capital or
credit facilities as a bottleneck. Fifteen per cent said lack of
larger premises and other facilities prevented their expansion.
Only some 11 per cent cited lack of demand as an important factor
constraining expansion. It is also worth noting that over 70 per
cent of the enterprises opted to buy land and/or construct/improve
business premises should they be provided with a financial
assistance of about 10,000 pesos. Finally, among the factors
preventing adoption of better methods, lack of capital turned out to
be the most important; about 76 per cent of the enterprises felt
so.

In conclusion, market imperfections may be an important factor
constraining the revenues of at least some small trade enterprises.
Since many of these small units are located in residential
structures and suffer from inadequate infrastructural facilities,
and since location plays an important role in competitions with the
formal sector, creation of market places in appropriate residential
locations with minimum urban services as is being done in Jakarta

could enhance the income situation for these entrepreneurs as well as improve the urban environment by segregating the commercial from residential areas. Even though these enterprises use relatively little fixed capital it is likely that they need assistance for working capital. To the extent that demand is not a major constraint and capital and infrastructure are, the above measures could facilitate the entry of new enterprises in this field. Though a majority of these enterprises do not engage hired labour, the few who do often do not pay the legal minimum wages. Since many of these workers do not acquire any technical skills on the job, as for example in the case of manufacturing, the conditions of work for wage employees in this sector needs a closer look.

THE INFORMAL SERVICES SECTOR

The sample included 535 enterprises in a wide range of service activities including some that can be considered as formal in terms of the capital intensity, the level of technical knowhow and organisation. As in the case of other activities, almost all these enterprises were in permanent structures, with access to electricity and/or water. More than half of them were located in the residence of the entrepreneurs. Only some 20 per cent however owned the premises, the rest rented them. The median value of rent paid was a little over 200 pesos per month. Virtually all the enterprises were accessible through motorable roads. A majority (61 per cent) explained their location in terms of proximity to their customers. One third of the enterprises reported that most of their workers lived within 30 minutes walking distance from the enterprise; and 30 per cent had their workers on the premises. Most of the enterprises had the necessary approval from the government authorities to operate and many were even subject to government inspection.

Employment, labour market and earnings

The sample units (535) provided employment to about 1,700 persons or about 3.2 persons per enterprise. Excluding the heads, 82 per cent of the workers (i.e., about 1,050 persons) were wage employees and the rest were unpaid (family) workers. Thus, wage employment plays an important role. For the two-thirds of the sample enterprises engaging wage workers, the average number of wage workers hired is about 1.9 persons per enterprise. Sixty-four per cent of wage workers were males and the rest females; further, 91 per cent of wage employees were on a full-time basis. In other words, only a few workers were on a part-time basis or were unpaid workers. Distribution of enterprises by size of employment (including the heads) shows that only a quarter of the total were single person units; 20 per cent each had two and three workers; 13 per cent had four persons; and the remaining 22 per cent had five or more workers. The median size is thus around 2.25 persons - smaller than the mean 3.2 noted earlier.

Labour turnover is a problem only to a small proportion of the enterprises. For example, only 7 per cent lost many or most of their employees during the year preceding the survey while another 26 per cent lost some or very few workers. Interestingly enough, nearly half of these workers seem to have switched to formal sector (including government) jobs and 20 per cent seem to have become self-employed. These findings imply at least some mobility between jobs.

As elsewhere, the enterprises generally do not have any difficulty in hiring labour; 66 per cent had no difficulty; 26 per cent had some and 8 per cent always had difficulty. In the case of skilled workers, however, 89 per cent experienced difficulties. Though the enterprises prefer to hire skilled labour, many are not averse to the idea of recruiting unskilled labour and training them on the job. Though there is no formal apprenticeship system as in the case of Africa, 15 per cent of the enterprises hiring unskilled labour did not pay wages at all while 44 per cent paid a reduced wage. One of the major disincentives in providing training to unskilled workers is that the entrepreneurs are unable to capture the benefits from such investments. Over 60 per cent of the entrepreneurs said that the workers trained by them tend to leave the enterprise within five years after training; only 38 per cent reported that they do not lose the workers trained by them. It is not therefore surprising that over 80 per cent of the sample felt that the Government can help in training workers.

In terms of the mode of wage payment, the Manila enterprises seem to be closer to the formal sector than elsewhere. Forty three per cent paid wages on a monthly basis; 20 per cent each paid on a weekly and daily basis. Only a few paid wages on an irregular basis (8 per cent) or piece-rate basis (9 per cent). Looking at the distribution of workers by daily cash wage rate, 57 per cent received less than 10 pesos per day, i.e. below the legal minimum; the median and mean cash wage were respectively 9.3 and 8.6 pesos per day - comparable to the trade sector. Wages in kind were not common; only 17 per cent of the workers received one peso or more per day. As elsewhere, women tend to receive lower wages than men; the average minimum and maximum wage paid to females were respectively 7.96 and 10.83 pesos per day as compared to 8.37 and 12.21 for males. With regard to incentives, 46 per cent of the enterprises did not increase the wage with the workers' experience. Also 90 per cent of the workers worked 8 hours a day or longer; and 52 per cent for longer than 6 days per week. These findings suggest there is considerable room for improving the conditions of work in this subsector.

What about the individual characteristics of the workers in this subsector? The average and median age of workers were respectively 42 and 37 years; in fact, 88 per cent were above 35 years, suggesting that very few youths have entered this sector as wage employees. Nevertheless a small proportion (0.5 per cent) of the workers were under the age of 10, either as wage employees or as unpaid family workers. Further these workers are not concentrated in a few enterprises; in 43 per cent of the sample units the youngest worker was under 10 years old. For 70 per cent of the enterprises, most of their workers had formal education. In terms of occupation, 36 per cent of the workers were classified as production and related workers (mainly in repair services) and 40 per cent as service workers.

Given the relatively low wage of workers in this sector, to what extent are they able to meet their minimum basic needs? First it is important to note that only 3 per cent of the workers had a secondary source of labour income. Second, 23 per cent of the workers did not have any immediate members of the family with them; of the remaining, about half had one additional immediate member of the family. The median household size including immediate members of the family was thus under two while the average was 3.3. Third, some 41 per cent of these workers had other household members. Fourth, the average size of the household including both immediate members of the family and others works out to 5.4 persons. Although no data are available on the earning status of other members of the household, the above data together with the average daily wage of 9 pesos (or 2,700 pesos per year at 300 days per year) imply a minimum average per capita income of 500 pesos per year for the workers' families, as compared to 5,059 pesos per capita in Greater Manila, noted earlier. If, however, one defines the household consisting of immediate members of the family only, then the average per capita income works out to 820 pesos per year. These findings taken together with the wage variations noted earlier suggest that many of the worker families fall below the poverty line.

Entrepreneurs and their earnings

The median and mean earnings of entrepreneurs work out to 150 and 318 pesos per week respectively. Although these figures include compensation for own capital and other family members as well, it is clear that on the average the entrepreneurs earn an income well above the legal minimum wage of ten pesos per day and that of wage workers. The level of earnings of heads showed considerable variations; perhaps some 20 per cent of the heads receive an income below ten pesos per day. The relatively higher level of earnings can partly be attributed to longer hours of work; two-thirds of the heads worked for longer than eight hours; and half for all seven days during the week.

In order to understand the significance of the above findings it will be useful to note a few pertinent data concerning the entrepreneurs. Nearly two-thirds of the heads were males; as in the case of workers, about 90 per cent of them are over 30 years old, the median age being around 42 years. Ninety seven per cent were literate, with formal schooling. In fact nearly three quarters of them had 10 years or more schooling - substantially higher than in other countries (except Kumasi) cited earlier - which is partly explained by the inclusion of several formal sector enterprises. What is perhaps more interesting is that there is no difference between males and females in terms of education. Although some 38 per cent of the heads were both outside Manila, most of them (86 per cent) had been in Manila for longer than 10 years. Thus, migration is relatively unimportant, particularly if it is defined in terms of under five years of residence in Manila. It is nevertheless interesting to note that over two-thirds of the migrants came from rural Luzon and rural Visayas suggesting that migration from other urban areas is relatively less important as in the case of other studies noted earlier. Although 74 per cent of them had not worked before migration, over 80 per cent of those who had worked were in farming related occupations.

With regard to occupational mobility, it is worth noting that for nearly two-thirds of the entrepreneurs the current occupation is the first one. Thus, the majority of the heads had not changed their job. Less than one quarter of the heads had ever used an employment agency to get a job. The main reason for lack of job mobility is of course the satisfaction with their current job. As a matter of fact, 78 per cent were unwilling to change their job even if new skills were taught to them. Similarly, with regard to geographical mobility, nearly 80 per cent of them were unwilling to move out of Manila either because it will affect the household earnings or because of travel costs and children's education.

Even though there was little occupational mobility, 43 per cent of the heads reported an increase in their earnings in contrast to 14 per cent reporting a decrease in recent years. The adequacy of earnings to meet the basic needs cannot be judged without taking into account other sources of income and the household size. A quarter of them had other sources of income exceeding 50 pesos per week. Also, 44 per cent of the heads had other earners in their households: 31 per cent, one additional earner and 13 per cent, 2 or more additional earners. About a quarter of the additional earners were also self-employed mainly in services, trade and manufacturing. Regarding the household size, the median was between six and seven, significantly higher than that for workers noted earlier.

Capital

In terms of the current value of fixed assets (excluding premises) the value of capital per enterprise showed enormous variations partly due to the inclusion of activities that do not belong to the informal sector. The mean and median values were respectively 11,300 and 4,000 pesos per enterprise. If, however, one excludes the formal sector activities such as photography studios, and medical and health services, then the capital variations are reduced considerably. Table 8 presents relevant data for activities that typically belong to the informal sector. The evidence suggests that on the average the amount of capital per enterprise in the service sector is about the same as in manufacturing noted earlier.

Nearly two-thirds of the enterprises acquired their capital equipment new and 26 per cent bought them second-hand. An overwhelming majority (93 per cent) financed their investment through own savings; formal lending agencies like banks played a negligible role. Virtually none of the sample enterprises rented any capital equipment. Reliance on own savings was even greater (99 per cent) for meeting working capital requirements.

Value added

The average total revenue per week was estimated to be around 1,400 pesos but the corresponding gross value added was around 990 pesos (table 2), the difference being the expenses on raw materials and services. Given the average size of the enterprise of 3.2 workers, the above implies an average value added per worker of 309 pesos per week - which is substantially higher than that in other sectors discussed earlier. The main reason for this is, as already noted, the inclusion of formal sector enterprises: some 12 per cent of the enterprises had a gross value added exceeding 1,500 pesos per week. If the typical informal sector activities alone are considered, then the average turns out to be only 550 pesos per week per enterprise (table 8).

Table 8: Capital, value added, earnings and wages in the informal service sector

Activity	(Pesos) per enterprise			Average daily wage	
	Capital equipment	Value added per week	Entrepreneurs' earnings per week	Males	Females
Electrical repairs (28)	10 935	731	284	8.22	-
Watch, clock and jewellery repair (23)	3 138	723	398	10.00	-
Footwear and leather goods repair (12)	2 400	626	162	5.62	-
Motor vehicles, etc., repair (83)	16 022	853	389	9.43	10.00
Other repairs (10)	1 461	363	186	6.38	-
Laundry services (11)	1 775	164	159	4.66	6.00
Barber and beauty shops (147)	5 405	354	162	6.45	6.26
All (314)	8 170	550	251	7.56	7.54

Note: Figures in parentheses indicate the number of sample enterprises.

Linkages

The question of linkages was briefly mentioned in the context of training and credit facilities. Since only a few sought credit from formal lending agencies they were asked if they had ever tried to seek such credit. Interestingly enough, 75 per cent of the enterprises had never tried; only 20 per cent had tried and obtained credit. Furthermore, 72 per cent believed that they can get credit while the remaining explained their non-belief in terms of non-recognition of the enterprise and complicated and stringent lending procedures.

The link between this sector and the Government was already noted in the context of licences and enforcement of government regulations. Another form of such linkages is through the payment of taxes. Ninety-two per cent said they paid taxes on what they produced and sold, while 59 per cent said they paid taxes on goods and services bought. These findings, unlike those in other cities, suggest that the sector has greater linkages with the Government. The amount of taxes paid varied from under 50 pesos per year to over 1,500 pesos, the median value being around 150 pesos.

Perhaps the most important forms of backward linkage is through the purchase of goods and services by the firm. About 90 per cent of the enterprises bought goods of which nearly half was obtained from other small enterprises while another 15 per cent bought from both households and small enterprises. Twenty one per cent however obtained their input requirements exclusively from the formal sector, viz., large enterprises and government agencies. In contrast, only 43 per cent of the enterprises bought any services at all, mostly (over 90 per cent) from households and/or small enterprises.

Regarding forward linkages, 96 per cent of the enterprises sold their services mainly to households and individuals and only 1.3 per cent depended on the formal sector. As in the case of manufacturing, 82 per cent of the households belonged to middle income group and 13 per cent to rich. Even though the direct linkage with the formal sector is small, the latter seems to exert an indirect influence on the informal sector through competition. For example, 29 per cent of the sample enterprises felt that their revenue was affected substantially through competition from larger ones. For one-third of the sample, such competition was detrimental but not to a significant extent. Among the reasons cited for this phenomenon, location of larger enterprises, cheaper price and better quality were the most important ones. With regard to the possibilities of diversifying the forward linkages, over half of the enterprises felt that the formal sector including government could buy more from them. Much of the differences in the pattern of backward and forward linkages between Manila and elsewhere seem to originate largely from the sampling procedures adopted, favouring relatively well established, larger enterprises.

Growth and expansion

As in the case of other activities, a majority of the service enterprises (71 per cent) had been in operation for longer than five years. Only a quarter of them however had increased the range of services provided. But in terms of quantity, 45 per cent of the enterprises had expanded; only 11 per cent had contracted. Employment however remained stable for 71 per cent of the enterprises while it increased for 16 per cent. Over one-third of the sample units had even introduced certain changes in their methods of production and operation.

Three-quarters of the enterprises cited capital as the major constraint in starting their business. However, with regard to expansion, only 31 per cent of the enterprises referred to lack of capital and credit facilities as an important constraint. For 26 per cent it was government licensing and regulations, for 14 per cent it was lack of larger premises and facilities and for 13 per cent it was the demand constraint. Lack of capital figured as a major constraint for 82 per cent of the enterprises wishing to improve their method of production and operation.

Summary and conclusions

The Manila informal sector study differs from others in many ways partly because the sampling frame was confined to well-established enterprises in fixed locations. Consequently, even though 60 per cent of the heads of enterprises had been born outside Manila, few had migrated in recent years. Also female participation was substantially higher - 57 per cent - mainly due to the dominance of trade activity in the sample and the use of unpaid family workers belonging to the entrepreneur's household. The median level of education was over 10 years. Since 41 per cent of the heads had switched occupations the informal sector seems to have offered some job mobility.[1] Under 14 per cent of the heads were below 30 years old, suggesting that few new entrants to the labour force have established their own enterprises - as compared to between 30 and 57 per cent noted earlier in other cities. These findings imply that it takes time to overcome various constraints in establishing one's own business.

Also, since the Manila sample enterprises were on the average older than elsewhere, they employed significantly more capital per worker and more workers. Only about half the enterprises were run with a single person; the average size was around three persons per enterprise. The manufacturing enterprises seem to compare favourably with their formal sector counterparts in terms of efficiency. As elsewhere significant income disparities exist between heads and workers. Most of the heads seem to earn incomes substantially above the legal minimum wage of 10 pesos per day (say, two or three times the latter). But a majority of the workers seem to earn a daily wage below the legal minimum; though the average is around the legal minimum in manufacturing and transport activities, it is significantly lower in trade and services. Females tend to receive a lower wage than males. And yet, as elsewhere, a large majority work full time, longer than eight hours a day and six days a week. These findings point to the scope for improving conditions of work and poverty alleviation. Since a majority of the heads also

----

[1] In another study on low-income communities in Metro Manila 54 per cent of those employed had held their first job for under two years. See Jose V. Abueva et al.: Metro Manila today and tomorrow (Quezon City, Institute of Philippine Culture, 1972), p. 173.

reported difficulties in hiring skilled labour, provision of skills could be an important factor in employment generation.[1]

In terms of physical environment, the Manila establishments seem to be quite well off as compared to other cities. Most of them are housed in permanent structures with access to both electricity and water. A majority rent their premises; and in trade many operate in residential premises. Most of them have easy access to households, the dominant source of demand. Further most of the demand for goods and services produced by this sector originates from the middle income groups and consequently the informal sector seems to be in competition with the formal sector. Though the evidence does not point to any direct linkage and exploitation by the formal sector, the latter seems to exert a negative influence on the informal sector partly tarough the occupation of choice locations within the city. In terms of backward linkages, few seem to depend directly on the formal sector. With regard to expansion, less than a sixth of the sample units experienced a decrease in demand in recent years; a significant proportion seem to have improved their methods of operation and the range of goods produced and sold. The major constraint in expansion seems to be access to capital, since over 90 per cent relied on own savings for such investment. Finally, few of the participants would consider moving out of Manila even if comparable opportunities are provided elsewhere.

Though these findings do not suggest that the plight of the informal sector in Manila is not as acute as in some of the cities discussed earlier they do point to the need for improving conditions of work, increasing the access to resources and markets and facilitating the acquisition of skills. Further, it seems more likely that the situation is worse in Manila too since informal sector participants in variable locations and of more recent origin were excluded from the sample.[2] For example, between 1963 and 1968 the squatter population of the metropolis is estimated to have grown by 171 per cent reaching a total squatter population of 770,000 in 1968.[3] And 93 per cent of the slum population in 1968 were estimated to be migrants, many earning a livelihood through odd jobs as cargadors, vendors, or collectors of scrap metals and the like, with a median household income of 150 pesos per month.[4] Evidence from other relevant studies[5] also suggest that the bulk of the urban poor and recent migrants to Manila rely on jobs in the informal sector
----

[1] Centre for Research and Communication: Principles and guidelines for area planning in the Tala Estate: Some considerations (Manila, 1976), Appendix for some examples of skills in shortage.

[2] McGee and Yeung: Hawkers in south-east Asian cities ..., op. cit.

[3] Abueva et al: Metro Manila today and tomorrow, op. cit., p. 96.

[4] ibid., pp. 97-98.

[5] Mary R. Hollenstiner: "Socio-economic themes and variations in a low income urban neighbourhood"; Jaime C. Laya et al: "An economic survey of a Manila squatter community: Agno-Leveriza area (1970)", in Papers and Proceedings of the Workshop on Manpower and Human Resources, Continuing Education Center, Los Banos, Laguna, 13-15 October 1972, Part II.

such as salesmen, vendors, peddlars, transport operators and domestic servants. Likewise another study[1] shows that scavenging as a source of employment is important in low income communities and arises due to the prevalence of high unemployment rates. Though it is not a preferred occupation, it seems to generate a minimum income of 8 pesos per day notwithstanding the competition facing them. Though scavenging activities contribute directly to the improvement of the urban environment and recycling of resources (waste paper, for example), scavengers in general seem to be subject to exploitation by the formal sector indirectly through the intermediaries. The results based on the Manila study do not therefore necessarily contradict the findings elsewhere or negate some of the hypotheses noted earlier; perhaps it is more appropriate to view them as referring to the informal sector in transition.

----

[1] William J. Keyes, S.J.: Manila scavengers: The struggle for urban survival, IPC Poverty Research Series No. 1 (Quezon City, Institute of Philippine Culture, 1974).

CHAPTER 11.   THE INFORMAL AND QUASI-FORMAL SECTORS IN CORDOBA

Carlos E. Sánchez,* Horacio Palmiero and Fernando Ferrero

Background

The town of Córdoba, capital of the province of the same name, is one of the three largest cities of Argentina;   located in the centre of the country.   Its population increased from 387,000 in 1947 to 802,000 in 1970; it is estimated to have risen to 875,000 in 1973 and 950,000 in 1976.   Thus, the annual rate of growth of population seems to have been reduced in recent years from 3.2 per cent during 1947-70 to 2.8 per cent during 1970-76.   Immigration is estimated to account for 54 per cent of the increase in population during 1947-70 period.[1]   Unemployment as a percentage of the labour force showed a corresponding rise from   2.5 per cent in 1947 to around 6 per cent in recent years.   Unemployment is about evenly divided among males and females but 85 per cent are young, under 29 years.   Incidence of unemployment is also higher among the less educated ones, and many of them are new entrants to the labour force.

Perhaps the distinguishing feature of economic growth in Córdoba during 1947-60 period was the emergence of the formal manufacturing sector.   Vast industrial complexes producing vehicles, tractors, engines and the like sprang up during 1953-60 leading to a quantum leap in output of engineering products;   the production index rose from 100 in 1953 to 4,691 in 1960.   Employment in the formal manufacturing sector showed a corresponding, though less spectacular, increase too.   During 1960-73, the increase in output and employment in manufacturing activities other than engineering was relatively more important.   Parallel to the above, the public sector employment in services also increased rapidly, exceeding the increase in economically active population substantially.   To give some idea about the levels of remuneration, the average wage for workers in provincial civil service was US$5,672 per year compared to US$1,300 per year legal minimum wage.

For the purpose of the present study, the urban economy of Córdoba was divided into three parts: (i) organised private sector with five or more employees;   (ii) public sector;   and (iii) unorganised private sector, employing fewer than five persons. Since not all the workers in the last category above earn a "low" income, it was further subdivided on the basis of income - those earning a high income either because of advanced skills, or because of high capital intensity or because of oligopolistic market environment - were termed as belonging to the "quasi-formal" sector and the rest with low incomes as belonging to the informal sector. In accordance with the above, the quasi-informal sector included: self-employed professionals like doctors, lawyers, etc.; small

----

* Professor Titular, Facultad de Ciencias Economicas, Universidad Nacional de Córdoba, Argentina.

[1] The share of urban population in Córdoba province has shown a steady increase from 22.4 per cent in 1869 to   75.1 per cent in 1970.

engineering units and manufacturing activities with significant
amounts of skills and investment; self-employed construction
workers including plumbers and electricians and the like; and
commercial activities with a substantial capital input. In addition
to these, the study also included certain activities which may not
necessarily be skill or capital intensive but nevertheless may earn
a high income because of their strategic locations within the city.

In contrast to the above, the informal sector included:
unskilled labour, mainly in construction-related activities;
domestic servants (mostly women); porters; gardeners and the like.
In other words, the informal sector in this study was defined to
include enterprises in the lower end of the spectrum characterised
by free entry, very little capital and skills, very small scale, job
and income uncertainty, etc. It will therefore be interesting to
see the implications of distinguishing between the quasi-informal as
opposed to purely informal activities.

The participants

The number of persons dependent on the quasi-formal and
informal activities in Córdoba - including owners and paid and
unpaid workers - was estimated to be 138,000 or 37.6 per cent of the
town's economically active population, divided between the two
subsectors in the ratio of three to two (or 84,000 and 54,000
respectively). About three quarters of those in the informal sector
were self-employed without a fixed address; 17 per cent were
employers and 9 per cent were paid or unpaid workers. If we exclude
paid and unpaid workers, 80 per cent of the heads of enterprises did
not have a fixed location. In contrast, 46 per cent of those in
quasi-formal activities were self-employed, 23 per cent were
employers and 31 per cent were wage employees.

Age and sex composition

One of the interesting conclusions emerging from the distinction between the informal and the quasi-formal sector is the
importance of females in the former. Sixty three per cent of the
employed population (both heads and wage workers) in the informal
sector were women as compared to only 23 per cent in the quasi-
formal sector. Thus, women's participation is relatively greater in
low income informal sector activities. It is also interesting to
note that women's participation is about the same both as heads of
enterprises and as (paid or unpaid) workers. In other words, the
distribution of women in these activities between "heads" and
"workers" is comparable to that of men.

Turning to age composition, first it is interesting to note
that, as elsewhere, only a third of all participants (i.e. 3,140)
are below 30 yeras; and the fraction is about the same for both
informal and quasi-formal activities. Further, the age composition
does not vary significantly between males and females. Are there
any differences in age between heads and workers? The proportion of
heads below 30 years is under a quarter of the total (i.e. 2,446) as
compared to a third for all participants suggesting that, as
elsewhere, the heads are somewhat older than workers. If the data
are broken down by informal and quasi-formal sectors, the proportion
of heads below 30 years is about 30 and 19 per cent respectively

suggesting that relatively few youth establish own enterprises in the quasi-formal sector. The median age of heads in both the sectors combined is a little over 40 years as compared to about 38 years for all participants suggesting that workers are somewhat younger but not so young as in the case of Africa noted earlier.

Schooling

As expected, a greater proportion of those in the quasi-formal sector were better educated; 39 per cent had eight years or more schooling as compared to only 18 per cent in the informal sector. But when compared to the economically active population in Córdoba town as a whole, the average level of education in the two sectors was much lower. For example, 56 per cent of those employed in Córdoba had eight or more years schooling. About one-fifth of those with eight years and over schooling in both sectors had technical as opposed to general education. The median level of education of women in the informal sector was somewhat lower than for men; but in the quasi-formal sector both men and women had about the same level of education. The median level of education (i.e. years of schooling) of entrepreneurs for both sectors combined was only around five years.

Migration

One of the debated issues in the context of the informal sector is whether it plays a significant role in absorbing migrants and, if so, does it also provide opportunities for advancement in terms of income and employment. The evidence from Córdoba sheds some light on this issue, as table 1 below shows:

Table 1: Distribution of immigrants between
quasi-formal and informal sectors
by duration of residence in Córdoba

Duration of residence (years)	Quasi-formal sector	Informal sector	Total	
Under 1	8.8	91.2	100.0	0.9
1- 5	45.7	54.3	100.0	10.2
6-10	50.8	49.2	100.0	14.3
10+	54.6	45.4	100.0	74.6
All	52.7	47.3	100.0	100.0

Note: Immigrants are defined as those born outside Córdoba.

Given that 55 per cent of the heads of enterprises in both the sectors combined were born outside Córdoba, the results are significant. They suggest that a greater proportion of recent migrants to Córdoba enter the informal rather than the quasi-formal sector. Since the proportion participating in the latter increases steadily with the duration of stay in Córdoba it also suggests some mobility from low income to higher income activities. The sex composition of natives and migrants does not seem to be significantly different. The rate of flow of migrants into Córdoba, however, seems to be slowing down. Surprisingly their median age is slightly higher than that of natives perhaps due to the fact that most of them had migrated 10 years or earlier. There are also some significant differences between natives and migrants in terms of age in the two sectors: in the informal sector 41 per cent of the natives were below 30 years as compared to 23 per cent among immigrants; and in the quasi-formal sector, 25 per cent of the natives were below 30 years in contrast to 14 per cent among migrants suggesting that a greater proportion of natives manage to establish own enterprises at a young age. The average level of education for migrants is somewhat lower than for the natives. For example, the proportion of migrants with 8 years or more schooling was 16 per cent in the informal and 34 per cent in the quasi-formal sector as compared to 18 and 39 per cent noted earlier for all heads (natives and migrants). Over one quarter of the migrants held temporary occupations like domestic servants, as own account workers compared to 20 per cent for natives.

Skills and occupation

Close to 60 per cent of the heads were estimated to be performing skilled work. But the proportion of skilled workers in the quasi-formal sector was much larger - 82 per cent - compared to 30 per cent in the informal sector. There seems to be some complementarity between the level of education and skills. For both sectors combined, the proportion of skilled workers in the three educational groups 0-3 years, 4-7 years and 8+ years were respectively 40, 58 and 70 per cent.

Table 2 below shows the distribution of heads of enterprises by occupation, separately for the two subsectors. Although the quasi-formal sector covers a wider range of occupations it is interesting to note that a good number of the heads are engaged as working proprietors (trade) and as sales workers. While it is true that a greater proportion of those in the quasi-formal sector are engaged as production, transport and construction workers, the evidence also suggests that the distinction between informal and quasi-formal sector cannot rest on occupational classifications, with the possible exception of "maids and domestic servants" who appear exclusively under the informal sector.

Table 2: Distribution of heads of enterprises
          by occupation

Occupation	Informal sector	Quasi-formal sector	Total
Professional	4 (..)	45 (3.4)	49 (2.0)
Managers	1 (..)	51 (3.8)	52 (2.1)
Clerical and related	-	16 (1.2)	16 (0.6)
Working proprietors (trade)	165 (14.7)	405 (30.5)	570 (23.3)
Sales workers	77 (6.9)	134 (10.1)	211 (8.6)
Working proprietors (hotel)	13 (1.1)	27 (2.0)	40 (1.6)
Maids, etc.	409 (36.5)	-	409 (16.7)
Barbers, beauticians, etc.	45 (4.0)	28 (2.1)	73 (3.0)
Tailoring	118 (10.5)	31 (2.3)	149 (6.1)
Wood and related manufacturing	1 (..)	34 (2.6)	35 (1.4)
Metalworkers	-	36 (2.7)	36 (1.5)
Fitters	6 (..)	54 (4.1)	60 (2.4)
Electricians, etc.	3 (..)	23 (1.7)	29 (1.2)
Plumbers, etc.	3 (..)	58 (4.4)	61 (2.5)
Painters	18 (1.6)	46 (3.5)	64 (2.6)
Bricklayers and other construction workers	54 (4.8)	155 (11.7)	209 (8.5)
Transport equipment operators	-	61 (4.6)	61 (2.5)
Other occupations	202 (18.0)	123 (9.3)	325 (13.3)
	1 119 (100.0)	1 327 (100.0)	2 446 (100.0)

Note: Figures in parentheses are percentages.

The study attempted to measure the extent of mobility in occupations and skills by comparing the survey data with the corresponding data for 1964. The occupational distribution did not show significant changes between the two periods. Compared to 28 per cent engaged as sales workers in 1964, 32 per cent were so employed at the time of the survey (1976). Those engaged as production workers showed a slight decrease from 28 to 24 per cent. What is perhaps more significant is the change in skill status. In all the major occupational groups the proportion of unskilled workers showed a significant decline between the two periods. The conclusion seems to be that there is a greater mobility within the same occupational groups (from informal to the formal sector for example), than between them. These findings are also consistent with the response on job satisfaction. Only one quarter of the heads were not satisfied with their current job although this proportion is higher (35 per cent) for those in the informal sector. Within the latter group, the more educated seem to be more dissatisfied; for example, 41 per cent of those with eight years or more schooling were dissatisfied with their present job as compared to 33 per cent among those with fewer than 3 years' schooling.

A question related to the above is the duration of employment in the same occupation. Only a third of those in the informal sector and 29 per cent of those in the quasi-formal sector had been in the same occupation for under five years. In other words, a majority did not change their job for at least five years. This seems to cast doubt on the extent of mobility from the informal to the quasi-formal sector.

The enterprise

The distribution of sampling units by major activity groups is presented in table 3 below. Personal services, trade and manufacturing account for over 90 per cent of the informal sector activities in Córdoba. Although construction plays a significant role within the quasi-formal sector it is surprising to see 16 per cent of the units engaged in the provision of personal services yielding significant incomes. Manufacturing in general is relatively less important in both the sectors.

Table 3: Distribution of informal and quasi-formal units by activity

	Informal sector	Quasi-formal sector	Total
Agriculture and related	12(1.1)	5(0.4)	17(0.7)
Manufacturing	171(15.3)	189(15.4)	360(15.4)
(Textile and related)	153(13.7)	61(5.0)	214(9.1)
Construction	83(7.4)	208(16.9)	291(12.4)
Trade and restaurants	219(19.6)	492(40.1)	711(30.3)
Transport, storage and communication	11(1.0)	73(5.9)	84(3.6)
Services	620(55.6)	261(21.2)	881(37.6)
(Personal services)	605(54.2)	195(15.9)	800(34.1)
Total	1 116(100.0)	1 228(100.0)	2 344(100.0)

Note: Figures in parentheses are percentages.

Within the informal sector, virtually all the units in manufacturing, 75 per cent of those in personal services and half of those in trade are headed by women. By contrast, in the quasi-formal sector, 85 per cent of manufacturing, 76 per cent of trade and 87 per cent of services enterprises are headed by men. The dominance of men in the quasi-formal sector and women in the informal sector has significant equity implications since the distinction between the two sectors hinges on the income criteria. It is not clear whether the women workers in the informal sector are secondary earners.

The structure of the sample units in terms of size is shown in table 4. Over three-quarters of them have own-account workers without any fixed location. Among those with fixed location, over two-thirds belonged to the quasi-formal sector. Whereas 70 per cent of such enterprises in the informal sector worked in their homes, a similar proportion of those in quasi-formal sector worked in non-residential premises. (Not shown in the table.) Except for those in trade and related activities, a large majority of the sample units do not have a fixed location. These findings suggest that investment in business premises is relatively unimportant for most of the enterprises.

Employment

Table 4 also shows that 40 per cent of the 549 establishments have no wage workers; thus, wage employment is important only to some 13 per cent of all sample units. And 91 per cent of those employing workers are in trade and services. Very few of the manufacturing units employed any workers - unlike in other cities cited earlier. In fact only 10 per cent of the workers, almost all in the quasi-formal sector, were in manufacturing. The total number of wage workers works out to 689 of which 83 per cent were in the quasi-formal sector. Total employment generated in all the 2,344 units was only 3,080.[1] Thus, the dominant feature of the informal sector in Córdoba seems to be the smallness of the enterprises in terms of numbers of workers.

Capital

The study unfortunately does not present data on capital and value added; but it does provide some information on the ownership of assets and entrepreneurs' earnings. Since the own-account workers without fixed location possess relatively little capital mainly in the form of tools and perhaps some inventories in the case of trade, the data on capital ownership pertains to establishments in fixed locations. With regard to assets in the form of premises, half of the informal sector enterprises operated in the residence owned by them; most of the remaining presumably rented their premises. But most of the informal sector units owned other kinds of fixed assets in use. In the case of the quasi-formal sector, one quarter of the enterprises owned their business premises and 18 per cent owned the residence in which they operated; most of the remainder apparently rented their premises. As in the case of the informal sector, most of these enterprises owned whatever fixed

---

[1] Since in a few cases the enterprise had more than one owner, the total number quoted above is smaller than 3,140 participants noted earlier.

Table 4: Distribution of the sample units by size and activity

	Enterprises with fixed location (size)							Own-account workers without fixed location	Total
	0	1	2	3	4	5	Total		
1. Agriculture and related	-	-	-	-	-	-	-	17 (100)	17 (100)
2. Manufacturing	5	6	7	1	4	6	29 (8)	331 (92)	360 (100)
3. Construction	-	-	-	-	1	-	1 (..)	290 (100)	291 (100)
4. Trade and restaurants	140	114	71	29	18	15	387 (54)	324 (46)	711 (100)
5. Transport, storage and communications	5	3	-	-	-	2	10 (12)	74 (88)	84 (100)
6. Services	68	19	20	9	3	3	122 (14)	759 (86)	881 (100)
Total	218	142	98	39	26	26	549 (23)	1 795 (77)	2 344 (100)

Note: Figures in parentheses are percentages. Size of enterprise excludes owners of business.

assets they used for business. Since the bulk of the enterprises in both sectors were in trade, construction and services, it is unlikely that investment in fixed assets in the form of tools and equipment was substantial.

Earnings and income inequalities

Turning to income of heads of these enterprises, it is clear from table 5 that a large majority of those in the informal sector belonged to the low-income category of under 80,000 pesos (or US$71) per month, which should of course be expected given the sampling procedures based on the income level. What is perhaps disquieting is that even within the quasi-formal sector a good number of the heads belong to the low-income category; since all of them are own-account workers without fixed location, their inclusion in the quasi-formal sector is a misclassification. Furthermore, it is also worth noting that only one quarter of the quasi-formal sector heads receive an income of over 400,000 pesos (or US$357) per month. These findings suggest that a majority of the heads in these two sectors combined, perhaps over two-thirds receive an income below the national per capita level which is estimated to have been around US$1,640 in 1973 (i.e. US$137 or 1,540 hundred pesos per month). Only a few received incomes comparable to the formal or the public sector. Making allowance for a median household size of four, these income figures suggest a much lower level of per capita income.

The data presented in table 5 also shows that there are significant disparities in the distribution of income even within the same groups of enterprises. Among own-account workers without a fixed location, a greater proportion (59 per cent) of the skilled entrepreneurs belong to medium and higher income categories as compared to the unskilled (23 per cent). Similar conclusions also hold for enterprises in fixed locations as well. Provision of skills could therefore play an important role in increasing the incomes of small entrepreneurs and improving income distribution.

Table 5: Distribution of heads of enterprises
by income level and skills (per cent)

	Income (hundreds of pesos per month)			
	Low under 800	Medium 801-4 000	High 4 000+	Total
Own-account workers without fixed location (1 760)				
Informal (896)	92.5	7.0	0.5	100.0
Quasi-formal (864)	24.1	55.1	20.8	100.0
Both (1 760)	58.9	30.6	10.5	100.0
skilled (891)	41.4	45.8	12.8	100.0
unskilled (869)	76.9	15.1	8.0	100.0
Heads of enterprises with fixed location (640)				
Informal (206)	100.0	-	-	100.0
Quasi-formal (434)	-	69.8	30.2	100.0
Both	32.2	47.3	20.5	100.0
skilled (453)	21.8	49.5	28.7	100.0
unskilled (187)	57.2	42.2	0.6	100.0
All enterprises (2 400)	51.8	35.1	13.1	100.0
Informal (1 102)	93.9	5.7	0.4	100.0
Quasi-formal (1 298)	16.0	60.0	24.0	100.0

Another interesting conclusion emerging from the study
pertains to inequalities in income distribution between men and
women. According to table 6, a greater proportion of female heads
of enterprises in Córdoba informal sector belong to low-income
groups as compared to men. For both the informal and the quasi-
formal sectors combined, 85 per cent of women belonged to the low-
income category as compared to only 39 per cent for men. The
relatively lower levels of mean income for females can be explained
partly in terms of the activities in which they participate, viz.
personal services and retail trade. Similar conclusions seem to
hold for heads of enterprises with fixed location as well; 56 per
cent of women were in the low-income group as against 23 per cent
for men.

Table 6: Distribution of heads of enterprises
by income level and sex (per cent)

	Income (hundreds of pesos per month)			
	Low under 800	Medium 801-4 000	High 4 000+	Total

I. Own-account workers without fixed location

Informal
Men	80.4	18.9	0.7	100.0
Women	97.8	1.9	0.3	100.0

Quasi-formal
Men	23.7	56.4	19.9	100.0
Women	26.0	48.1	26.0	100.0

Both
Men	39.0	46.2	14.8	100.0
Women	85.0	10.1	4.9	100.0

II. Heads of enterprises with fixed location

Informal
Men	100.0	-	-	100.0
Women	100.0	-	-	100.0

Quasi-formal
Men	-	65.7	34.3	100.0
Women	-	88.5	11.5	100.0

Both
Men	23.1	50.5	26.4	100.0
Women	55.9	39.0	5.1	100.0

Linkages

The Córdoba study, as studies elsewhere have shown, suggests
that households and individuals provide the major market for their
goods and services. Eighty two per cent of the informal sector
units and 72 per cent of those in the quasi-formal sector sell
directly to the final consumers; only 13 and 16 per cent
respectively relied on intermediaries. Quite naturally, 92 per cent
of those relying on intermediaries were own-account workers without
a fixed location. Perhaps lack of premises and direct access to
market force them to rely on intermediaries, implying that at least
some of these units are unable to realise their full income
potential. With regard to linkages with the Government, 93 per cent
of the establishments in fixed location were subject to registration
and inspection.

Growth and expansion

The data on age structure of these units provide some
indications about growth of this sector. The proportion of

enterprises that emerged during the year preceding the survey was
6.1 per cent. This seems to suggest that the number had been
growing at a "gross" rate of perhaps 6.5 per cent per year (i.e. 6.1
over 93.9). Nearly one-third of the sample units had come into
existence during the five years preceding. A breakdown of the data
separately by activity and type of enterprise is presented in table
7. One of the interesting findings is that the rate of growth of
own-account enterprises without fixed location seems to be
substantially higher as compared to that for establishments in fixed
locations. The most obvious explanation for this phenomenon seems
to be that there are few constraints if any to entry in the former
category. Further, trade and "other" activities seem to be growing
faster in both types of enterprises. These findings also imply
difficulties in access to business premises in choice locations
closer to markets or central parts of the city. In other words,
access to markets could be an important consideration in opting for
variable locations. Lastly, only a handful of enterprises with two
or more workers had come into existence in recent years suggesting
that employment growth if any occurred primarily through entry of
new enterprises rather than through increase in wage employment as
elsewhere.

Table 7: Distribution of enterprises by activity
and age of business (per cent)

Age of business (years)	Manu-factur-ing	Construc-tion	Trade	Services*	Other*	Total
own-account workers without fixed location						
Under 1	10.0	3.4	10.5	4.2	10.9	6.8
1- 2	4.8	7.9	8.0	10.9	11.7	8.9
2- 5	21.4	5.2	15.4	16.5	20.4	15.7
5-10	13.6	20.3	24.7	25.1	29.2	22.4
10+	50.2	63.1	41.4	43.2	27.7	46.2
All	100.0	100.0	100.0	100.0	100.0	100.0
	(331)	(290)	(324)	(713)	(137)	(1 795)
establishments in fixed locations						
Under 1	-	-	4.4	1.7	7.1	3.6
1- 2	3.4	-	9.3	1.7	14.3	7.5
2- 5	13.8	-	24.5	16.1	42.8	22.6
5-10	6.9	100.0	20.7	21.2	21.4	20.2
10+	75.9	-	41.1	59.3	14.3	46.1
All	100.0	100.0	100.0	100.0	100.0	100.0
	(29)	(1)	(387)	(118)	(14)	(549)

* Insurance, real estate and related services are included
under "other" category which also includes primary activities
and transport.

Note: Figures in parentheses indicate the number of sample
units.

Turning to the question of expansion, only 20 per cent of the informal sector and 53 per cent of the quasi-formal sector establishments having fixed locations showed interest in expanding their business. In the first case non-availability of loans at reasonable rates of interest, lack of suitable premises and lack of demand were cited as the constraints preventing expansion by 100, 93 and 40 per cent respectively of those interested in expansion. In the case of the quasi-formal sector, however, lack of demand figured as the most important factor (70 per cent); only 48 and 18 per cent respectively, of the enterprises, complained that credit and premises were limiting factors.[1] With regard to access to credit from banks there seems to be one major difference between the informal and the quasi-formal sectors: only 6 per cent of the former enterprises ever obtained a bank loan as compared to 86 per cent in the latter. Consistent with the above, 71 per cent of those in the informal sector did not believe they can get bank credit (compared to only 14 per cent in the other case) because they lacked the collateral necessary and because of the absence of favourable government policies.

Informal sector and urban environment

Statistics concerning living conditions in 1965 suggest that the housing condition in Córdoba was reasonably good as compared to Africa, for example; 83 per cent of the dwelling units were estimated to be independent units and only 8 per cent were "shacks and temporary" structures. In terms of access to utilities, 83 per cent had running water, 95 per cent had toilet facilities and 91 per cent had electricity. But in terms of occupancy rates, 29 per cent of the dwellings fell below the international standards and were overcrowded. These statistics are also reflected in the sample data. Comparing the living conditions of informal and quasi-formal sector participants, few differences are to be noted: own residential premises: 70 per cent in informal sector and 65 per cent in quasi-formal sector; rented: 24 and 28 per cent; rent-free: 15 and 6 per cent respectively. In other words, not only most of the households participating in the two sectors have access to basic urban amenities but a majority also own their own premises (including land).

Notwithstanding the above positive features of Córdoba, a minority of the city population lived in what are known as "emergency towns" or "poverty towns" according to the 1970 Population Census. The residents of these shanty towns or slum dwellers belonged to the fringe of the informal sector, some 80 per cent of them working as domestic servants or casual labourers with little vocational training or capital. It is also interesting to note that 54 per cent of the population in these towns is under 20 years as compared to 36 per cent for the whole of Córdoba. It is also interesting to note that only 42 per cent were immigrants; three-quarters of the native population were under 20 years old because most of them were born to immigrants in Córdoba. As against the average household size of four for the city, it is seven in the slums. In terms of schooling, only 11 per cent completed the primary level. Also of those working, 84 per cent were independent workers and 16 per cent were wage workers; and half of the employed

----

[1] The reasons cited are not mutually exclusive.

did not have a regular source of income. With regard to income, most of the slum dwellers earned between 25 and 85 per cent of the legal minimum wage, the average being 56 per cent. These findings not only emphasise the close link between poverty, employment and environment but also the constraints to upward mobility even within the informal sector.

Conclusions

Though a third of all informal sector participants in Córdoba are under 30 years of age, as elsewhere, only a quarter of the heads of enterprises belonged to this group. The proportion of younger heads was even smaller, only 19 per cent, in the quasi-informal sector which generates relatively higher incomes. Women's participation in the Córdoba informal sector seems to be relatively greater as compared to other cities noted earlier: 38 per cent as compared to 25 per cent in Jakarta and Freetown, 15 per cent in Lagos, 12 per cent in Colombo and 11 per cent in Kano. But a large majority of those engaged in low-income activities, 63 per cent, were women as against only 23 per cent in the quasi-formal sector, which is also reflected in the distribution of heads by earnings. Relatively more skilled heads received relatively higher incomes. In terms of education, the Córdoba informal sector is not very different from other cities noted earlier; the majority had under 8 years of schooling but a greater proportion of less educated (and unskilled) ones participated in low-income activities or what is described in this study as purely informal sector. Education and skill acquisition seem to be complementary.

With regard to job mobility, only some 30 per cent of the heads had changed their jobs during the five years preceding the survey; further mobility seems to be restricted to similar occupational groups. Unlike in Africa, there seems to be little migration to Córdoba in recent years which may partly be explained by rising unemployment and deceleration in economic growth in the region. Consequently, most of the immigrant heads in the informal sector were residents of Córdoba for 10 years or longer. Nevertheless, the study suggests that a greater proportion of the recent immigrants participated in the low-income informal sector as against a large majority of older migrants in the quasi-formal sector indicating that longer duration of stay in the city contributes to some upward mobility.

Notwithstanding the substantial economic transformation that took place in Córdoba during the 1950s and 1960s, the informal and quasi-formal activities in the city are not dominated by manufacturing but by trade, construction and service activities. Both the level of capital utilisation and the income generated are significantly lower than those in the formal sector. In fact, a large majority of the participants in the two sectors seem to be earning below the legal minimum wage.

Most of the informal sector units in Córdoba did not have any hired workers; only 14 per cent provided wage employment. Thus, the informal sector is mainly a source of self-employment rather than wage employment. Eighty-nine per cent of males and 75 per cent of females worked full-time. Only a small fraction of the sample units operated in fix location implying lack of access to markets in choice locations is an important factor constraining their income and expansion. A greater proportion of those in low-income activities (70 per cent) operated in their own residential premises.

Though the level of income generated in the sector was substantially lower relative to that of the formal sector, the living conditions and access to urban amenities were significatnly better as compared to African cities, for example. Since much of the recent growth in informal sector units is occurring in low-income activities without fixed location, there seems to be an urgent need to improve the physical environment, notably access to business premises. Evidence based on shanty town dwellers suggests a close link between employment, poverty and environment. It would therefore seem necessary to initiate programmes that can simultaneously tackle all these three factors.

Although credit facilities and provision of appropriate infrastructure in the form of premises with direct access to markets could play an important role in promoting income and productivity in this sector, the dominance of trade and personal service activities coupled with demand constraint would seem to limit the scope for action along these lines. Perhaps a programme to diversify the skills (and hence activities) followed by appropriate linkages to formal sector activities seems to hold greater promise in the context of productive employment generation in Córdoba.

CHAPTER 12. THE URBAN INFORMAL SECTOR AND INDUSTRIAL DEVELOPMENT IN A SMALL CITY: THE CASE OF CAMPINAS (BRAZIL)

Manoel Tosta Berlinck, José Murari Bovo
and Luiz Carlos Cintra*

The city of Campinas, located 94 kilometres from Sao Paulo, is an intermediate urban centre within the municipio of Campinas whose population in 1970 was around 376,000. Located in the centre of a region specialising in plantation crops, Campinas served as the "mouth of the sertas" through which agricultural production was funnelled for onward transmission to domestic and international markets. Consequently, it acquired considerable investment in the form of infrastructure during the last century. Though industries began to appear towards the end of the nineteenth century it was not until 1950 that a profound change in industrial structure began to take place.

The total population of the municipio of Campinas increased at an annual rate of 1.6 per cent between 1940 and 1950; but the rate of increase shot up to 3.7 per cent per year during 1950-60 and 5.5 per cent per year during 1960-70. Correspondingly, the share of rural populations in the municipio decreased from 40 per cent in 1940 to 13 per cent in 1970. Evidently migration played an important role in the process. The share of agriculture in total employment in this region decreased from 39 per cent in 1960 to 9 per cent in 1970 while that of industry increased from 21 to 48 per cent during the same period. The massive economic transformation however came to an end by 1973 when the rates of growth of employment showed a substantial drop in most of the sectors. Nevertheless the study of the informal sector in Campinas should prove to be quite interesting, particularly in the context of migration and a decline in relative importance of agriculture.

The universe covered by the study included own-account workers (with or without unpaid family labour) and small enterprises with fewer than ten wage workers. The study is based on a sample of 500 units, divided in the ratio of 20:40:40 between industry, commerce and services respectively. The interesting feature of this study is that it analysed the data collected with particular reference to the size of the unit where size was measured in terms of capital owned. Thus, the sample units were stratified into three groups: I – capital up to Cr$10,000 (or about US$930) per unit; II - capital between Cr$10,000 and 50,000 (i.e. US$930-4,650); and III – Cr$50,000 and above (or US$4,650+).

Table 1 shows the distribution of sampling units within each major group as well as by the capital size of the units. Within the service sector, repair services accounted for 46.5 per cent, construction and transport services for 12 per cent and the remainder, other services.

----

* Instituto de Filosifia e Ciências Humanas, Universidade Estadual de Campinas, Brazil.

Table 1: Distribution of sample units by activity
and capital size (per cent)

| Activity | Capital size (Cr$'000) | | | | All units |
	I (under 10)	II (10- 50)	III (50+)	Total	
A. Industry	14.6	17.5	67.9	100.0	100.0
1. Tailoring	91.7	8.3	-	100.0	11.7
2. Garments	11.1	22.2	66.7	100.0	8.7
3. Metallurgy	3.2	29.1	67.7	100.0	30.1
4. Printing and publishing	-	10.0	90.0	100.0	9.7
5. Carpentry	-	15.4	84.6	100.0	12.7
6. Other	7.2	10.8	82.0	100.0	27.1
B. Commerce	20.7	26.4	52.9	100.0	100.0
1. Bars and groceries	11.0	29.7	59.3	100.0	43.7
2. Apparel and haberdashery	8.3	33.3	58.4	100.0	11.5
3. News stands	68.0	32.0	-	100.0	11.9
4. Peddlars	80.0	20.0	-	100.0	7.2
5. Other	3.7	16.9	79.4	100.0	25.7
C. Services	37.3	43.2	19.5	100.0	100.0
1. Shoe repair	75.9	20.7	3.4	100.0	15.7
2. Auto repair	6.1	45.5	48.4	100.0	17.8
3. Barber, beauty shops	38.9	51.9	9.2	100.0	29.1
4. Other	32.7	43.0	24.3	100.0	37.4
TOTAL (A+B+C)	26.0	31.0	43.0	100.0	

A striking feature of these units in Campinas is that they use substantially larger amount of capital as compared to the informal sector units in other cities presented earlier. Only a quarter of the enterprises used under US$930 worth of fixed assets; as many as 43 per cent had over US$4,650. Of course the larger units also employ more labour as will be shown later. With the exception of tailoring (most of them are run by own-account workers), the industrial units used relatively larger amounts of capital. In commerce, except for news stands and peddlars operated by own-account workers, other units used relatively larger amounts of capital. In the service sector, most of the units engaged in the production of personal and social services used relatively small amounts of capital.

It should not therefore come as a surprise that 93 per cent of the units had a fixed place of work; 94 per cent operated in legal structures, mostly in non-residential premises; most of the structures were permanent, with masonry construction, had electricity and water, and were easily accessible. As should be expected, the few which did not conform to the above description belonged to stratum I with little capital. Among the few who did not operate in a fixed structure, 60 per cent had motorised vehicles and 20 per cent, non-motorised vehicles. Lastly, 90 per cent of the units were legally registered with appropriate authorities.

Though the use of capital has already been emphasised, it is nevertheless worth noting that only 13 per cent of the sample units did not possess or use any capital equipment or tools. Virtually all the units owned the machinery and equipment used by them. In 81 per cent of the cases they were acquired through own savings; in only 8 per cent of these cases the purchase of equipment was financed by private banks. In this respect, Campinas does not differ from other studies cited earlier.

Heads of enterprises

Eighty-eight per cent of the heads of these units were males. Fifty six per cent of the heads were between 30 and 49 years old; 22 per cent each belonged to under 30 and above 49 years groups. Median age thus seems to have been around 40 years. With regard to schooling, 2.5 per cent of the heads were illiterate; 15 per cent had incomplete primary education and 41 per cent had primary level education. Considering the amount of capital possessed, it is remarkable that only 40 per cent of the heads had beyond primary-level education.

Turning to the role of migration, only 22 per cent were born in the city of Campinas; 73 per cent had come from other parts of Brazil and the rest from abroad. Over two-thirds (68 per cent) of those born outside had lived in the city for longer than ten years. Thus, as in the case of Córdoba, only a small proportion of the heads of enterprises were recent migrants (i.e. those who came to Campinas within the ten years preceding the date of survey). Further a majority (73 per cent) of those born outside Campinas had lived in an urban area before migration; in other words, unlike in other cities noted earlier, few came from rural areas.

One of the interesting findings of the study pertains to occupational mobility. Eighty-six per cent of the heads had been in an occupation different from the current one. About three-quarters of them were in fact wage workers in industry, commerce and services; and the remaining were own-account workers. In otherwords, the informal sector in Campinas as defined in this study seems to have played an important role in providing better income opportunities for many wage workers in the formal sector. It is further interesting to note that a majority of those who did switch to the informal sector did not encounter any difficulty. Unlike in other cities, over one half of the heads overcame the problem of initial capital by accumulating their savings through wage employment. It would thus seem that these entrepreneurs entered the formal sector in order to acquire skills and capital before actually establishing their own enterprises. For the remainder, the initial capital came from own savings through self-employment, or from friends and relatives. Only 2 per cent relied on banks. Finally, 60 per cent of those who acquired their capital through wage employment were in capital strata I and II.

Table 2 shows the distribution of sample units by the level of income received by the head and by capital size of the unit.

Consistent with the amount of capital used by these units, the
income earned by these heads is substantially higher than that
earned by entrepreneurs in other cities discussed earlier. The bulk
of them (72 per cent) were in the range of 1,000 to 5,000 cruzeiros
(or US$93 to US$464) per month; only 10 per cent earned under US$93
per month, the median being around US$310. Given the national GNP
per capita of US$1,140 (or about 1,023 cruzeiros per month) in
1976,[1] 90 per cent of the heads received a higher level of income.
Likewise a large majority of the heads were above the legal minimum
wage income. As should be expected, those with less capital
dominated the lowest income bracket; 72 per cent in the latter
bracket belonged to capital stratum I. Conversely, heads in higher
income brackets mostly belonged to capital strata II and III.

Employment

Of the 500 sample units, 232 (or 46 per cent) were one-person
enterprises run by own-account workers. Of the remainder, 85 units
did not employ any wage workers but had unpaid family workers - 120
persons to be precise. Thus, only 183 units engaged wage workers
and some of them had unpaid family workers as well. The total
number of wage workers in them was 616; and the number of unpaid
family workers, 132. Total employment generated in the sample units
was thus 252 family workers plus 616 wage workers in addition to 500
entrepreneurs or 1,368 persons. The average size of the enterprise
thus works out to 2.74 persons.

Table 2: Distribution of sample units by amount
          of capital and monthly income per unit
          (per cent)

Amount of capital (Cr$'000)	Monthly income				
	Up to Cr$1 000	From 1 001 to 5 000	From 5 001 to 10 000	More than 10 000	Total
Stratum I (under 10)	(72) 29	(26) 68	(3) 2	(4) 1	(26) 100
Stratum II (10-50)	(14) 5	(27) 83	(22) 11	(4) 1	(31) 100
Stratum III (50+)	(14) 3	(37) 60	(75) 25	(92) 12	(43) 100
TOTAL	(100) 10	(100) 72	(100) 15	(100) 5	(100) 100

Note: Cr$10.77 = US$1, on the average in 1976.

Figures in parentheses are column percentages.

Table 3 below shows the size distribution of enterprises with
wage employees (i.e. 183 units). It is clear that a majority of

[1] World Bank: World Development Report, 1978, op. cit., p. 77.

them, 61 per cent, had between one and three wage workers; only a few (16 per cent) had seven or more wage workers. But from the last column of the table it is evident that only 30 per cent of the wage employment originates in such small enterprises. The table also shows the distribution of workers by age and sex. As elsewhere, relatively few females (16 per cent) participated as wage employees. The proportion of wage employees under 18 years of age is however quite significant - about 30 per cent. If the data on wage workers are broken down by the amount of capital owned by enterprises, 89 per cent of all wage workers were employed by those in capital stratum III, i.e., over 50,000 cruzeiros. In other words, most of the wage employment in the Campinas informal sector is provided by enterprises with more capital. Further, since only a few hired workers on a part-time or temporary basis, most of the wage employees were also full-time workers.

Table 3: <u>Distribution of enterprises and wage workers by size of enterprise</u>

Size (number of wage workers per enterprise)	Sample units with wage workers		Distribution of wage workers (per cent)					
	No.	Per cent	Under 18 years of age		18+ years		Total	Column
			M	F	M	F		
1 to 3	112	61.2	24	8	59	9	100.0	30
4 to 6	42	23.0	25	8	59	8	100.0	32
7 to 10	29	58.8	23	3	62	12	100.0	38
All	183	100.0	24	6	60	10	100.0	100 (616)

Note: M - Males; F - Females; figure in parentheses refers to absolute number of workers.

With regard to supply of labour, about half the enterprises hiring workers had difficulty in getting skilled labour. Only a quarter of the wage workers seem to have come from rural areas. Also, most of the wage workers (76 per cent) had worked earlier with either small or large enterprises;[1] only 11 per cent were unemployed before. Turning to wage payment, almost all the

[1] The mobility from formal sector wage employment to self-employment in the informal sector may at least partly be attributed to the prevailing legislation concerning enterprises and workers. Thus, for example, large enterprises are known to prefer subcontracting to own account workers rather than hiring workers themselves in order to avoid expenses on social security and the like foreseen in the labour legislation.

enterprises paid wages in cash; and 60 per cent of the enterprises revise the wage on an annual basis and 13 per cent on a semi-annual basis.

Linkages and constraints

Limited access to credit from banks for starting an enterprise was already mentioned. Likewise, 96 per cent of the sample units relied on own funds for their current expenditures. Although 55 per cent of the units never tried to get credit, of those who did, over 60 per cent did not encounter any obstacles. This suggests that access to credit is a problem only to some enterprises and most of them felt that stringent requirements prevented them from getting credit. Of course 87 per cent of those who tried to get credit and did not encounter any obstacles belonged to larger firms with more capital viz., strata II and III. Nearly three-quarters of those in stratum I with little capital did not even try to get credit.

With regard to other forms of backward linkages, 90 per cent of the manufacturing units obtained their raw materials from (small, medium and large) enterprises and only 10 per cent depended on households/individuals. In fact, 34 per cent depended on large enterprises alone, 22 per cent on small enterprises and 34 per cent on both. There seems to be some market imperfection in obtaining raw materials; a third of those relying exclusively on large enterprises bought their raw material requirements from a single large enterprise. In any case, these findings suggest a significant amount of integration of these activities in Campinas with the rest of the economy. Among the units engaged in commerce, 99 per cent relied on small and large enterprises (31 per cent on large only, 29 per cent on small only and 39 per cent on both). Here again, 22 per cent of the sample units relied on a single enterprise (large or small) for their merchandise.

One of the interesting features of the above linkages is their variation with the size of enterprise. With regard to industrial units, only two-thirds of those in capital stratum I bought their inputs from enterprises, large or small, in contrast to 96 per cent in stratum III. Another interesting finding is that 44 per cent of those in stratum II relied on a single enterprise for their raw material needs. But in the case of trade enterprises, 52 per cent of those in capital stratum I (little capital) obtained their merchandise from a single enterprise, large or small. It is not clear whether these units are subject to subordination by those on whom they depend; but it does raise a question for further examination.

Turning to forward linkages, 83 per cent of the units sold their goods and services mainly to households; only 12 per cent sold exclusively to small or large enterprises. As should be expected, the link with households was stronger for units in (low capital) stratum I. In terms of geographical area, 90 per cent of the clientele were located in the town or municipio of Campinas. These findings suggest that the survival of this sector in Campinas depends primarily on local household incomes as in the case of other cities discussed earlier.

Growth, expansion and attitudes
towards government policies

Though it is difficult to judge the rate of growth of informal sector units in Campinas in recent years, the data available suggest that it is not far different from other cities/towns discussed earlier. Fifty-five per cent of the sample units in Campinas had come into existence during the five years preceding the date of survey as compared to 69 per cent in Freetown, 66 per cent in Lagos, 62 per cent in Jakarta and 51 per cent in Kumasi. Twenty-two per cent were between five and ten years old and 23 per cent over ten years.

The study also attempted to measure the extent of improvements effected by these units. About one-quarter of them had significant improvements and a third had small improvements in the business premises during the year preceding the survey. But the proportion reporting such improvements was higher in those with more capital: 35 per cent in stratum I as against 70 per cent in stratum III. Similarly 10 per cent had improved the method of production/operation significantly and 12 per cent had done so to a lesser extent; for the majority (77 per cent) there was no change. A greater proportion of those reporting improvement, of course, belonged to higher capital strata. About one-half of the enterprises had improved the quality of their products and a majority of them were larger enterprises. Finally, with regard to demand, 44 per cent had experienced an increase and 50 per cent did not experience any change in recent years. Of those in the expansionary phase, 55, 26 and 19 per cent were respectively in strata III, II and I suggesting that larger enterprises had a greater chance of expansion.

When asked about the changes in volume of capital invested during the five years preceding the date of survey, 22 per cent of the units reported a substantial increase and 51 per cent, a small increase; for 25 per cent, there was no change. Here again, 71 per cent of the units reporting a substantial increase in capital belonged to the (highest capital) stratum III; only 21 and 8 per cent respectively to strata II and I. Consistent with these results, 14 per cent of the units had a substantial increase in net revenue and 48 per cent, a small increase; only 7 per cent reported a decrease. Over two-thirds of those with substantial increases in income belonged to (highest capital) stratum III as opposed to 14 per cent in stratum I. In conclusion, the Campinas study suggests that enterprises with most capital tended to grow and effect improvements in business.

With regard to constraints on expansion, decrease or elimination of taxes was desired by two-thirds of the units; a greater proportion of them of course belonged to higher capital strata. Competition in general did not pose a threat to expansion. For two-thirds of the enterprises, competition did not affect their income.

Conclusions

Given that less than 2 per cent of the population of the municipio of Campinas were living in slums (at the time of the survey), coupled with the finding that a large majority of the selected enterprises had significant amounts of capital yielding an income well above that implied by the legal minimum wage to their heads suggests that the informal sector in Campinas is substantially better off as compared to other cities cited thus far.

The informal sector in Campinas seems comparable to that in other cities discussed earlier in many respects. Women's participation is quite small, only 12 per cent among the heads and 16 per cent among wage workers. Unpaid family labour plays an important role. Only 22 per cent of the heads were under 30 years of age. Median level of education of the heads was only around primary level. Though migration is important in the sense that 78 per cent of the heads were born outside Campinas, as in the case of Córdoba, very few were recent migrants; over two-thirds had been in the city for longer than ten years. Also very few migrated from rural areas.

The Campinas study is significant and interesting from certain points of view. First, a large majority of the heads had experienced occupational mobility. Perhaps this is largely related to the massive transformation from agriculture to industry, commerce and services that took place in the region. Second, the average amount of capital possessed and income earned by these entrepreneurs was substantially higher than in the cities noted earlier. What is more interesting is that few encountered any obstacles either in switching occupations or in starting their own enterprises and this seems mainly due to the fact that many had accumulated skills and capital from formal sector wage employment before entering the informal sector. The study is also significant in that the sector not only generated respectable levels of income to entrepreneurs but also experienced few constraints to growth and expansion. A large majority experienced increase in volume of capital, however small it may be; only 6 per cent of the enterprises experienced a decline in business; also 62 per cent realised increases in net revenue in the years preceding the date of survey. Over half had improved their business premises. Access to credit from the banks was however a problem to many as in other cities. Taxes seem to pose a constraint to expansion to a majority of the sample enterprises. The findings above seem to cast doubt on the hypothesis that the informal sector is involutionary.

As elsewhere a large majority of the enterprises sold their output directly to households and individuals. But unlike in other cities, a majority of these industrial units obtained their raw material requirements from large enterprises (formal sector) partly or exclusively. In many cases they seem to depend on a single large enterprise suggesting at least some market imperfections. Somewhat similar results were reported for informal units in commerce.

Finally, unlike many other cities, almost all of the informal sector enterprises in Campinas had fixed location and access to markets. In fact almost all of them were legal and a majority even paid taxes to the Government. Also, most of them worked longer hours and six days a week. The relatively better physical conditions and environment in which the Campinas informal sector operates can partly be attributed to little recent migration and partly to the mobility of entrepreneurs from formal sector wage employment to the informal sector.

The findings based on Campinas differ somewhat from those

emerging from a study on Belo Horizonte,[1] also in Brazil. The two are not, strictly speaking, comparable, because the latter is based on the household survey data and the definition of the informal sector hinges on the contribution to social security by workers and includes domestic servants. Furthermore, Belo Horizonte is the third largest city in Brazil. Nevertheless, the study shows: (a) a relatively larger fraction of the workforce in poor households depend on the informal sector; (b) informal sector plays an important role in absorbing migrant labour; (c) migrants tend to move from the informal to the formal sector as their duration of residence increases; (d) earnings in the informal sector are significantly lower, sometimes up to 65 per cent; and (e) the informal sector provides employment not only for the secondary earners but also for the heads of households. Part of the differences in findings between Campinas and Belo Horizonte can be attributed to the approach adopted by these two studies, notably the exclusion of domestic service activities in the former. Also the role of migration seems to be more important in Belo Horizonte, partly due to the fact that the study was carried out in 1972.[2] More importantly, the conclusions based on the Campinas study seem to reflect its location close to a large industrial centre like Sao Paulo. Thus, the two studies seem to complement rather than contradict each other. The evidence suggests that the role of the informal sector is highly dependent on the size of the town/city, the role of migration and the stage and rate of economic development of the region.

----

[1] Thomas W. Merrick: "Employment and earnings in the informal sector in Brazil: The case of Belo Horizonte", in Journal of Developing Areas, Apr. 1976, pp. 337-354.

[2] Population in Belo Horizonte increased at 6.2 per cent per year during the 1950-70 period as compared with 4.6 per cent per year in the municipio of Campinas. And yet the metropolitan Belo Horizonte attracted only one-fifth of those who left the State of Minas Gerais (where the city is located), the most populous State in Brazil. Sixty-eight per cent of males and 71 per cent of females in the active population of the city were migrants.

PART III

Implications for environment and development policies
S.V. Sethuraman

The implications of promoting employment through the urban informal sector for the urban environment in the Third World countries were briefly mentioned in Chapter 3. Conversely, policies to improve the urban environment have significant implications for employment generation in the urban informal sector. It is therefore interesting to ask to what extent the two objectives - employment creation and improving the environment in urban areas - are mutually consistent. Is there a set of policies which can contribute to the achievement of both the objectives simultaneously? If not what are the alternatives for combining employment policies with environment policies? This chapter reviews the evidence emerging from the studies presented in Part II and assesses their implications for the above issues.

Environmental implications of promoting the informal sector can be discussed at two levels at least. In the narrow sense of the term they can focus on the immediate environment in which the informal sector participants themselves live and work. In a broader sense one can talk about the environmental implications for the city or region or even country as a whole. Accordingly, the discussion below is divided into three parts: the first part focusing on the immediate environment of the informal sector participants themselves; the second part discusses the role of the informal sector in recycling waste materials and its contribution to environment; and the last part describes the link between migration and the informal sector and its environmental implications for regional or national development in general.

The term environment again can be defined as narrowly or as broadly as one wishes. In its broader sense "environment" can be taken to mean "the biosphere, or simply nature, including human beings".[1] Thus, environment protection involves a whole range of issues including consumption patterns, time and space uses, resource profiles and technological choices.[2] Alternatively, environment can simply be defined to include various forms of pollution including the physical milieu in which people live and work. In the discussion below the word environment embraces both the above senses of the term in view of their short- and long-run policy implications.

Informal sector participants and environment

One of the problems confronting the informal sector enterprises is the access to premises and supporting infrastructural
----

[1] UNCTAD: Development, environment and technology: Towards a technology for self-reliance, study prepared by Johan Galtung for UNCTAD with financial support of the UNEP (New York, United Nations, 1979), p. 4.

[2] See, for example, I. Sachs: Developing in harmony with nature: Consumption patterns, time and space uses, resource profiles and technological choices; and J. Pajestka: Spatial development patterns and sound environment development, Papers presented at the UNEP/ECE Regional Seminar on Alternative Patterns of Development and Lifestyles, Ljubljana (Yugoslavia), 3-8 December 1979.

facilities. A related problem is their access to suitable locations
within the city. Evidence from Part II suggests that the proportion
of sample enterprises without even a fixed location to carry on
their business was as follows: 34 per cent in Colombo; 25 per cent
in Jakarta; 24 per cent in Kano; 23 per cent in Cordoba; 20 per cent
in Freetown; 8 per cent in Lagos; and 7 per cent in Campinas. Among
those in fixed locations, a significant proportion neither owned nor
rented their locations implying that they occupied public (or
private) space, notably in city centres, legally or illegally; for
example, 19 per cent in Freetown and 11 per cent in Lagos reported
so. In Kumasi though 100 per cent of the enterprises belonged to
this category, thanks to the policies of local authorities, the land
was legal and approved. One of the consequences of the above is
that the enterprises either do not possess any premises (i.e.
structures) at all or they operate in temporary sheds and structures
that are easy to dismantle at the request of the public authorities
(or private owners). For example, in Colombo half the enterprises
had no premises at all and 14 per cent used some kind of premises
free of charge; even those who owned or rented their premises
operated in poor physical structures. Among informal trade
enterprises in Manila, 20 per cent were in temporary structures; in
Lagos, a third of the sample enterprises reported so.

Another dimension of the problem relates to location of the
enterprises within the city; of those in fixed location many operate
in residential areas. This is particularly the case in Colombo,
Jakarta, Manila and Lagos, where a majority were so reported. In
fact many in fixed locations operated in their own residential
premises: 46 per cent in Jakarta; 50 per cent or more in trade and
services sectors of Manila; 67 per cent of those in Kano; 61 per
cent in Lagos; and 70 per cent in the informal sector (low-income
activities) of Cordoba. With regard to supporting urban services,
except in the case of Manila and Campinas, only a few had both
electricity and water: 25 per cent in Lagos; 37 per cent in Kano; 20
per cent in Kumasi; and virtually none in Colombo.

Since there are significant links between workplace and
residence, it will be useful to look at the living conditions. In
Jakarta, for example, only 30 per cent of the households dependent
on the informal sector for employment lived in "permanent"
structures; 84 per cent of them had electricity; 38 per cent had
water; and 16 per cent neither. Though 61 per cent owned their
dwellings, 14 per cent neither owned nor rented and 6 per cent
shared the accommodation. The situation was worse for those in
temporary structures. In fact 70 per cent of them were claimed to
be "illegal".

The brief survey of evidence should not come as a surprise,
since the informal sector has emerged primarily in search of
employment and hence income. It is also consistent with the
findings reported in World Housing Survey cited in Chapter I. Most
other similar studies cited elsewhere in this volume also suggest
similar evidence. In particular the study on hawkers and vendors in
selected South-East Asian cities[1] is quite striking in this respect.
What are the implications of the above for improving the physical

----

[1] McGee and Yeung: Hawkers in South-East Asian cities ..., op.
cit., table 2.

environment in which the informal sector operates? These enterprises have very little investment in the form of business premises. This is understandable in view of their low level of income. Perhaps a more important reason is their preference to operate in central locations within the city where the property values are substantially higher rather than in the periphery. Also the enterprises may not find suitable space for constructing their premises even if they have the necessary investment funds - and this explains why a significant proportion of them occupy available public or private land on a temporary basis, legally or otherwise. Thus, uncertainty associated with the tenure could also act as a constraint on investment in premises. The question then is why do they prefer to operate in such locations where they cannot afford to have suitable premises with supporting facilities in the form of electricity, water, drainage and the like? The reason seems to be the close link between the location and income opportunities, as the evidence below shows.[1]

First it should be recalled that most of the informal sector enterprises produce goods and services for consumption by households and individuals; and second they deal with their clientele directly rather than through intermediaries. Also given the competition among enterprises to reach a limited market for their goods and services it is quite natural that they try to minimise the cost for their clientele in acquiring the goods and services by offering them where and when they want and thereby maximise their net revenues. The evidence from various studies shows that an overwhelming proportion of sample enterprises sold their goods and services to households and individuals rather than to enterprises: 81 per cent in Freetown; 87 per cent in Lagos and Kano; 72 per cent in Kumasi; 80 per cent in Manila; 82 per cent in the informal sector and 72 per cent in the quasi-formal sector in Cordoba; and 83 per cent in Campinas. More than half the clientele in Lagos and most of the customers in Colombo for example are reported to live within 20 minutes walking distance from the location of the enterprise.

The informal sector entrepreneurs also seem to minimise the cost of reaching their enterprises by choosing their residential locations close to the enterprise.[2] Two-thirds of the heads of enterprises in Colombo lived within 3 kilometres from their enterprise; in Jakarta 46 per cent lived in the business premises itself and 43 per cent within a kilometre distance. In Lagos 31 per cent of the heads lived in the business premises and 47 per cent in the same neighbourhood.

In addition to the above, there are also significant backward linkages which prompt the enterprises to choose central city locations. Lack of working capital often implies buying inputs from other small retailers in small quantities as and when required. Likewise linkages take the form of buying supporting services such

----

[1] The reluctance to give up locations in city centres could also be attributed to increase in urban land prices far above that of other commodities. See United Nations: World Housing Survey, 1974, op. cit., pp. 63-64.

[2] To some extent it is also motivated by the need for secondary earners in the household to participate in economic activities in central districts.

as transport, welding and electrical repair from other small enterprises. Finally, to those who do hire workers, availability of labour at short notice seems to be an important consideration too in choosing central city locations.

The complex nexus of linkages described above seems to pose some conflicts between policies designed to improve the urban physical environment on the one hand and those aimed at improving employment and incomes in the informal sector on the other. The environmental consequences of crowding the informal sector activities in central city locations cannot be over-emphasised. In so far as public space, including footpaths, are occupied by these enterprises they cause traffic congestions, inconvenience to pedestrians and even pollution of the environment depending on the nature of the activity. Since the participants tend to live close to their work space, it also implies increased densities in residential locations, notably in low-income neighbourhoods or slums. Implications of such population concentrations coupled with poor urban services in these locations to urban environment are well known. In other words, the physical conditions of work and living and environment are closely related.

One consequence of the above is that any effort to improve the urban environment by severing the linkages could affect the income and employment situation in the informal sector. Urban authorities in many developing countries have attempted at least two types of solutions to cope with the problem above. The first may be described as policies and action towards the informal sector itself and the second aimed at the slum and squatter settlements. Policies and action towards the informal sector, as one study on hawkers and vendors puts it, may be classified into three categories: locational, structural and educational. Locational measures included interference with the ecological patterns, e.g. removal or relocation of petty enterprises and/or customers through squatter clearance and the like. Structural actions are aimed at eliminating or developing the economic base of the hawkers, e.g. introduction of alternative distributive outlets or encouraging alternative employment opportunities. Educational actions are designed to educate hawkers and the like about the environmental consequences.[1] In the South-East Asian context these three types of interventions varied somewhat in terms of their impact on these activities ranging from negative to mildly positive to favourable. Based on equity considerations, local authorities in some of these cities have also modified their attitude towards hawkers in recent years showing greater tolerance if not positive support. Similar attempts have been made in other parts of the Third World as well.[2]

Parallel to the above measures focused directly on selected subsectors of the informal sector, cities in most developing

----

[1] McGee and Yeung: Hawkers in South-East Asian cities ..., op. cit., Chapter 3.

[2] See, for example, S.V. Sethuraman: Employment promotion in the informal sector in Ghana (Geneva, ILO, 1977; mimeographed World Employment Programme research working paper; restricted); Development of informal sector in Java, UNDP/ILO Technical Report 1 (INS/72/030) (Geneva, 1976); and Ray Bromley: "The locational behaviour of Colombian street traders: observations and hypotheses" (unpublished manuscript, 1977).

countries have also sought to improve the housing situation through
a variety of policies and action programmes. In so far as their
major focus has been on slums and squatter settlements, their
implications for the informal sector cannot be ignored. It is
beyond the scope of this work to go into details of such measures;
nevertheless a brief reference to them seems relevant and useful.
"Government policies with respect to slum and squatter settlements
can be grouped under three broad headings: laissez-faire policies,
restrictive or preventive policies, and supportive policies."[1] While
laissez-faire policies tend to ignore slum and squatter areas,
restrictive policies seek to eliminate or reduce low-income areas
either by denying the basic urban services or through eviction of
residents and relocating them elsewhere and slum and squatter
clearance. Supportive policies on the other hand attempt to
integrate slum and squatter residents in the socio-economic network
surrounding the area; it may take the form of improving the existing
facilities or providing urban land and housing for new settlements
or promoting self-help housing. Considering the close links between
the informal sector on the one hand and the living conditions of its
participants on the other, restrictive policies described above
clearly are unfavourable to the informal sector. It is not
therefore surprising that "attempts to deal with these problems
through massive resettlement and public housing have proved to be of
little success".[1] The one clear pattern to emerge from present
policies and programmes is the rejection, at least in principle, of
automatic slum clearance as a viable policy alternative ... The
second notable trend is that, given the pressing developmental needs
of developing countries and their limited resources, it is unlikely
that they will consider the massive construction of conventional
public housing as a viable policy option. ... On the other hand, it
is likely ... that a combination of aided self-help and squatter
upgrading will be used to improve low-income living conditions".[1]
These trends in thinking are quite significant in so far as they
minimise the negative effects on employment and incomes in the
informal sector.

The search for compromise solutions along the lines indicated
above is indeed a significant step in the right direction; it
represents an effort to arrive at policy measures compromising
income and employment creation in the informal sector on the one
hand and improving the urban physical environment on the other. It
is increasingly realised that such efforts should constitute a part
of the integrated urban development plans. Improving the urban
physical environment also implies at the same time fulfilling the
basic human needs through greater access to urban services and
assurance of tenure and hence cannot be separated from the social
and economic circumstances of households.

Parallel to the above there have been attempts by urban
authorities in developing countries to seek compromise solutions
with regard to policies and action concerning the informal sector
itself. In some countries such as Malaysia it has taken the form of
revisions in policies towards the informal sector including liberal

---

[1] Habitat News, Apr. 1980, p. 14.

licensing and educational policies.[1] In others such as Ghana (Accra and Kumasi) it took the form of providing urban land in suitable locations for clusters of informal sector activities and selling built premises in the form of wooden kiosks;[2] these measures represent efforts to relieve urban congestion in central city locations without destroying the income and employment opportunities of the informal sector. Singapore is another interesting case where new hawker centres were created along with a major public housing programme away from the city centres. In more recent years Jakarta has created market centres with a view to housing informal trade activities.

Based on the knowledge from various informal sector surveys the ILO has proposed measures to integrate urban informal sector activities with the conventional urban development project framework whereby clusters of homogeneous informal sector activities can be created in given locations within the city.[3] Such an approach to physically integrate the urban informal sector with urban development planning has several positive features. First, by earmarking suitable locations within the city, it is possible to extend the concept of sites and services and provide for public investment in the form of minimum infrastructure and supporting services conforming to the required environmental standards. Secondly, activities can be separated in terms of their environmental implications, notably the nature and extent of pollution. Thirdly, it contributes to separation of commercial from residential activities and it can be incorporated into the urban land-use planning or the master plans. Fourthly, by providing minimum premises in legally approved locations the approach reduces uncertainty associated with the tenure and encourages private investment both in improving the premises and in acquiring fixed assets.

The approach also contributes to informal sector development in terms of employment and incomes. First, it does not attempt to alienate the informal sector from its markets. Second, by bringing the various informal sector units (located in or outside the residential premises, scattered in or outside the slum and squatter areas) into visible clusters it facilitates the expansion of markets for their goods and services and their employment and income

---

[1] McGee and Yeung: Hawkers in South-East Asian cities ..., op. cit., Chapter 3, for more details.

[2] S.V. Sethuraman: Employment promotion in the informal sector in Ghana (Geneva, ILO, 1977; mimeographed World Employment Programme research working paper; restricted).

[3] H. Lubell: "Manila urban development project: Support to small enterprises" (Geneva, ILO, 1977) (unpublished manuscript); S.V. Sethuraman: "Employment promotion through cottage industries in Madras Metropolitan Area" (Geneva, ILO, 1977) (unpublished manuscript); idem: "Assisting the informal sector enterprises in Jakarta" (Geneva, ILO, 1977) (unpublished manuscript). See also Carolyn Muench: "Planning for informal sector enterprises", in The Informal Sector in Kenya, Occasional Paper No. 25, Institute for Development Studies, University of Nairobi (Nairobi, Jan. 1978) for some efforts along these lines in Nairobi.

potential.[1] For example, a cluster of construction-related
activities can be readily involved directly in low-income housing
activities and the like. Third, it facilitates the provision of
skills and technology and thereby ensuring the quality and standards
vital to compete with the formal sector successfully; not only can
skills and technology be provided in situ but also at lower unit
costs. Fourth, with a legally approved site for business within the
city, the collateral requirements for obtaining credit from banks
and the like can be considerably simplified.

The above solutions to combine policy prescriptions regarding
employment creation in the urban informal sector and improving the
urban environment no doubt pose some problems. As a recent report
observed, "In most urban areas, scarcity of land at reasonable
prices and in close proximity to employment opportunities is the
crux of the housing problem. Income is an important determinant of
housing supply, and in most developing countries prices have
outstripped wages which in effect means that while income remains at
low levels the cost of shelter is constantly rising and becoming
beyond the reach of low-income families."[2] Thus, one of the most
obvious problems is finding the necessary space within the cities in
suitable locations. In this context it is worth recalling that
besides capital, location of business within a city is an important
determinant of business income (see for example Chapter 11). This
implies selection of construction technologies that are both space
saving and labour using.

Another problem relates to financing, affordability and cost
recovery. With regard to upgrading of slums and squatter areas it
is generally recognised that the costs can be substantially lower if
the problem of shelter is essentially left to the residents and
outside intervention is limited to self-help assistance, adaptation
of building codes and standards, provision of credit and security of
tenure. According to a survey based on 69 less developed countries,
self-help methods would seem to reduce housing costs by 33 per cent
on the average; if families also participated in production of
building materials a further reduction of up to 70 per cent seems
possible.[3] Even so, the cost involved in the provision of public
utilities, community services, land acquisition and the like can be
quite substantial. Thus, it would seem necessary to complement the
above efforts through choice of appropriate technologies designed to
lower the costs notably through greater reliance on indigenous
construction materials. Also, in order to facilitate the
involvement of informal sector in these activities, technologies
must be simpler. The recent experience of the World Bank in this
context is encouraging and worth noting. For example, the Kampong

----

[1] In trade and services activities, creation of clusters or
market centres mixing durable and non-durable commodities could lead
to an expansion of the market for informal sector goods and services
by attracting customers from all income groups. See McGee and
Yeung: Hawkers and vendors in South-East Asian cities ..., op. cit.,
for more on design of such clusters.

[2] United Nations, Centre for Human Settlements (HABITAT):
Science and technology in human settlements (Nairobi, June 1979), p.
13.

[3] United Nations: World Housing Survey, 1974, op. cit., p. 105.

Improvement Programmes in Indonesia sponsored by the World Bank have successfully reached over 4 million inhabitants of the poorest quarters in five cities at a cost of only US$45 per person.[1] The Bank experience also shows that there need not be any conflict between policies to improve the urban physical environment and urban employment creation in the informal sector. "The evident expansion of commerce and small-scale enterprises in project sites also indicates a significant addition to local output and employment, even though net employment gains from a project cannot be measured because of the wide secondary effects."[1]

Notwithstanding the considerable potential for combining employment and environment policies through direct involvement of the people themselves in a more significant way, the emerging evidence from the studies in Part II suggests that construction plays a relatively unimportant role in the informal sector. Since much of the slum and squatter housing is created by the people themselves, does it mean that the informal sector makes no contribution to construction? The apparent contradiction is, however, partly explained by the fact that most such construction activities in the slums and squatter areas are undertaken by the occupants themselves without necessarily involving hired labour from the informal sector. In other words, the sample surveys captured only those construction activities where significant construction services were offered in the market on a more or less regular basis. It is also understandable, given the quality of such constructions and low purchasing power of the urban slum dwellers, and hence their desire to economise money spent on such construction through a do-it-yourself approach. Also, as in the case of Indonesia, much of the construction activity in the slums is carried out through the conventional labour exchange methods. The findings therefore do not necessarily imply that the informal sector does not contribute to improvements in the urban physical environments; rather it poses a challenge to the development of the informal sector. On the one hand, it implies expanding the capacity of the informal sector in terms of skills, tools and technologies and, on the other, adoption of appropriate construction technologies[2] and increasing their participation in slum and squatter improvement through explicit policies and assistance measures.

Among the constraints restricting the scope for informal sector participation perhaps the most important pertains to the

----

[1] World Bank: Report, Sep.-Oct. 1979, p. 3. As in the case of Jakarta the Bank has attempted to introduce "more economical standards of design and construction for services and dwelling than those of conventional 'low-cost' housing schemes in the Philippines".

[2] For example, in the Philippines the direct and indirect employment content of conventional housing is estimated at 45 to 49 per cent of cost as compared to 35 per cent in prefabricated techniques adopted by the National Housing Corporation. See Alan Stretton: "Independent foremen and the construction of formal sector housing in the Greater Manila Area", in P.J. Rimmer et al. (eds.): Food, shelter and transport in south-east Asia and the Pacific, op. cit., p. 164.

availability of construction materials. As the World Housing Survey showed, many developing countries lack the necessary building materials; many African -countries imported between 50 and 60 per cent of the building materials. In the Asian region imported building materials were estimated to account for 30 per cent of construction costs on the average.[1] Given that the informal sector enterprises lack access to credit, it is not surprising that the sector's contribution to housing has been limited and confined to recycling of waste materials that are poor substitutes. The policy implication emerging from the above seems to be that there is a need to promote informal sector enterprises in production of suitable construction materials.

Perhaps the most important contribution of the informal sector to improvement in the urban physical environment is indirect via increased incomes of its participants. Though tax revenues and surcharges or provision of utilities are important means of meeting the costs of upgrading the urban physical environment, direct payments from the residents still remain an important source of cost recovery. It is also important from the point of view of urban authorities for otherwise such programmes will not be considered as viable and self-sustaining.

In this context it is worth noting that many slum dwellers not only pay for utilities such as water but also at a higher rate than those who are better off. For example in Kano migrants in poor localities were reported to pay 3 Nairas per 1,000 gallons of water as compared to 2 Nairas elsewhere in the city (Chaper 6). In Karachi the very poor are reported as paying "20 times more for their water (from itinerant water carriers) than the well-to-do who receive piped water".[2] Similar findings are reported for Jakarta.[3] In other words, the urban poor can and do pay for urban services.

Though not all urban poor are in the informal sector, the close link between the participants in this sector and the poor physical environment in which they work and live implies that improving their incomes could, by increasing their ability to pay, increase the effective demand for better housing and related services. In some cases, however, initial income may be a poor guide; for example the experience in the Nairobi low-income housing schemes shows that plot owners frequently prefer construction of a room that can be rented out for cash income rather than build for themselves.[4] Likewise, tenure plays an important role in investment decisions relating to housing; to the extent that uncertainties associated with tenure are eliminated, housing policies could encourage savings and investment in housing. Also, aided self-help housing schemes coupled with cost-reducing innovations seem to play an important role in stimulating private investment by residents as

----

[1] United Nations: World Housing Survey, 1974, op. cit., p. 97.

[2] Barbara Ward: Progress for a small planet (New York, 1979), p. 233.

[3] S.V. Sethuraman: Jakarta: Urban development and employment (Geneva, ILO, 1976), p. 150.

[4] J.T. Winpenny: "Housing the poor" (unpublished manuscript, 1979).

well.[1] Further, since the evidence presented in Part II suggests that informal sector enterprises rely on own savings for investment in business, programmes to assist them with easy access to credit for business investment could result in diversion of at least part of the savings to investment in housing. Policies and measures to assist the informal sector presented later in Chapter 14 must therefore be viewed as complementing the policies for improving the urban physical environment.[2]

The various measures discussed above focus on combining the objectives of employment and income generation in the informal sector and urban physical environment without severing the links between residential and work locations. Since income opportunities in the informal sector heavily depend on demand for its goods and services from households, it is clear that the enterprises be located close to the source of demand, i.e. in central locations within the city. But does it necessarily mean that the participants should also live close to their workplaces? Provision of cheaper and more efficient public transport facilities would seem to offer an alternative solution whereby the living conditions can be improved independently of the physical environment surrounding the workplace. The argument is valid to the extent that land in the periphery is cheaper and that new settlements can be better designed and implemented to meet the environmental objectives. But it is not clear that the resulting cost of housing and related services makes a substantial difference to the residents as compared to costs of upgrading in the city. Further, the time involved in transporting informal sector participants from the periphery to the centre is likely to be quite significant given the long hours of work in the informal sector. For example, in Freetown 94 per cent of the heads worked for eight hours or more per day; similar figures are reported elsewhere. More important, the cost of transport is likely to be a significant proportion of their daily earnings. In other words, such a policy is unlikely to be successful unless accompanied by substantial transport subsidies. But the fact that some 28 per cent of the informal sector entrepreneurs in Colombo[3] lived outside but worked in the city thanks to subsidised public transport facilities would seem to suggest that this policy option needs further examination.

Another issue related to the above is the merits of using formal vis-à-vis informal means of transport. While the latter is relatively more labour intensive and hence generates more employment and income in the informal sector, it would also seem to worsen traffic congestion. On efficiency grounds, informal transport activities seem to compare favourably with their formal sector counterparts. But the issue is much more complex owing to the presence of secondary employment effects, market distortions

----

[1] World Bank: Report, op. cit., p. 3, for details on Manila experience.

[2] H. Lubell and S.V. Sethuraman: Income and employment-generating policies for lower-income urban settlements (ILO), Paper presented at the Ad-Hoc Expert Group Meeting on Strategies for the Improvement of Different Types of Lower-income Settlements, United Nations, New York, 28 November-2 December 1977.

[3] See Chapter 8.

(notably easy access to credit and imports in the formal sector) and differential consequences for environment.[1]

Informal sector as a source for recycling waste materials

One of the virtues of the informal sector is its ability to recycle waste materials into productive use. Given the paucity of initial capital, premises and skills, it is not surprising that a significant proportion of the informal sector enterprises in many cities are engaged in the collection of waste materials ranging from scrap metals to cigarette butts including used bottles, waste paper, spent batteries and the like. Some of these materials such as waste paper find their way through to large manufacturing enterprises while most of the rest are transformed into commodities for daily use, notably by the lower-income groups, within the informal sector. Given the low opportunity cost of labour and scarcity of relevant raw materials, imported or domestic, it is not surprising that these activities are profitable. In the case of Dakar (Senegal)[2] the items include: used clothing, shoes, plastic materials, tin cans and newspapers. Used clothing and shoes are sold as they are or after mending and alterations. Tin cans, once cleaned, are used in the manufacture of aluminium wares. Similarly, a variety of wooden cases, packing materials and containers are recycled in appropriate forms for constructing residential and/or work premises. Many wards in Dakar's African districts are estimated to have between 25 and 60 per cent wooden houses; some shantytowns are 100 per cent wooden constructions. Likewise, steel drums (oil containers) are recycled in the form of roofing materials, walls and the like. Even old butane canisters are given a new lease of life as petrol lamps since many dwellings do not have access to electricity. The large steel barrels, estimated to cost 250 CFA francs each, from which a metalworker can make four or five average-sized charcoal cooking stoves in a day and sell them at 150 CFA francs each, thus making a daily profit of between 350 and 500 CFA francs. Even if one makes an allowance for other costs, the worker's net daily earnings are quite substantial. Similar examples can be cited in the case of beds, mattresses and the like. In most of these cases the informal sector is able to emulate the products manufactured by the formal sector by using recycled materials; thus it is able to cut down the costs of production substantially and sell the output cheaper. While the formal sector products are expensive and beyond the reach of the lower-income groups, the comparable products but of lower quality are designed for lower-income groups.[3]

----

[1] See P.J. Rimmer: "The future of Trishaw enterprises in Penang"; and Dean Forbes: "Urban-rural interdependence: The Trishaw riders of Ujing Pandung", in P.J. Rimmer et al. (eds.): Food, shelter and transport in south-east Asia and the Pacific, op. cit. See also Chapter 10 on Manila in this volume.

[2] Gerry: Petty producers and the urban economy: a case study of Dakar, op. cit.

[3] ibid., for more details. See also Sethuraman: Employment promotion in the informal sector in Ghana, op. cit., for some evidence on recycling of waste materials through the informal sector in Ghana; and Gustav F. Papanek: "The poor of Jakarta", in Economic Development and Cultural Change, Oct. 1975, pp. 1-28.

Though recyling of waste materials is by no means a dominant feature of the informal sector, it undoubtedly forms a major component, notably in certain types of activities. In certain activities of Nairobi, for example, 77 per cent of the establishments are reported to be using partly or exclusively recycled materials.[1] Recycling occurs not only in raw materials but also in capital goods. The Lagos study estimated that about 10 per cent of the sample enterprises with capital equipment acquired them second-hand. Similarly, in Manila, some 38 per cent of the enterprises acquired their capital equipment second-hand or reconstructed them.

One aspect of the recycling problem that is of direct consequence to improvement in the urban physical environment pertains to garbage collection. In Cali (Colombia), for example, some 1,200 to 1,700 garbage pickers earn their livelihood through recycling materials collected from garbage dumps, from streets and from households and enterprises.[2] They seem to earn a daily income ranging from 25 to 100 pesos (or US$1-3), the average being perhaps 70 pesos as compared to the legal minimum wage of 62 pesos per day. It is estimated that in Colombia in 1974 waste paper constituted a third of the raw material requirements in the paper industry, equivalent to 112,000 tons of which half came through garbage collections. In Cali alone some 15,000 tons of waste paper per year is collected by garbage pickers. Though they seemingly operate independently, in reality they are caught in a hierarchical network involving the formal sector which buys much of the recycled materials. Another study on Manila scavengers also suggests similar findings and emphasises the role of market distortions in providing little incentive to the informal sector.[3] The question of promoting such informal sector activities with due recognition of their role in improving the urban environment must therefore take into account the nature of relationships between the formal and the informal sectors as well as the scope for providing incentives to the latter.

The evidence presented above also suggests the scope for involving the informal sector in a more direct way in improving the urban physical environment. As a recent report argued, "Local governments could convert some of their own operations so as to utilise more labour-intensive practices. For example, solid and sanitary wastes could be collected from slum and squatter settlements by handcarts, and labour-intensive methods could be used for picking, sorting and recycling use-solid wastes".[4] Much, however, will depend on the kind of incentives and local government support extended to participation in such activities.
----

[1] Chana and Morrison: "Nairobi's informal economic sector", op. cit., p. 128.

[2] Chris Birkbeck: "Garbage, industry and the 'vultures' of Cali, Colombia", in Bromley and Gerry (eds.): Casual work and poverty in third world cities, op. cit. See also Juan Mosque-Alcaino and Ray Bromley: "The bottle buyer - an occupational autobiography", ibid.

[3] William J. Keyes, S.J.: Manila scavengers: The struggle for urban survival, IPC Poverty Research Series No. 1 (Quezon City, Institute of Philippines Culture, 1974).

Habitat News, Apr. 1980, p. 16.

Recycling of waste materials, besides contributing to employment and physical environment also leads to conservation of resources. For example, by reusing scrap metals it is estimated that up to 90 per cent of energy can be saved.[1] Similarly, by recycling waste paper a considerable amount of forest resources and water can be conserved besides reducing industrial pollution.[2] While many developed countries have taken a number of steps ranging from legislative action to incentives in the form of taxes and subsidies to promote recycling of used materials, one of the major hurdles continues to be the collection and sorting out of such materials for further processing.[2] Though attempts based on sophisticated technologies are under way, it is generally recognised that garbage separation is indeed a highly labour-intensive process. It is in this context that the informal sector plays a key role in developing countries. Since much of the garbage-recycling problem originates from the level and pattern of consumption which in turn is related to the level of income, the recycling role of the informal sector is particularly important in large cities of the Third World. Since most of these activities are carried out without state intervention or support, explicit incentives to them would enhance their contribution to the environment.

Migration, informal sector and the urban environment

The discussion above suggests a number of policy instruments for combining urban employment and environment objectives. Measures to upgrade slum and squatter areas and provide basic urban sources can promote employment and incomes in the informal sector. And, conversely, policies to promote the informal sector can, directly and indirectly, contribute to improvement in the urban physical environment. But, in the longer run, such policies can have only a limited impact unless accompanied by other measures, since half the urban population increase in developing countries is estimated to be due to migration (and perhaps a greater proportion in large cities), particularly from rural to urban areas. The need to slow down if not arrest this trend cannot therefore be over-emphasised.

The evidence emerging from Part II suggests a strong link between migration and the informal sector. The proportion of informal sector participants born outside the city where they live and work was: 78 per cent in Freetown; 95 per cent in Lagos; 35 per cent in Kano; 14 per cent in Colombo; 60 per cent in Jakarta; 33 per cent in Manila; 55 per cent in Cordoba; and 78 per cent in Campinas. In many cities, notably in Asia and Latin America, a majority of the migrants had been living in the city for longer than ten years; 79 per cent in Colombo; 61 per cent in Jakarta; 86 per cent in Manila; 75 per cent in Cordoba; and 68 per cent in Campinas. In Africa, however, a majority of the migrants seem to have arrived in recent years: 55 per cent in Lagos and 37 per cent in Kano had been living in the city for under ten years; and in Freetown, 48 per cent. These findings are consistent with other evidence suggesting that

----

[1] Ward: Progress for a small planet, op. cit., p. 93.

[2] ibid., Chapters 5 to 7.

migration in recent years is particularly important in African cities.[1]

In some cities such as Jakarta a significant proportion of the informal sector participants belong to the category of "circular migrants", migrating on a seasonal basis.[2] Unfavourable policies toward the informal sector, restrictive policies towards migration, poor living and working conditions as well as income opportunities in rural areas would seem to explain the growing importance of circular migration. One of the consequences of this phenomenon has been on the urban physical environment since the circular migrants view their presence in the city as temporary and hence tend to share the available shelter in slums rather than create their own. Policies to improve urban environment through employment decentralisation discussed below are therefore of particular significance to this group.

The consequences of migration for urban physical environment essentially depend on how soon the migrants get a job, the level of income earned and the capacity of the urban infrastructure to expand, absorb and accommodate the migrants, notably the response from urban authorities. In this context, it is worth noting that migrants generally have a shorter waiting period before finding a job in the city and lower rate of unemployment as compared to the natives, partly because they cannot afford to remain openly unemployed for long periods. The evidence presented in Part II as well as other studies on migration show that migrants derive considerable economic benefits after migration. For example, 41 per cent of the participants in Kano, 45 per cent in Freetown, 70 per cent in Lagos, 64 per cent in Jakarta and 74 per cent in the Manila service sector were reported to be unemployed before migration. For many others migration implied a switch from low-paid and uncertain jobs in agriculture to better-paid and more permanent jobs in non-agriculture. Migration and duration of stay in the city seem to offer significant opportunities for upward mobility. To the extent that policies and measures to promote the informal sector also contributes to greater business expansion and job mobility, it follows that migrants will be able to increase their capacity to pay for the housing and other related services and in a shorter time.

----

[1] Evidence from other African countries suggests the following. The proportion of informal sector participants born outside the city was: 76 per cent in Dakar; 74 per cent in Ouagadougou; 67 per cent among garagists, 94 per cent among tailors, 87 per cent among traders in Abidjan; 95 per cent among "menuisiers" in Yaoundé; and 94 per cent in Nairobi. Source: M.P. van Dijk: "Le secteur non-structuré: Dakar (Sénegal)" (ILO, JASPA, 1977); idem: "Le secteur non-structuré: Ouagadougou (Haute Volta) (ILO, JASPA, 1977); Marc Penouil: "Activités de transition et activités informelles: 4 études sectorielles à Abidjan et Yaoundé", Mar. 1979 (unpublished manuscript); and Chana and Morrison: Nairobi's informal economic sector, op. cit.

[2] Lea Jellinek: "Circular migration and the Pondak dwelling system: A case study of ice-cream traders in Jakarta", in P.J. Rimmer et al. (eds.): Food, shelter and transport in south-east Asia and the Pacific, op. cit.

It was mentioned in Chapter 3 that the case for limiting the size of the city in terms of population seems to rest primarily on equity and environment rather than on efficiency grounds.[1] Besides encroachment on cultivable land surrounding the urban areas, migration contributes to increased population densities notably in selected geographical locations within the city. For example, in the case of Kano in Nigeria migrants originating from certain areas tend to concentrate in particular locations either because of ethnical affinity or because of close links between the "sponsors" and the new migrants or simply to economise the cost of living by sharing accommodation. Congestion and insanitary conditions and the tendency to gather grimy tenements around the place of work coupled with other forms of pollution are cited as reasons for increased urban mortality.[2] Besides economic policies, socio-cultural factors play a vital role in contributing to such environmental consequences. Perhaps more important is the speed with which the urban authorities respond to the emerging trends and the quality and adequacy of the response. If past experience is any guide few developing countries have demonstrated their willingness and capacity to deal with the situation satisfactorily.[3] Besides resource constraints, managerial capacity on the part of urban authorities would seem to be a limiting factor too. In addition to finding the land necessary for the new arrivals, the authorities must expand the prevailing transportation facilities. Further, the cost of providing shelter and other supporting urban services seems to be higher in urban than in rural areas; urban housing is more dependent upon the man-made environment than upon natural environment.

In view of these and other problems it would seem necessary to contain the growth of large urban areas in developing countries through appropriate population redistribution and employment decentralisation policies. Though migrants in the informal sector benefit through migration and absorb the associated costs in terms of poor living and working conditions, they also impose "costs" on others already living in the city by competing for the existing

[1] Some available evidence suggests that even efficiency considerations are important. For example, in India one study shows that cities with a population range of 130-300,000 are considered as the least cost option for industrial growth. See O.P. Mathur: "The problem of regional disparities: An analysis of Indian policies and programmes", in Growth pole strategy and regional development planning in Asia (Nagoya, United Nations Centre for Regional Development, 1976).

[2] United Nations: The determinants and consequences of population trends, Vol. I (New York, 1973), p. 145.

[3] See, for example, A. Ramachandran: "Human settlements and the New International Development Strategy", in UNCHS-Habitat Occasional Papers OP-1 (New York, 1979); and World Bank: World Development Report, 1979, op. cit., pp. 78-79. For a good discussion of the prevailing policies and approaches to the problem of urbanisation and its consequences see United Nations: Habitat: urban slums and squatter settlements in the third world, UN Conference on Human Settlements, Vancouver, Canada, 31 May-11 June 1976, A/Conf.70/RPC/9 (1975). See also United Nations: Social aspects of housing and urban development (New York, 1967).

urban facilities. As noted in Chapter 3, some would justify this phenomenon on grounds of equity - that it is one of the most effective ways of redistributing income, wealth and opportunities. Notwithstanding these arguments it is doubtful that large cities can absorb much of the additions to urban population envisaged for the future in developing countries without other consequences noted earlier.

It is in this context that the growth pole approach as a tool for regional development assumes considerable importance. Growth pole approach based exclusively on decentralisation of large and medium industries away from large urban centres may not per se discourage migration flows to primate cities. Rather it should be integrated within a larger regional planning framework aimed at revitalising the rural environment by bringing about a symbiosis of agricultural and industrial development. Such an approach should also allow for greater involvement of small-scale activities in view of their implication for the adoption of appropriate technologies and employment decentralisation.

It was noted earlier that an overwhelming proportion of the demand for informal sector goods and services orginates through households. To the extent that household incomes are generated in the formal sector (e.g. wage employment), it is obvious that there are limitations in shifting the informal sector activities away from primate cities (where formal sector dominates) or in encouraging such activities in smaller urban centres. It is not surprising that only a small proportion of the informal sector participants - 14 per cent for example in Jakarta and 20-23 per cent in Manila - showed interest in moving out of the city. But where the market is not confined to the city itself, the scope for decentralising economic activities would seem to be greater. For example, in certain activities such as soap and match manufacturing, decentralised production through small-scale enterprises is not only feasible but also seems economical owing to low capital intensity.[1] Also, since construction generates significant direct and indirect employment, it would seem possible to decentralise employment by manipulating construction activities in favour of secondary urban centres.[2] Besides demand constraints, availability of building materials and skills locally are however important factors limiting the scope along these lines.[3]

----

[1] See Chapter 14 for further discussion on efficiency of small enterprises. See also Ward: Progress for a small planet, op. cit., Chapter 20.

[2] R. Paul Shaw: "Bending the urban flow: a construction-migration strategy", in International Labour Review, July-Aug. 1980. See also O.H.G. Koenigsberger: "The absorption of newcomers in the cities of the third world", in ODI Review, No. 1, 1976, p. 79, which suggests an "outstandingly high employment-generation potential of low-income housing", based on an input-output analysis of the construction sector in Colombo, Sri Lanka.

[3] M.A. Johnstone: "Unconventional housing in West Malaysian cities: A preliminary survey" in Rimmer et al. (eds.): Food, shelter and transport in south-east Asia and the Pacific, op. cit., pp. 123-124, where it is shown that building costs in secondary urban centres are higher than in large cities.

Besides market linkages, one of the key factors motivating migrants to move to the cities, particularly in Africa, is access to training and skills. For example, two-thirds of the informal sector participants in Kumasi were apprentices; similar evidence emerges from other cities in Africa. Another important reason for being in primate cities seems to be the availability of greater choice in occupations and greater job insurance in terms of alternative employment opportunities. Measures to decentralise employment opportunities must therefore take into account all the factors noted above.

How does decentralised development contribute to environment? It was already mentioned that by directing migration flows away from primate cities, it should be possible to arrest the deterioration if not ameliorate the urban environment. But decentralised development could also contribute to other broader environmental goals such as shaping the lifestyles, conservation of resources, reducing regional income disparities and more efficient use of resources. But, in order to realise these objectives, it would seem necessary to emphasise the role of small-scale activities or the informal sector where the poor and jobless create their own employment. In so far as small enterprises use more labour-intensive techniques of production,[1] (and presumably less commercial sources of energy) than the large ones, it is clear that they generate relatively more employment. A basic-needs-oriented development strategy would also seem to provide greater opportunities for small enterprises' participation in development. The evidence based on various studies also suggests that the informal sector places a greater reliance on indigenous rather than imported resources. Finally, the informal sector seems to offer greater opportunities for human resource development through on-the-job training and apprenticeship system.

To conclude, the deterioration of the urban environment in the Third World would seem to be mainly the result of the current approach to and emphasis on development. Failure to generate adequate and balanced distribution of employment opportunities would seem to have played a major role in causing "excessive" urbanisation. Likewise, inadequate and slow response on the part of the urban authorities would seem to have aggravated the concern for the urban environment. It seems also clear that there are severe limitations to decentralisation of the development process in the short and medium run, for it calls for a radical shift in the approach to development besides other constraints. While efforts along these directions must pursue, it is evident that other solutions to remedy the worsening urban environment must be found in the short and medium run.

Development of the urban informal sector would seem to be a first step in this direction. It could not only contribute to an improvement in the urban environment directly through participation in the creation of urban services and in improving the physical environment but also indirectly through increased purchasing power of a substantial part of the urban poor. Likewise, policies and measures to improve the urban physical environment could, by involving the informal sector to a greater degree, contribute to urban employment creation. Thus, urban employment and environment objectives need not necessarily conflict with each other; what is required is a judicious combination of relevant policies.

----

[1] See various chapters in Part II and also Chapter 14.

CHAPTER 14. SUMMARY AND CONCLUSIONS: IMPLICATIONS
FOR POLICY AND ACTION

The unprecedented rate of increase in the Third World urban
population witnessed in recent years is expected to continue: from
about 275 million in 1950 it is projected to exceed 2 billion by the
turn of the present century. Though it is primarily a reflection of
the rate of increase in total population, since roughly half this
increase has been due to migration from rural areas in search of
employment and income opportunities, it also reflects the poor rate
of labour absorption in rural areas. Notwithstanding the
considerable expansion in the formal sector and government-related
activity in urban centres of developing countries, these sectors
have failed to absorb all the additions to the labour force imposed
on them. Consequently, the rate of urban unemployment in these
countries has tended to exceed that in rural areas. But open
unemployment in urban areas increased but little when compared to
the massive additions to the urban labour force noted above. The
bulk of the new entrants to the urban labour force seems to create
its own employment by engaging in the production and distribution of
goods and services through a variety of small-scale activities. The
survey of evidence from many developing countries suggests that
anywhere between 20 and 70 per cent of urban employment is to be
found in such activities or the so-called "informal" sector.

The changing urban scene in the Third World, though a natural
response under the circumstances, has nevertheless elevated the
concern of policy makers on a number of fronts - excessive
concentration of population in primate cities, increased population
densities and their negative consequences for environment, higher
cost of basic urban services, regional income disparities - as
already noted in the last chapter. It not only underlines the need
for population control. More importantly, it reflects the failure
of development policies followed hitherto. It is beyond the scope
of this volume to assess the merits and weaknesses of rural
development policies but it is clear that there is a need to promote
employment in rural areas, notably through the development of non-
farm activities, besides agricultural development. It would also
seem necessary to incorporate regional development perspectives into
national development strategies. Finally, the growing importance of
the urban informal sector as a source of employment calls for a re-
examination of the development approach, stressing mainly the
relatively capital-intensive formal sector even though these
countries are relatively labour-abundant and the consequent tendency
to limit the benefits of development to certain sectors or sections
of population.

Parallel to the above, the emerging importance of the informal
sector has also drawn the attention of the development community to
what is happening within the informal sector - the whole range of
adjustment problems, the conditions under which labour is being
absorbed and its potential to absorb further increases in the labour
force. It is in this context that the ILO, under the World
Employement Programme, launched a series of survey studies to
understand the role played by this sector in employment and income
generation, in the satisfaction of basic needs, in improving the
conditions of work and environment.

A word about the concept and definition. The growing
importance of the informal sector as a major source of urban

employment in the Third World countries is now widely acknowledged. And yet little is known about this sector - its contribution to employment, income and environment or its potentials. More importantly, the informal sector concept, notwithstanding the widespread use of the term, had itself remained vague and slippery, leading to widely differing if not contradictory interpretation of the findings about this sector. This is inevitable in any new area of research; it only underlines the complexity of the subject.

The term "informal sector" is generally understood to represent a number of small-scale economic activities. But it will be misleading to label them as small-scale "enterprises", for the following reasons. Since the informal sector in this volume is viewed primarily as a manifestation of the emerging employment situation in these countries, those entering such small-scale activities in urban areas are motivated mainly by employment and income rather than profit. Since the entrants to this sector are generally poor, ill-educated, ill-trained and often migrants, it is clear that they are neither capitalists seeking profitable investment outlets nor entrepreneurs in the usual sense. Their horizon seems to be limited to immediate employment and income generation for themselves. It must, however, be admitted that many of them do, however, attempt and even succeed in breaking the initial barriers and evolve into small-scale enterprises with significant amounts of capital and skills over time and presumably with greater orientation toward profits. In other words, the urban informal sector must be viewed as consisting of mainly small-scale units engaged in the production and distribution of goods that are still in a process of evolution rather than as a group of small-scale enterprises with substantial capital and managerial inputs. The rationale for such a distinction, needless to say, also stems from its operational and policy significance. It implies, for example, that the assumptions common to a programme on small enterprise development are not, in general valid for informal sector development; policies to promote this sector must go well beyond and identify and remedy the factors constraining its evolution, including the milieu in which it functions.

The above conceptualisation of the urban informal sector, while helpful, nevertheless leaves the question of definition unanswered. Yet some definition demarcating the boundaries of this sector is necessary both from an operational and research point of view. Perhaps the most important observable characteristic emerging from the above framework that can serve as a tool in isolating economic activities belonging to the informal sector from the whole spectrum is the scale of operation. Though scale can be measured in a variety of alternative ways, including value of capital, business turnover and the like, since they are usually highly correlated, the most convenient yardstick for measuring the scale seems to be the number of persons engaged in the activity. Viewing the urban economy as a continuum of units of production and distribution, all those with ten or less number of persons were generally classified as belonging to the informal sector universe (though there were exceptions) for purposes of the present volume. The choice of ten persons per establishment is no doubt arbitrary, as any other equivalent measure will be; the rationale for this choice stemmed from the prevailing systems of data collection in the Third World countries in general. Further, it was based on the belief that establishments with more than ten persons are unlikely to have emerged mainly with an employment motive; they are likely to possess significant capital and skill inputs. Since such an assumption risks the exclusion of at least some truly informal sector activities in the sense described above (notably in Africa where masters engage a number of apprentices), additional criteria were used to minimise such errors. The above procedure implied, if any, the risk of including units that may not belong to the informal sector. In this sense the evidence presented in this volume covers at least some enterprises that typically do not belong to the informal sector.

Turning to the evidence emerging from various studies in Part II, the physical conditions in which the informal sector units operate, the role of the sector in recycling used materials and its contribution to urban environment and the relation between migration and employment in this sector were presented in the last chapter. The discussion below therefore focuses on other aspects of the informal sector and thus complements the above.

Female participation in the informal sector seems surprisingly small. The proportion of women participating in this sector was: 25 per cent in Freetown; 11 per cent in Kano; 15 per cent in Lagos; 12 per cent in Colombo; 25 per cent in Jakarta; 38 per cent in Cordoba and 12 per cent in Campinas. In Manila, however, 57 per cent of the enterpreneurs, mostly in trade, were females. Though, in some cases, female participation seems to be underestimated owing to sampling design, dominance of males in the informal sector is, in general, noticeable in Africa, Asia and Latin America. In specific activities, notably in trade and domestic service, female participation is significantly higher than in others.

It is sometimes suggested that the informal sector is a source of employment mainly for secondary earners or older persons. The evidence from Part II does not seem to support this view. The proportion of heads in the informal sector units below 30 years was: 38 per cent for males and 30 per cent for females in Freetown; 53 per cent in Kumasi; 38 per cent in Colombo; 14 per cent in Manila; 24 per cent in Cordoba; and 22 per cent in Campinas.[1] The corresponding figures for heads and workers combined tend to be higher since wage earners are generally younger than heads of establishments. This is understandable since establishment of enterprises generally requires some capital and skills besides the necessary "contacts" and thus a certain amount of time is required to overcome these constraints. The median age of heads was: 35 years in Freetown; 27 years in Kano (for heads and workers); 28 years in Kumasi; 35 years in Colombo; 36 years in Jakarta (heads and workers); 30 years for heads in transport and 42 years for heads in services in Manila; 41 years for heads in Cordoba; and 40 years for heads in Campinas. Thus, most of the heads in the informal sector seem to be in their prime age; those in Africa tend to be younger and this is partly related to the rate of migration. This evidence also suggests some scope for upward mobility from wage

----

[1] Some studies have reported an even higher proportion of younger heads of enterprises. For example, 62 per cent of tailors, 43 per cent of traders, 58 per cent of garagists in the Abidjan informal sector and 75 per cent of "menuisiers" in the Yaoundé informal sector were reported to be under 30 years of age. See Penouil: "Activités de transition et activités informelles", op. cit.

earners to heads since the latter tend to earn more, as will be shown later. It is nevertheless important to remember that a significant proportion of wage earners seem to have remained as such, suggesting that they lack such opportunities.

What about education? The median level of schooling of participants was: under six years in Freetown; six years (mean) in Lagos; nine years in Kumasi (mostly manufacturing); four years in Colombo; three years in Jakarta; over ten years in Manila; and primary level in Campinas. With the exception of Kumasi and Manila (where the sample design excluded very small-scale activities), these findings suggest that the informal sector absorbs persons with relatively little education. In contrast, the average level of schooling of those openly unemployed seems to be significantly higher, as can be discerned from other sources of evidence. Here again, there seems to be little regional difference, if any.

The importance of migration in informal sector employment was already discussed in the last chapter. Migrants in the informal sector, as most other studies on migration show, tend to be younger and are mostly males. The average level of schooling of migrants in this sector is generally lower as compared to that of natives of the city, with the exception of Kano. Though a substantial proportion of the migrants in the informal sector were unemployed or outside the labour force before migration (Chapter 13), the limited evidence available suggests that, for many, it was a switch from agriculture to non-agricultural occupations. Also, much of such migration occurred from rural areas. These findings imply that the informal sector not only provides jobs for the jobless but also facilitates the switch to non-agricultural occupations. No doubt it also reflects poor income and employment opportunities in rural areas. Finally, in certain cities such as Freetown, as much as a third of the migrants in the sector came from neighbouring countries; the corresponding proportion in Lagos was 5 per cent and, in Kumasi, 8 per cent. Similar evidence is reported from other studies in francophone Africa.[1] Thus, migration from neighbouring countries in search of opportunities in the urban informal sector is an important feature, particularly in Africa. It was also noted in the last chapter that a greater proportion of the migrant entrepreneurs in the informal sector in Africa had arrived in the city recently, unlike in Asia and Latin America. These findings imply that not only migration is important but also that the informal sector provides significant opportunities for self-employment to recent migrants.

One consequence of the above has been the rapid growth in the number of informal sector units in these cities. In Africa, 59 per cent of the enterprises in Freetown, 52 per cent in Kumasi and 66 per cent in Lagos were established during the five years preceding the date of survey. Results from other studies suggest: in Bamako (Mali), 55 per cent; in Nouakchott (Mauritania), 81 per cent; in Lomé (Togo), 63 per cent; in Yaoundé (Cameroon), 81 per cent; and in Kigali, 60 per cent. Similar results are reported by studies in Abidjan as well. In contrast, the corresponding percentages in Asia

---

[1] In the Abidjan informal sector, for example, 50 per cent of garagists and traders and 74 per cent of tailors were reported to be foreigners. See Marc Penouil: "Activités de transition et activités informelles", op. cit.

and Latin America were: 37 per cent in Colombo, 62 per cent in Jakarta; 29 per cent in services and 33 per cent in Manila; 32 per cent in Cordoba and 55 per cent in Campinas.[1] The slightly higher proportions in Jakarta and Campinas seem to be explained by the relatively greater importance of migration; 60 per cent of the entrepreneurs in Jakarta and 78 per cent of those in Campinas were reported to be born outside as compared to 14 per cent in Colombo, 33 per cent in Manila (services) and 55 per cent in Cordoba. Growth in the size of the informal sector thus appears to be closely related to the extent and pace of migration. In so far as migration itself is motivated by economic growth in and around the urban areas, growth of the informal sector is at least partly explained by the growth of the formal sector.

Turning to the size distribution of enterprises, of course by definition they are small; nevertheless, size measured in terms of number of persons engaged, including the head, the family workers, wage earners and the apprentices varied significantly. That the informal sector provides self-employment to many is also borne out by these studies. The proportion of sample units that had only one person, viz. the owner alone, was: 74 per cent in Freetown; 50 per cent in Lagos; 67 per cent in Kano; 85 per cent in Colombo; 90 per cent in Jakarta; 58 per cent in trade and 25 per cent in service sectors of Manila; 40 per cent in Cordoba and 46 per cent in Campinas. A greater proportion of those with workers (including apprentices) tended to concentrate in manufacturing, repair and related activities where the scope for capital and skill accumulation is greater. Also, those with additional workers are more likely to be found in older enterprises, suggesting the process of evolution noted earlier. The average number of persons per unit, though varying somewhat between different cities, activities and years of establishment, was generally under five, the typical size being around one to two. These findings have implications for operational activity designed to assist the sector since it has to cope with a large number of micro units; in other words, it imposes limitations on the capacity to absorb assistance, cost of providing assistance, designing the nature of assistance and so on.

It also follows from the above that wage employment in the informal sector is relatively less important. The proportion of females among workers is also low: 16 per cent in Freetown; 21 per cent in Jakarta; 34, 50 and 36 per cent in manufacturing, trade and services sectors of Manila. For example, few family workers are engaged; most of the wage earners participate on a full-time basis. Apprentices constitute a significant proportion of workers, mainly in Africa.

Wages paid to workers showed considerable variations in all the studies. How does the average wage compare with the respective legal minimum? In Freetown, the average wage paid to full-time workers was a little over 11 leones per month - substantially lower than the legal minimum of 30 leones per month. It was 35 nairas per month (for males) in Lagos, as compared to the legal minimum of 60 nairas; in fact, the maximum wage paid was only 52 nairas per month. The situation in Kano was somewhat similar; for

---

[1] In Ahmedabad (India), the proportion of enterprises less than five years old was estimated to be 35 per cent. See Papola: The informal sector in an urban economy ..., op. cit.

entrepreneurs and wage earners combined, the median income was under 60 nairas - the legal minimum wage per month. The median wage of paid employees in Jakarta was around Rp.500 per day - substantially lower than the minimum paid in the formal sector. The average wage per day for workers in the Manila informal sector varied between 8 and 10 pesos, depending on the subsector (i.e. manufacturing, trade or services) which may be compared to the legal minimum daily wage of 10 pesos at the time of the survey. If one talks about the informal sector as a whole, the evidence above seems to suggest that a majority of the wage-earning employees in this sector receive wages below the legal minimum. It must, however, be noted that the "average" masks more than it reveals, for wages show systematic variation between different activities. In almost all cases, the wage rate in manufacturing exceeded that in trade or (household) services. Besides some evidence presented in Part II of the volume, the results based on the "modern" informal sector (i.e. production and repair services) in francophone Africa clearly suggest that a majority of skilled workers received above the legal minimum wage. Finally, the evidence also shows that the rate of remuneration for women workers is significantly lower than for men.

The share of urban employment in developing countries, as noted earlier, is anywhere between 20 and 70 per cent, depending on the case in question and the definition adopted, the typical figure being in the range 40-50 per cent. Rapid growth in the number of informal sector units suggests that employment in this sector has also been increasing. While the role of the informal sector in labour absorption has been increasingly recognised in recent years, its contribution to income generation is much less obvious. This again is partly related to non-availability of statistics about the sector and partly due to the problems of measuring the relevant magnitudes.[1] Some bold attempts to measure income generated in the informal sector suggest the following. The proportion of urban regional income attributable to the informal sector in some cities is: 33 per cent in Asuncion (Paraguay); 25 per cent in San Salvador (El Salvador); 30 per cent in Lima (Peru); and 28 per cent in Ahmedabad (India) (Chapter 1). In Lagos, gross value added in the informal sector in 1976 (Chapter 5) seems to have been around 380 million nairas (or US$650 million), as compared to a value added figure of 134 million nairas in 1972 in large establishments (i.e. ten persons or more)in Lagos State;[2] even if one makes allowance for growth and inflation between 1972 and 1976, the contribution of the informal sector is indeed impressive. The Jakarta informal sector appears to have contributed around US$400 million in 1976 (Chapter 9), as compared to an estimated value of GDP in the region in the remaining sectors of about US$940 million, i.e. 30 per cent of the total income generated in the Jakarta region. The scanty evidence above is no more than an indication of the extent of this sector's contribution to urban regional incomes; in view of the importance of such measures for development planning, the need for further research in this area cannot be over-emphasised. What is significant about these findings is that it takes so little capital per worker in generating this income, as will be seen below.
----

[1] Harry Schimmler: "Towards distinguishing between traditional and modern activities in the national accounts of developing countries", in Development Centre Papers (Paris, OECD, 1979), for more on this.

[2] O.J. Fapohunda and H. Lubell: Lagos: Urban development and employment (Geneva, ILO, 1978), p. 10.

Even though the informal sector units operate in a poor physical environment, as noted in Chapter 13, a large majority of them - about 80 per cent or more - possessed at least some capital; the few who did not were mainly in services. Some writers have drawn attention to the fact that the informal sector units often use capital rented to them by intermediaries or petty capitalists. But the studies reported in this volume suggest that it is not a widespread phenomenon. Though renting of capital goods is reported in a few cases, most of the sample units claimed ownership of their assets. The amount of capital per worker showed substantial variations, not only between cities, but also between size of enterprise, age of business and type of activity.

In Freetown, capital per worker, on the average, was only around 36 leones (or about $36) and the median value was even lower, suggesting that not only capital requirements are very low but also that they vary between enterprises. The median value of fixed assets in Lagos is estimated to be 250 nairas (or $400) per enterprise, as compared to a mean of 450 nairas. Given the average size of enterprise of 2.1 persons, the average capital-labour ratio turns out to be about 210 nairas (or about $330), which is considerably higher than in Freetown, mainly due to the dominance of trade activities in the latter. The Kano study suggests a very skewed distribution of enterprises by level of capital - the median was only 50 nairas as compared to a mean of 282 nairas per enterprise, with an average capital-labour ratio of about 157 nairas (or $250). In Kumasi, where the sample was exclusively based on manufacturing and repair services, the capital per enterprise was substantially higher - median, 400 cedis and mean, 780 cedis; but since they engaged a large number of apprentices too, the average capital-labour ratio was only 176 cedis (or about $200). In the case of Manila, 23 per cent of the sample enterprises had under 1,000 pesos of fixed assets but the median was around 6,000 pesos. Given the average size of enterprise of 3.2 persons, it implies a capital-labour ratio of around 2,000 pesos or under $300 per worker. Again, it showed substantial variations between activities - lower in trade and higher in manufacturing and transport. Among the studies presented in Part II, Campinas was an exception; by virtue of the sample design adopted, 43 per cent of the establishments belonged to the stratum where capital per enterprise exceeded 50,000 cruzeiros (or US$4,650); consequently, the average capital-labour ratio was well over $1,000. The findings above thus tend to confirm the evidence from other studies noted in Chapter 3. In particular, they emphasise the low capital requirements for creating jobs in the informal sector; it is only a fraction of what is required in the formal sector.

What about the value added in these enterprises? The gross value added per worker in selected cities was approximately: 52 leones per month in Freetown; 69 nairas per month in Lagos. 85 cedis per month in Kumasi; Rp.30,000 per month (median) in Jakarta and 350 pesos per month in manufacturing; 640 pesos per month in trade and 720 pesos per month in services sectors of Manila. Both the sampling procedures and methods of estimation adopted, noted in the respective chapters, suggest that the figures quoted above are only indicative of the probable order of magnitude. They nevertheless show that the average value added per worker in the informal sector is somewhere in the range of US$600 to US$1,200 per year - substantially higher than the average capital per worker noted above.

Since a large majority of the informal sector enterprises in most cities are operated by single individuals, without any additional workers, the figures above also reflect the level of earnings realised by their heads. Average net return to the heads of enterprises in different cities was estimated to be approximately: 92 leones per month in Freetown; 99 nairas per month in Lagos; 105 nairas per month (for heads and workers combined) in Kano; 78 cedis per month in Kumasi; Rs.500 per month (median) in Colombo; Rs.34,000 per month in Jakarta; 500 pesos per month in trade and 900 pesos per month in services in Manila; US$120 per month (median) in Cordoba; and $310 per month (median) in Campinas. These figures hint that the average earnings range between US$60 and 300 per month in various cities — substantially higher than the legal minimum wage quoted earlier. Given the conditions in which the enterprises operate and the level of physical and human capital used, the level of earnings above is by no means insignificant. As in the case of capital and value added, the averages mask substantial variations between activities. Nevertheless, it is significant to note that, unlike wage earners, a majority of the entrepreneurs earned an income substantially higher than that implied by the legal minimum wage and comparable to incomes in the formal sector. For example, in Kumasi, the median value of earnings of masters was 40 cedis per week as compared to the legal minimum wage of 2 cedis per day and the formal sector wage for comparable labour was 80 cedis per month. Since most ent鈥巖epreneurs not only own the assets but also many in Africa engage apprentices, the level of earnings reflects not only labour income but also returns to capital and training imparted. In short, notwithstanding the low level of investment, the informal sector generates respectable levels of income to the entrepreneurs. At the same time, one must not lose sight of the fact that there are substantial income variations within the informal sector.

It was hypothesised earlier that the informal sector is mainly a source of self-employment; those entering the sector are generally poor and hence lack the necessary capital to start their own business. It was further hypothesised that, besides capital, entrants to this sector are in general confronted with constraints limiting their access to resources and markets, including skills. The studies presented in this volume, as do others on this subject, generally confirm these hypotheses. With regard to constraints in starting their own business, an overwhelming proportion of the sample enterprises reported capital as one of the major constraints. Most of them relied on their own savings, though a few also resorted to borrowing from friends and relatives. A very small proportion, if at all, sought and obtained credit from banks and other such formal sources. In fact, many did not even believe that they can get such credit. In some cases (e.g. Kumasi and Campinas), however, the entrepreneurs had shifted from wage employment in the formal sector to self-employment in the informal sector and thus were able to accumulate the savings and skills necessary to start their own business. Where apprentices played an important role, mainly in Africa, apprenticeship fees would seem to contribute in a significant way to capital accumulation as well. Parallel to the above, the enterprises have also made efforts to minimise the cost of capital investments through recycling of old capital equipment by reconstructing them or even through self-construction where feasible and appropriate.

With regard to access to skills, the studies clearly show that formal sources of training such as government training institutions play a minimal role. An overwhelming majority obtained their skills through the apprenticeship system or on-the-job training, mainly in the informal sector itself. As for raw materials and services, very few reported buying them from large enterprises or wholesalers; most of them relied on retailers, notably those within the informal sector. This is understandable, given the small scale of operation and lack of access to working capital to buy raw materials in bulk quantities. This became evident when data were tabulated by type of activity, age of enterprise and scale of operation; there seems to be some tendency for larger enterprises, particularly in manufacuring, and older ones to rely on the formal sector. It is no doubt true that a substantial part of the raw materials (including spare parts) does originate from the formal sector, notably in certain activities and in Africa, but there seems to be little direct backward linkage with the formal sector. Similar conclusions emerge with regard to forward linkages. As already noted in the last chapter, physical access to markets is indeed a problem to many enterprises owing to spatial limitations. Also, by virtue of the type of goods and services produced, most of the enterprises deal directly with the households and some through other small enterprises. There seems to be little, if any domination by the formal sector. These findings, though they do not necessarily deny the constraints on access to resources and markets and hence tend to raise the cost of inputs and lower the price of outputs, question the general proposition that the informal sector is "exploited" by the formal sector. Evidence emerging from various studies suggests that the latter phenomenon, if true, is confined to a few activities in selected cases.

Turning to the question of capital accumulation and growth in the informal sector, it is clear that there are indeed a number of constraints, perhaps the most important of all being capital itself. Generally speaking, lack of capital was cited as the most important constraint and thus many sought government assistance in this area. To some extent, uncertainties associated with poor physical location posed some problems in improving the premises and business expansion. It is ofter argued that there is little scope for promoting the informal sector since they generally compete for the same market; perhaps this is true in certain activities such as trade where each enterprise attempts to increase its market's share. But the evidence suggests that demand was a constraint to expansion only to a minority of enterprises. The proportion of sample enterprises reporting a decrease in demand for their products was: 34 per cent in Freetown; 4 per cent in Lagos; 12 per cent in manufacturing; 10 per cent in trade and 16 per cent in services sectors of Manila; 40 per cent in Cordoba; and 6 per cent in Campinas. Whether demand will be a constraining factor in future expansion of the informal sector as a whole is, however, a moot question and will be discussed later.

Despite the generally hostile policy environment and factor and product market imperfections in which the informal sector operates, enterprises belonging to this sector seem to have done reasonably well. In Campinas, for example, 73 per cent of the enterprises had expanded in terms of capital and 62 per cent had improved their incomes. In the services sector of Manila, 43 per cent of heads realised an increase in earnings in recent years and only 14 per cent a decrease. In Freetown, as in other cases, a greater proportion of the older enterprises was in manufacturing and other related activities requiring more capital and skills, and the older enterprises tended to employ more workers as well. If one ranks the sample enterprises by size of capital, the the average age of enterprises in the bottom decile turns out to be 4 years in Kumasi, 2.8 years in Freetown and Lagos as compared to 4.9, 3.9 and 3.3 years respectively in the top decile. Another way of looking at it is to compare the capital-labour ratio in the top decile with the average; the ratio of the former to the latter in manufacturing and repairs is estimated to be: 3.7 in Freetown; 4.8 in Kumasi; 6.3 in Lagos; 4.9 in Bamako; 5.5 in Kigali; 3.9 in Lomé; and 2.3 in Nouakchott.[1] Needless to say, data based on one-shot surveys such as reported here are not the best to answer the question – whether informal sector enterprises accumulate capital and grow over time?[2] Further, the potential for its growth obviously depends on a number of factors, including the stage of growth of the economy, the role assigned to the formal vis-à-vis the informal sector and other development policies. All that can be inferred from the findings above is that growth in the informal sector could be evolutionary.

Whether growth in the informal sector is evolutionary or involutionary depends on another dimension as well: the number of enterprises. From the age structure of informal sector enterprises noted earlier, it is obvious that the number of enterprises has been growing rapidly in most cities. It is also clear that a greater proportion of the new entrants tend to be concentrated in the tertiary activities requiring relatively little capital and skills. There also seems to be some mobility between activities, notably from tertiary to secondary activities requiring more capital and skills. In fact, a major part of the employment growth in the informal sector seems to be not in older enterprises hiring more labour but in the growth of the number of small, i.e. single-person enterprises. It is this phenomenon that lends support to the view that growth in the sector is involutionary, implying that labour absorption is followed by decreasing real incomes to its participants. Given the one-shot nature of the sample surveys, the only feasible approach that could throw light on the issue was to ask whether entry of new enterprises led to greater competition, decrease in demand and decrease in income for those already in business.

With regard to competition, there is some evidence to suggest that it does pose a threat to incomes for at least those engaged in trade and services. For example, in Freetown, where the number of enterprises in trade and services increased very rapidly, 84 per cent of the heads complained of increased competition and its negative effect on income. Similarly, in Jakarta, where the tertiary activities are important, 50 per cent of the heads reported competition as a factor hurting their revenue. Also, in the Manila trade sector, 80 per cent of the heads (and 29 per cent in services) cited competition as a problem affecting their revenue. It is therefore likely that involutionary tendencies do exist, notably where growth in number of units has been rapid and tertiary activities are dominant.
----

[1] Nihan: Le secteur non-structuré - significations, aire d'extension du concept et application expérimentale, op. cit., p. 18.

[2] See also Chapter 3 for some evidence based on Nairobi, Lomé and Ahmedabad.

As for changes in demand at enterprise level, it was already noted that only a minority experienced a decrease. Changes in income of heads would also seem to follow the pattern above. What has been the response of heads to this trend? The only discernible response seems to be to diversify the products or, better still, move into different activities. Here again, besides capital, lack of know-how and skills play an important role. In so far as investment in skills is negatively correlated to age of heads, it is primarily the younger ones that are motivated to respond. These findings seem to imply the need for vocational guidance besides other forms of assistance to new entrants in this sector. In this context it is also worth recalling that at least some heads of enterprises (e.g. in Kumasi, Campinas, Manila) moved from formal sector wage employment to self-employment in the informal sector (particularly manufacturing), hinting that the income potential in selected informal sector activities is higher. In other words, it seems difficult to label growth in this sector as evolutionary or involutionary without taking into account other factors.

Another question related to the above is whether the informal sector provides opportunities for upward mobility to its participants. It was noted earlier that migrants in the sector benefited significantly either by securing jobs or by moving into better paying jobs. Though not all the new entrants succeed in creating their own enterprise and hence entering the sector as wage earners or apprentices with low incomes, many in fact successfully establish themselves as petty entrepreneurs and in a fairly short period of time, as in the case of Kano. In Freetown, 62 per cent of the former employees were reported to have become self-employed in the same line of business as before and 8 per cent in different activities. In Lagos, some 80 per cent of the heads were satisfied with their current job and were not keen to change; among the apprentices a majority tend to leave the enterprises in which they work in search of better opportunities as soon as they complete their training. Kumasi's study showed a positive relationship between education and earnings of entrepreneurs; likewise, those moving from the formal to the informal sector earned 85 cedis per week as compared to 77 cedis per week for the rest. In Jakarta, though nearly two-thirds of the participants were still in their first jobs, a third of the remainder had changed their jobs but in the same occupational category, but many after learning additional skills. Also, the tendency to learn skills before changing jobs seems to be greater among those with a few years of schooling as compared to illiterates. Two-thirds of the participants were satisfied with their current jobs while most of the rest were looking for better jobs, particularly the better educated ones. As in the above cases, 82 per cent of those in trade and 78 per cent in services sectors of Manila were not keen to change their jobs. In Cordoba though some three-quarters of the heads were satisfied with their current job, whatever occupational mobility there was among workers was confined to the same occupational category. The impression one gets from the above is that there is some upward mobility within the informal sector; in any case, there is little evidence to show that the participants in this sector hold out for better jobs in the formal sector. In other words, virtually all of them seem to view the informal sector as a permanent source of employment and income.

One final question of interest to policy makers is whether the informal sector is also economically efficient. One of the reasons

favouring the emphasis on the formal sector in development planning
has been its ability to generate surplus for investment and hence
foster economic growth. It is clear from the evidence above that
the informal sector enterprises use very little capital even though
it generates respectable levels of income for a majority of the
petty entrepreneurs and for a substantial part of its workers. Most
important of all, it provides a means of livelihood to many who
would otherwise be jobless. The capital used by them is mostly
generated from within; far from draining the scarce resources of
the economy, it contributes to resource mobilisation. As one study
argued:

> Many of the structures (the largest component of reproducible
> fixed capital) used by smaller firms for productive purposes
> are homes built for living purposes, or extensions which are,
> to a large extent, own-account produced. Similarly, tools and
> equipment used are also, to a certain extent, home-produced.
> Unlike capital in the capital-intensive sector, and like
> agricultural capital, much of the capital is produced as part
> and parcel of or mere extensions of the activities of the
> small firms and does not represent drains on the capital
> market. And since many raw materials used in the structures
> and equipment of small units are likely to be indigenously
> produced, pressures on the balance of payments are not
> generated.[1]

In addition to reliance on indigenous materials, one should
also remember the role of this sector in recuperating and recycling
discarded materials and equipment, as noted in the last chapter.
Thus, the informal sector in the Third World cities would seem to
have emerged without imposing any strain on the available investment
resources.

Given the constraints on capital and other resources noted
above and their implications for sub-optimal levels of employment
and output and for exploitative forms of relationships discussed in
Chapter 3, it is natural to think in terms of augmenting the
resources available to this sector among other promotional measures.
Some evidence cited in Chapter 3 suggests that there need not be any
conflict between output and employment following allocation of
additional resources to the informal sector. In Ghana, for example,
capital required per worker was estimated to be 11 per cent of that
in the formal sector, even though it generated a value added per
worker of 19 per cent. Among the studies in Part II, the informal
manufacturing sector in Manila suggests that it generates both more
value added and employment than the organised sector in the country.
A similar comparison but within the informal sector between
different size groups based on Kumasi data, however, suggested a
trade-off between employment and value added as size of the
enterprise increased - larger ones generated more employment and
less value added for a given investment. In all such comparisons,
however, there is one drawback; besides measurement problems, since
the informal sector also generates skills besides producing goods
and services, value-added estimates are biased downwards owing to
the exclusion of human capital formation. Larger enterprises have

----

[1] Harry T. Oshima: "Labour force 'Explosion' and the labour-intensive sector in Asian growth", in Economic Development and Cultural Change, Jan. 1971, p. 167.

more apprentices and hence generate more skills as well. Based on such scattered evidence it would be hazardous to conclude that the informal sector is efficient; all that one can conclude at this stage is that such a proposition is highly plausible and cannot be rejected. Obviously, this is one of the areas for further research.

The survey studies in Part II, though not focused on income distribution, poverty and basic needs as such, did throw some light on these issues. First, the informal sector generates income and employment to many poor, but not all those dependent on the sector are poor for, as already noted, a significant proportion of the participants do receive incomes comparable to the minimum in the formal sector, or above the national per capita level. Second, even within the informal sector, incomes are not evenly distributed. Significant income inequalities exist between men and women, between different activities and between workers, apprentices and entrepreneurs. Income variation is also due to differences in occupation, age, education of participants. The number of years in business and the physical location of the business within the city also explain differences in income of heads. Third, the types of goods and services produced are, by and large, those demanded by poor and medium-income households and most of them can be interpreted as basic-needs items. Fourth, the poor physical conditions of living and workplace discussed in Chapter 13 suggests that a majority of the informal sector participants have not been able to satisfy their minimum needs in terms of shelter and related services. Fifth, reasonable levels of income generated in this sector do not necessarily imply that the households concerned are above the poverty line. For example, in Lagos, even though the entrepreneurs earned about 100 nairas per month - well above the legal minimum wage of 60 nairas - a majority of them had dependents, some 80 per cent of them children under 14 years. Large household size coupled with the absence of additional earners in the family tends to reduce the income per capita substantially. These findings, in other words, emphasise the challenge ahead: whether development of the informal sector can increase income and employment levels sufficiently to eliminate urban poverty in the Third World cities.

Implications for policy

The emergence of the urban informal sector as a major source of employment and income in the Third World cities in recent years is primarily a manifestation of increasing pressure of population growth juxtaposed against the inadequate growth of employment and income opportunities in rural areas and small urban centres on the one hand, and in the formal and government sectors of the urban economy on the other. The swelling size of this sector in terms of employment is at least partly explained by rapid internal migration which in turn is mainly a response to concentration of development effort in big cities. That the urban informal sector acts as a safety valve to the multitude of jobless and underemployed in the countryside is therefore a reality that the policy makers in these countries ought to recognise. Neither the participants in this sector nor the policy makers now believe that adequate well paid jobs in the formal or the government sectors will be forthcoming and that the informal sector will disappear over time. That the sector deserves to be recognised and supported is increasingly accepted albeit reluctantly by many countries. This ambivalence is at least

partly due to legitimate fears that promotion of the urban informal
sector could worsen rather than improve the problems associated with
"urban explosion".

Policies aimed at containing the population growth should no
doubt form the cornerstone of any development strategy. Given the
inelastic supply of land, the key input in agriculture, it is clear
that even if far-reaching changes in agrarian structure and more
advanced agricultural technologies are introduced, agriculture
offers only limited possibilities for labour absorption. The need
for promoting non-farm employment particularly in rural areas and
small towns cannot therefore be over-emphasised. This implies no
doubt a significant departure from the development policies followed
hitherto in many developing countries where much of the development
efforts has been concentrated in primate cities.

Development strategies emphasising the above aspects however
are unlikely to yield desired results, notably with regard to the
problems of urban "explosion", except in the longer run. Both the
magnitude of the urban problems in developing countries and the rate
at which population is increasing in urban areas (mainly large
cities) call for solutions within the urban context that will make
an impact in the near future. Yet, in order to minimise attraction
of additional migration, it is imperative that such solutions avoid
any open subsidies; in other words, as in the case of self-help
housing programmes, it would seem necessary to stress on solutions
of a self-help character to the extent possible. Such an approach
would also appear inevitable in view of the limited availability of
resources at the disposal of urban authorities.

While it is important to stress on the need to harness human
energy and motivation, it will be naive to believe that self-help
approach per se will cure all the ills haunting the sector. In so
far as the relatively low level of incomes is mainly the consequence
of the status assigned to this sector within the over-all
development strategy, notably the importance attached to the formal
sector, obviously the solutions proposed must go well beyond the
informal sector itself. In other words, though informal sector is
identified in this volume as a subsector of the urban economy
deserving attention for purposes of research and policy, it does not
follow that the policies and measures proposed to develop this
sector can be independent of the economic system in which the
informal sector co-exists with its formal counterpart. It should
also be clear from the brief resumé of evidence above that informal
sector is not a homogeneous entity; measures to promote this sector
will obviously vary with the type of activity and a number of other
factors as the discussion below shows.

Some of the policies pertaining to employment and urban
environment were discussed in the last chapter. The evidence
emerging from this volume suggests a number of policies and measures
both within and outside the informal sector with a view to improving
not only employment and incomes but also the conditions of work and
job and social security. Some of them are no doubt tentative since
the evidence on which they are based is rather limited. These
include adjustment policies designed not only to minimise the
adjustment problems confronting the participants in this sector but
also to regulate the structure and growth of the sector. In
addition there are policies affecting allocation of resources within
the informal sector and between the informal and the formal sectors.

Finally there are policies and measures to bring about the structural changes notably with regard to the institutions relating to this sector.

One of the first measures to assist the informal sector, as the Kenya employment mission report argued in 1972, seems to be a change in the policy environment in which the sector operates. Though an ambivalent situation exists in many countries, some have adopted a more tolerant if not positive attitude toward this sector. Clearly there is a greater need to appreciate the merits of the sector; unless positive and sympathetic policies are adopted it may not be possible to mount various forms of assistance. It does not however imply that all informal sector units, irrespective of their location or nature, be legalised in their present form. Where these measures clearly conflict with other development objectives (e.g., environment and social) it would seem necessary to search for suitable compromises not excluding measures to transform or diversify certain activities. As a corollary to this, it seems desirable to facilitate registration of the units which in turn will generate the necessary statistics for planning purposes. The main aim of such a change in policy environment is not only to eliminate restrictions preventing fuller participation by the informal sector but also to foster its growth over time. Such changes in attitude may be reflected in national plan documents assigning an explicit and important role to this sector; but is not a sufficient condition. It may also include modifications in prevailing policies and attitudes at regional or local government levels that have a direct responsibility for this sector on a day-to-day basis. The important consequence of such a change seems to be on the access to resources and markets. It is clear that the problem of "access" is at least partly derived from the prevailing policies and attitudes toward this sector though the existing socio-economic structure also plays a very important role.

The informal sector provides opportunities for those previously employed in rural areas (mostly in agriculture), and those unemployed or outside the labour force. In so far as skill is a determinant of the activities in which they enter, access to skills plays an important role in shaping the structure of the informal sector. Since lack of skills could constrain mobility between occupations and/or activities, access to skills, both in physical and economic terms would seem to hold the key to upward mobility. It is in this context the apprenticeship system within the informal sector in many African countries deserves to be noted. The scope for improving such systems where they exist and introducing suitable alternatives where they are absent therefore deserve further examination. In particular such measures may include reorientation of the existing formal and informal training facilities, upgrading the quality of training and introduction of new skills for which demand is rising. In so far as the motivation for investment in skills is stronger among youth, such policies will be of particular significance to new entrants to the labour force.

Besides skills capital is also a major constraint both in starting own business and in expansion or diversification into more productive lines. Lack of working capital tends to limit both the size of business and its profitability owing to higher input costs obtained through retailers and cash flow problems. Often capital and skills are complementary. Poor access to capital may also increase the vulnerability of the small enterprises by encouraging a patron-client relationship with intermediaries that is not always favourable. Policies to reorient the existing credit sources, notably the banks, therefore deserve greater attention. More importantly, changes in lending procedures and credit availability must take into account the needs and absorptive capacity of the participants in the sector. Further credit policies must be co-ordinated with training policies to ensure complementarity between capital and skills.

The role of infrastructural facilities and suitable locations for informal sector enterprises within the cities was already referred to. Positive policies recognising the informal sector and greater access to capital will no doubt contribute to a reduction in uncertainty and risk and encourage suitable infrastructure investment by the entrepreneurs themselves. Measures to promote self-construction of premises through assistance in provision of cheap building materials and knowhow could also prove effective. It is however equally important to co-ordinate these measures by suitable changes in the prevailing master plans for cities not only to meet the environmental objectives but also to facilitate the informal sector's physical access to various markets for it is one of the important determinants of income inequality.

In the same vein the need for improving the informal sector's access to improved technologies, tools and technical knowhow, particularly in manufacturing cannot be over emphasised. To the extent the formal sector plays an important role in transfer of technology either through workers switching from formal to informal sector or through subcontracting ways and means of strengthening such links deserve greater attention too. Where such linkages are weak or absent the scope for introducing suitable institutional mechanisms needs to be explored.

Finally, though lack of capital and skills are important factors restricting mobility from low income tertiary activities to more productive manufacturing activities within the informal sector, inadequate or imperfect information on the relative profitabilities of various activities would also seem to be a significant factor. Since a substantial number of the participants are young and at the beginning of their career, measures such as vocational counselling could prove to be an important means for promoting productive employment and regulating the structure of employment in the informal sector. In other words such measures could serve as tools for planning utilisation of human resources in the Third World countries.

It will be naive to belive that measures suggested above to facilitate entry, expansion and mobility between occupations/activities will per se lead to "development" of the informal sector. No doubt they will minimise the time required for informal sector units to evolve into small-scale enterprises by according them equal access to factor and product markets comparable to that available to the formal sector. But it is important to recognise the need for policy intervention in other areas as well since after all the informal sector coexists with the formal sector. The problems of coexistence of the two sectors may arise in the factor markets where both compete for the same resources or in the product markets where they both compete for the same market.

With regard to capital, it was noted earlier that the informal sector by and large mobilises the resources required within itself and much of the capital goods are indigenous and often self-built or recycled. It may be possible to augment the credit available to this sector through banks and other formal channels through explicit policies on grounds of both equity and efficiency. Similar measures may prove effective in the case of foreign exchange, raw materials and intermediate goods, imported or domestic. But relaxing the supply constraints per se may not be adequate; it may often be necessary to take additional measures to eliminate market imperfections. These may include the creation of a supply channel in the public sector or a suitable organisation within the informal sector.

But in certain cases it may well be necessary to go beyond the above measures to consider solutions affecting formal vis-à-vis informal sectors. For instance, it is not uncommon to find informal sector units, owing to the traditional skills and knowhow, rely heavily on certain traditional raw materials like leather, metal and wood. With the growing shortage of these materials few often succeed in acquiring the skills and technology necessary to replace them by modern substitutes such as vinyl, plastic and other materials. Consequently either their final products are not competitive with comparable formal sector products and/or that they are forced to stop production. To some extent the informal sector enterprises overcome such shortages by recuperating and recycling waste materials. Obviously, in such situations, there is a need to assist the informal sector in improving their technological capacity by providing the necessary skills, tools and knowhow. Where such a course of action is not feasible, particularly in the short run, what are the alternatives? To the extent the shortage of traditional raw materials is caused by exports it would seem necessary to reconsider the export policies in relation to loss of employment in the informal sector. It is also possible that the formal sector firms cause such shortages by bidding away the scarce materials, in which case it raises a question: should the formal sector firms be forbidden or restrained from using such materials on grounds of equity if not efficiency?

Though the discussion above refers in particular to traditional raw materials, it has wider relevance. In principle such a situation can arise when factor supplies are inelastic or when the market for final products is limited. Besides favourable policy environment accorded to the formal sector firms, scale and technology factors would seem to offer particular advantage to the formal sector. One consequence of this is to limit the scope for evolutionary growth in the informal sector. Various policies and measures to facilitate access to markets and resources suggested earlier will no doubt discourage informal sector units being lured into direct exploitative forms of relationships with the formal sector. To the extent subtle forms of domination by the formal sector such as those described above are important clearly it poses a dilemma to policy makers. It is thus argued that unless the formal-informal sector relationships are so altered, much of the efforts to promote the informal sector may not per se yield the desired results. Potential conflicts between policies toward these sectors are no doubt valid in certain activities and in certain countries; but the evidence emerging from this volume seem to question that it is a widespread phenomenon. In a situation where the formal sector is numerically small (e.g., in many cities of Africa), where the demand for goods and services is rising rapidly or where the factor supplies are not totally inelastic such problems are relatively less important. Inasmuch as the formal sector is projected to grow faster, such conflicts are bound to sharpen over time unless accompanied by other measures. It is for this reason that development strategies recognise the interdependence between the two sectors. In short, this is an area that deserves scrutiny by policy makers.

Turning to the demand aspects, it was mentioned in the last chapter that the scope for greater involvement of the informal sector in the provision of shelter and other related urban services must be explored. In some activities the informal sector is playing a positive role in providing import substitutes however imperfect they may be. The scope for expanding this role of the informal sector through appropriate incentives is therefore worth considering. The evidence presented in this volume suggests that the bulk of the demand for this sector's goods and services originates from households. To the extent that the development strategies stress income redistribution and basic needs satisfaction it seems likely that the demand for informal sector's output will increase too. More importantly, since these goods can generally be produced with relatively simple technologies and small scale of operations, there is greater scope for participation by the informal sector. In some countries such as India attempts have been made to provide sheltered markets for small enterprises by reserving the production of certain items exclusively to the small-scale sector. Another measure to increase the demand prospects has been, as the Kenya employment mission report argued, to strengthen linkages between the informal and the formal sectors through subcontracting from the latter. It is however important, for reasons already noted, that such linkages are not detrimental to the interest of the informal sector. Finally, removal of restrictions on informal sector activities could also make a significant contribution. The essence of these measures is of course to link the informal sector with the growth sectors on the one hand and to restructure the demand pattern in favour of this sector. These measures are not only desirable but also seem necessary to foster evolutionary growth of this sector.

One implication of such an approach is to encourage the development of manufacturing, construction and related activities rather than trade and services. The rationale for this stems from the fact that there are limitations to promoting tertiary activities unless the aggregate demand itself increases substantially; for otherwise it could only contribute to an involutionary growth, a larger number of enterprises sharing a given market. To the extent there are possibilities for redistributing the demand from the formal to the informal sector (e.g., sale of consumer goods through formal sector outlets as opposed to informal sector enterprises) there may be exceptions.

The wide range of policies and measures suggested above stress the need to assist the informal sector participants to help themselves more effectively. But they also underline the need to reorient development strategies and restructure the socio-economic relationships, notably those between the formal and the informal sectors. Autonomous solutions aimed at the informal sector alone can have only a limited impact. These conclusions, in other words, echo the interdependent nature of the solutions underlying the current debate on new national and international economic and social order. They in essence argue in favour of a new deal for the informal sector.

Besides contributing to higher levels of income for the urban poor and evolutionary growth the various elements of the development strategy noted above would also seem to make a significant contribution to other objectives. Since the informal sector provides a training ground to many, it contributes to investment in human capital. By increasing the level of incomes and by promoting mobility between occupations it could significantly improve the conditions of work to many, notably the wage workers a majority of whom currently receive wages below the legal minimum. It would also facilitate the introduction of a programme to improve job and social security that is self-sustaining. To realise these objectives it would no doubt be necessary to take additional measures in terms of improving the working environment, reducing occupational hazards and the like.

To the extent labour market inefficiencies are the consequence of imperfections in other markets, measures suggested above to facilite mobility will significantly improve the functioning of the labour market. It would nevertheless seem necessary to consider additional measures notably to improve the extent of women's participation and their conditions of work because (a) women's participation in the informal sector is substantially lower than for males; (b) they are highly concentrated in low productive tertiary activities; and (c) their level of remuneration is significantly lower than for males.

Implications for action

It was mentioned earlier that the need to distinguish informal sector units from small enterprises in their usual sense arises from operational implications. Though there is much in common between the two in terms of specific programme inputs such as credit, training, resources, technology and the like, the fact that informal sector units are not headed by entrepreneurs but by people with little or no education and the fact that their orientation is primarily employment rather than profit suggests that the approach to assist the informal sector must be different. For one thing the informal sector participants, though interested in receiving various forms of assistance, seem to have little hope in receiving them. Many seem to suspect the willingness or ability of the local authorities to assist them. This should not come as a surprise given that the public policies toward this sector in many countries have been hostile and hence eroded their credibility. It would therefore seem important to reverse the situation through changes in policies and attitudes. It also implies that voluntary agencies could play a useful role in assisting the informal sector.

The characteristics of the informal sector participants also suggest that they cannot always articulate and define their needs. Often it seems necessary to work with such small units with a view to helping them define their needs. Such an approach is also inevitable in order to identify the complementarities between various forms of assistance (e.g., credit, skills, tools, technology, marketing, infrastructure) and providing a package that is tailor made to suit their needs. In this context it is also worth noting that though some attempts have been made in the past to assist this sector, they have not always yielded the desired results. Though such shortcomings are partly due to lack of clear focus on the needs, failure to judge the capacity of informal sector units to absorb assistance provided would also seem to have played a vital role. Any programme to assist this sector cannot assume that the informal sector units will automatically reach the authorities assisting them; both the small scale of operation coupled with the uncertainty of receiving assistance would seem to discourage them from approaching the authorities. In other words, unlike the programmes for small enterprise development, those focused on informal sector would have to build confidence, assist them in defining their needs, identify the interrelationships between various forms of assistance, assess their capacity for absorption of assistance and hence reach them rather than vice versa.

Many countries have reconsidered various policies affecting the informal sector. Some have gone beyond to provide specific forms of assistance such as provision of space or premises in the form of "kiosks" for informal sector units (e.g., Ghana). Others have attempted to extend credit through special programmes for weaker sections of the population (e.g., India). Still others have sought to provide skills as a means of occupational mobility (e.g., Philippines). Few have sought to eliminate marketing constraints (e.g., Jakarta in Indonesia). Attempts have also been made to organise informal sector units. Special programmes to create production-cum-training centres have also been considered in some cases, notably to facilitate women's participation. Several voluntary agencies and other bodies such as ACCION International have also sought to promote programmes for the informal sector in selected countries.[1] Agencies such as the USAID, under specially conceived programmes like PISCES (programme for investment in the small capital enterprise sector) have also attempted in recent years to formulate action programmes for the informal sector.[2] The World Bank, particularly under the urban development projects, has also been making efforts to reach small enterprises with a view to increasing employment and alleviating urban poverty.

Though these efforts are significant few of them recognise the subtle differences in approach necessary to promote the informal sector. It is in this context that the ILO is currently focusing on initiating suitable operational activities. Besides giving the orientation outlined earlier, such efforts recognise the need to promote institutions with a multidisciplinary dimension and outlook within the respective countries. They also emphasise the need to disseminate information on the subject to policy makers to bring about the necessary changes in development strategies and thus the ILO has organised regional seminars on the subject.[3] Further, development of the informal sector embraces a number of objectives

----

[1] See for example: José Gentil Schreiber: Small business development in Brazil: A study of the UNO program (New York, ACCION International, 1976).

[2] See Urban Edge, June 1980, for more details.

[3] S.V. Sethuraman: "The urban informal sector in Africa", in International Labour Review, Nov.-Dec. 1977, for a brief summary on the West African regional seminar on the informal sector held in Ghana in 1977. Another seminar, organised jointly by the ILO and OCAM (Organisation Commune Africaine et Mauricienne), is due to be held in Ouagadougou (Upper Volta) in November 1980 for French-speaking Africa.

besides employment promotion; for example they include promotion of suitable organisations to enhance people's participation, improvement in conditions of work and environment and in social security. Consequently the ILO is placing considerable emphasis on this sector in its activities over the years to come.[1] In order to facilitate this task the ILO is currently in the process of developing suitable pilot projects in selected slums of Bombay (India) and in selected countries of French-speaking Africa (Kigali in Rwanda, Lomé in Togo, Bamako in Mali, Djibouti, etc.). It is hoped that these efforts will throw considerable light not only on the possible approaches and their limitations but also on the national capacities to cope with the problem and the replicability of the solutions on a wider scale.

Future research

As stated at the outset, the evidence emerging from various studies perhaps raises more questions than answers. In particular they point to the need for further research in many areas where a settled body of conclusions are yet to emerge. In concluding this volume it may be useful to identify some of these key areas for further investigation. Firstly, the extent to which informal sector development conflicts with the development of formal sector is unclear. Besides efficiency considerations, what kind of policy measures are required and for what types of activities? What are the factors that sharpen such conflicts? What are their implications for growth and income distribution? How do the rates of return to capital compare between the two sectors? Secondly, on the demand side, what are the prospects for increasing the demand for informal sector goods and services? How does a basic needs oriented development strategy influence the informal sector's future? What are the income elasticities of demand confronting the two sectors? How does income redistribution policy affect the informal sector? Third, the evidence suggests a significant variation in incomes and wages within the informal sector. What are its implications for policies towards arresting internal migration? Fourth, how do the prospects vary with the size of the city, the structure of the formal and informal sectors, the stage of economic development, the extent of dependence on international trade? Finally, what factors account for the success of those within the informal sector and whether they lend themselves to suitable policy intervention?

----

[1] ILO: Medium-term plan, 1982-87 (Geneva, 1980).

APPENDIX TABLES

Table 1.

Income inequality among households and population in rural and urban areas of selected developing countries.

Table 2.

Income inequality among economically active population and income recipients in rural and urban areas of selected developing countries.

Table 3.

Proportion of total income received by the urban poor in selected developing countries.

Table 4.

Estimated share of urban labour force in the informal sector in selected cities of the Third World.

Table 1: Income inequality* among households and population in rural and urban areas of selected developing countries

Country	Year	Distribution of households			Distribution of population		
		National	Rural	Urban	National	Rural	Urban
A. 1. Argentina	'61	0.433		0.385			
2. Chile	'68	0.506	0.428	0.455			
3. Mexico	'63	0.573	0.531	0.471			
	'63	0.546	0.482	0.524			
4. Venezuela	'62	0.544	0.461	0.438			
	'62		0.452	0.442			
B. 1. Bangladesh	63/64	0.373	0.351	0.502	0.173	0.164	0.254
	66/67	0.342	0.334	0.399			
2. India	'60	0.473	0.454	0.530			
	64/65	0.421	0.370	0.480			
	67/68	0.478	0.477	0.465			
3. Malaysia	67/68	0.554	0.464	0.516			
	'70	0.519	0.476	0.504			
	'70	0.518		0.508			
4. Pakistan	63/64	0.386	0.362	0.443	0.222	0.190	0.261
	66/67	0.355	0.328	0.391	0.207	0.166	0.266
	68/69	0.336	0.302	0.385	0.208	0.163	0.245
	69/70	0.336	0.304	0.367	0.186	0.146	0.239
	70/71	0.333	0.298	0.364			
5. Philippines	'61	0.504	0.412	0.526			
	'65	0.510	0.426	0.530			
	'71	0.494	0.466	0.458			

6. Sri Lanka	69/70	0.373	0.352	0.410
	69/70	0.377		0.414
7. Thailand	62/63		0.440	0.466
	'70		0.448	0.385
8. Rep. of Korea	'66	0.265	0.306	0.323
	'70	0.384	0.314	
	'71	0.360	0.310	0.338
C. 1. Cyprus	'66		0.193	0.318

* Gini coefficient.

Source: Shail Jain: Size distribution of income: a comparison of data (World Bank, Washington, 1975).

Table 2: Income inequality[1] among economically active population and income recipients in rural and urban areas of selected developing countries

Country	Year	Distribution of economically active population			Distribution of income recipients		
		National	Rural	Urban	National	Rural	Urban
A. 1. Argentina	'61				0.490		0.411[2]
2. Brazil	'60	0.654	0.434	0.485	0.590		
	'70	0.641	0.448	0.556	0.646		
3. Colombia	'62	0.483			0.525		
	'64	0.647			0.594	0.592	
	'70	0.556			0.562		0.552
	'70					0.476	0.547
4. Panama	'70				0.448		0.421[3]
	'72				0.426		0.419[3]
B. 1. India	61/64				0.488	0.335	0.529
	63/65				0.467	0.328	0.493
2. Malaysia	'70				0.513	0.473	0.520
3. Sri Lanka	'63				0.508	0.468	0.541
	'73				0.409	0.373	0.399

[1] Gini coefficient.

[2] Buenos Aires City.

[3] Metropolitan area.

Table 3: Proportion of total income received by the urban poor* in selected developing countries

(per cent)

A. Bottom 50 per cent of households

1.	Argentina	'61	24.5	8.	Pakistan	63/64 22.0
						66/67 24.6
						68/69 25.1
						69/70 26.2
						70/71 26.2
2.	Chile	'68	19.7			
3.	Mexico	'63	19.2	9.	Philippines	'61 16.4
		'63	15.7			'65 16.8
						'71 19.7
4.	Venezuela	'62	21.0	10.	Sri Lanka	69/70 23.0
		'62	20.6			69/70 22.1
5.	Bangladesh	63/64	18.8	11.	Thailand	62/63 19.2
		66/67	23.7			'70 23.7
6.	India	'60	17.4	12.	Rep. of Korea	'66 28.2
		64/65	20.4			'71 27.8
		67/68	20.5			
7.	Malaysia	67/68	18.8			
		'70	18.2			
		'70	17.4			

B. Bottom 50 per cent of income recipients

1.	Argentina	'61	23.1	3.	Panama	'70 22.3
						'72 23.1
2.	Colombia	'64	13.8	4.	India	61/64 20.7
		'70	15.9			63/65 21.2
		'70	15.0			'70 17.0
				5.	Malaysia	
				6.	Sri Lanka	'63 15.8
						'73 23.4

* Bottom 50 per cent of households (or income recipients).

Table 4: Estimated share of urban labour force in the informal
          sector in selected developing countries

Area	Year	Per cent

Africa

Area	Year	Per cent
Abidjan (Ivory Coast)	1970	31
Lagos (Nigeria)	1976	50
Kumasi (Ghana)	1974	60/70
Nairobi (Kenya)	1972	44
Urban areas (Senegal)	1976	50
Urban areas (Tunisia)	1977	34

Asia

Area	Year	Per cent
Calcutta (India)	1971	40/50
Ahmedabad (India)	1971	47
Jakarta (Indonesia)	1976	45
Colombo (Sri Lanka)	1971	19
Urban areas in West Malaysia (Malaysia)	1970	35
Singapore	1970	23
Urban areas (Thailand)	1976	26
Urban areas (Pakistan)	1972	69

Latin America

Area	Year	Per cent
Cordoba (Argentina)	1976	38
Sao Paulo (Brazil)	1976	43
Urban areas (Brazil)	1970	30
Rio de Janeiro (Brazil)	1972	24
Belo Horizonte (Brazil)	1972	31
Urban areas (Chile)	1968	39
Bogota (Colombia)	1970	43
Santo Domingo (Dominican Republic)	1973	50
Guayaquil (Ecuador)	1970	48
Quito (Ecuador)	1970	48
San Salvador (El Salvador)	1974	41
Federal district and State of Mexico	1970	27
Mexico D.F., Guadalajara and Monterey	1970	42
Asuncion (Paraguay)	1973	57
Urban areas (Peru)	1970	60
Urban areas (Venezuela)	1974	44
Caracas (Venezuela)	1974	40
Kingston (Jamaica)	1974	33

Sources:

(1) PREALC: Sector informal, p. 30.

(2) Kalmann Schaefer: Sao Paulo: Urban development and employment (Geneva, ILC, 1976), p. 67.

(3) H. Joshi, H. Lubell and J. Mouly: Abidjan: Urban development and employ-ment in the Ivory Coast (Geneva, ILO, 1976), p. 54.

(4) Marga Institute: The informal sector of Colombo (Sri Lanka) (Colombo, ILO, 1978), p. 26.

(5) Donald Lee and A.G. Othman: "The urban informal sector: A glimpse of the Malaysian experience", in ASEAN Seminar on informal Sector, Jakarta, 11-16 December 1978.

(6) Chia Lin Sien and Chia Siow Yue: "The informal sector in Singapore", ibid.

(7) S. Tambunlertchai et al.: "The urban informal sector in Thailand", ibid.

(8) M. Irfan: "The informal sector in Pakistan" (unpublished manuscript), p. 3.

(9) M.P. van Dijk: Développement du secteur non-structuré au Sénégal: une étude de son context et son potentiel, JASPA (Dakar, ILO, 1977), p. 1.

(10) PREALC: Guidelines for action in the informal sector of Central Kingston, PREALC Working Paper No. 101 (Santiago, ILO, 1976), p. 6.

(11) Biplab Durgupta: "Calcutta's informal sector", in Bulletin (Insitute of Development Studies, University of Sussex). Oct. 1973, p. 67.

(12) Mahomond Drira: Le secteur non-structuré dans l'économie tunisienne d'après le recensement des établissements, Paper presented at the Seminar: La petite production marchande en milieu urbain africain, organised by IEDES, Paris, March 1979.

(13) Victor Tokman: "Technologia para el sector informal urbano", PREALC Documento occasional No. 4, Jan. 1978, table 1.

INFORMAL SECTOR:

SELECTIVE BIBLIOGRAPHY

ACCION International/AITEC: <u>Assisting the smallest economic</u> <u>activities of the urban poor: Final workshop report</u>, PISCES Phase I (Mass., Apr. 1980, mimeographed).

Aryee, George, A.: <u>Effects of formal education and training on the</u> <u>intensity of employment in the informal sector: a case study</u> <u>of Kumasi, Ghana</u> (Geneva, ILO, 1976; mimeographed World Employment Programme research working paper; restricted).

-- <u>Small-scale manufacturing activities: A study of the inter-</u> <u>relationships between the formal and the informal sectors in</u> <u>Kumasi, Ghana</u> (Geneva, idem, 1977; mimeographed World Employment Programme research working paper; restricted).

Berlinck, M.T., Boro, J.M., and Cintra, L.C.: <u>Development of the</u> <u>economy of compinas: the informal sector</u> (Geneva, ILO, 1977; mimeographed World Employment Programme research working paper; restricted).

Bienefeld, M.: "The informal sector and peripheral capitalism: The case of Tanzania", in <u>Institute of Development Studies</u> <u>Bulletin</u>, Feb. 1975.

Bose, A.N.: <u>Calcutta and rural Bengal: Small sector symbiosis</u> (Calcutta, ILO, 1978, published in 1974 as <u>The informal sector</u> <u>in the Calcutta metropolitan economy</u>; Geneva, idem; mimeographed World Employment Programme research working paper; restricted).

Breman, J.: "A dualistic labour system? A critique of the 'informal sector' concept", in <u>Economic and Political Weekly</u>, Nov.-Dec. 1976.

Birkbeck, Chris: "Self-employed proletarians in an informal factory: The case of Cali's garbage dump", in <u>World Development</u>, Sep.-Oct. 1978.

Bromley, R.J.: <u>The locational behaviour of Colombian street traders:</u> <u>Observations and hypotheses</u>, Paper presented at the "Urban poverty session" of the International Congress of Latin-Americanist Geographers, paipa, Colombia, 8-12 Aug. 1977.

-- "Organisation, regulation and exploitation in the so-called 'urban informal sector': The street traders of Cali, Colombia", in <u>World Development</u>, Sep.-Oct. 1978. Bromley, R.J., and Gerry, Chris: <u>Casual work and poverty in third world</u> <u>cities</u> (1979).

Cavalcanti, Clovis, and Duarte, Renate: <u>A procura de espaço na</u> <u>economia urbana: O sector informal de Fortaleza</u>, SUDANE/FUNDAJ (Recife, Brazil, 1980), Series Populaçáo e Emprego 10, Vol. 1. Cavalcanti, Clovis: <u>Viabilidade do Sector Informal: A demanda</u> <u>de paquenos serviços no Grande Recife</u>, Instituto Joaquim Nabuco de Pequisas Sociais, Ministério da Educaçáo e Cultura, Series Estudos e Pesquèsas 11 (Recife, Brazil, 1978).

Chana, Tara, and Morrison, Hunter: "Nairobi's informal economic sector", in Ekistics 257, Aug. 1975, pp. 120-130.

Van Dijk, M.P.: <u>De informele sector van Ougadougou en Dakar</u> (Vrije universiteit te Amsterdam), Nov. 1980.

Papohunda, O.J.: The informal sector of Lagos (Geneva, ILO, 1978; mimeographed World Employment Programme research working paper; restricted).

Faragó, G.: "Employment promotion in Nairobi's informal sector" (Nairobi, unpublished manuscript, 1978).

Fowler, D.A.: The informal sector of Freetown (Sierra Leone) (Geneva, ILO, 1978; mimeographed World Employment Programme research working paper; restricted).

Friedman, J., and Sullivan, F.: "The absorption of labour in the urban economy: The case of developing countries", in Economic Development and Cultural Change, Apr. 1974.

Fuenzalida, Luis, A.: Labour intensity and micro-business: A view from Bahia, Brazil (Mass., Acclon International, 1976).

Gerry, Chris: "Petty production and capitalistic production in Dakar: The crisis of the self-employed", in World Development, Sep.-Oct. 1978.

-- Petty producers and the urban economy: A case study of Dakar (Geneva, ILO, 1974; mimeographed World Employment Programme research working paper; restricted).

Godfrey, M.: "Rural-urban migration in a Lewis-model context", in The Manchester School of Economic and Social Studies, Sep. 1979.

Guisinger, Stephen, and Irfan, Mohammed: "Pakistan's informal sector", in Journal of Development Studies, July 1980.

Hakam, Ali N.: Technology diffusion from the formal to the informal sector: The case of the auto-repair industry in Ghana (Geneva, ILO, 1978; mimeographed World Employment Programme research working paper; restricted).

Hart, K.: "Informal income opportunities and urban employment in Ghana", in Journal of Modern African Studies, Mar. 1973.

Hinderink, J., and Sterkenberg, J.: Anatomy of an African town - A socio-economic study of Cape Coast, Ghana (Utrecht, 1975).

Hollensteiner, Mary R.: "Penetrating the grey areas: Urban workers in the tertiary sector", in Philippine Labour Review, First Quarter, 1978.

House, William J.: Nairobi's informal sector: A reservoir of dynamic entrepreneurs or a residual pool of surplus labour? Working paper No. 347, Institute of Development Studies (University of Nairobi, 1979).

-- "Nairobi's informal sector", in Tonykillick (ed.): The Kenyan economy: Readings in performance problems and policies (Nairobi, forthcoming).

Hugon, P., Abadie, N.L., and Morice, A.: Petite production marchande et l'emploi dans le secteur "informel": Le cas africain (Paris, Institut d'étude du développement économique et social, Université de Paris I, 1977), p. 272.

Human Resources Development Centre (Indonesia): ASEAN Seminar on "Informal Sector", Jakarta, 11-16 December 1978, sponsored by the Government of Indonesia (jointly with the ILO and other organisations) (Jakarta, 1978).

Industrial Survey and Promotion Centre, Ministry of Commerce and Industry: Development plan 1979-83: Programme implementation-Development of the informal sector (Nairobi, 1979), p. 106.

Institute for Development Studies, University of Nairobi: The Informal Sector in Kenya, occasional paper No. 25 (Nairobi, 1977).

Institute for Development Studies, University of Sussex: "The informal sector and marginal groups", in Bulletin, Oct. 1973.

ILO: Employment, incomes and equality: A strategy for increasing productive employment in Kenya (Geneva, 1973).

-- "Training workers in the backward sectors of the economy", in International Labour Review, Sep.-Oct. 1977.

-- Jobs and skills programmes for Africa: Propositions pour une politique intégrale de développement de la petite entreprise à Ougadougou, Haute-Volta (Rapport provisoire) (Addis Ababa, Oct. 1979).

-- Jobs and skills programme for Africa: Employment, incomes and production in the informal sector in the Gambia (Addis Ababa, 1980).

-- PREALC: Políticas hacia el sector informal urbano, documento de trabajo PREALC/116, June 1977, p. 19.

- -- PREALC: Sector informal: funcionamiento y políticas (Santiago, 1978).

-- UNDP: Development of informal sector in Java, Indonesia, Report prepared by S.V. Sethuraman under the ILO/UNDP project No. INS/72/030 (Geneva, 1976).

Jellinek, Lea: "Circular migration and the Pondok dwelling system: A case study of ice-cream traders in Jakarta", in P.J. Rimmer et al. (eds.): Food, shelter and transport in South-East Asia and the Pacific (Canberra, 1978).

Joshi, H., Lubell, H., and Mouly, J.: "The urban informal sector", in Abidjan: Urban development and employment in the Ivory Coast (Geneva, ILO, 1976), Chapter 3.

Jurado, G.M., et al.: The informal sector of Manila (Geneva, ILO, 1978; mimeographed World Employment Programme research working paper; restricted).

Keyes, S.J., and William J.: Manila scavengers: The struggle for urban survival, Institute of Philippine Culture Poverty Research Series No. 1 (Quezon City, 1974).

King, K.: "Kenya's informal machine makers: A study of small-scale industry in Kenya's emergent artisan society", in World Development, Apr.-May 1974.

-- African artisan: Education and the informal sector in Kenya (London, 1977).

Koenigsberger, O.H.: "The absorption of newcomers in the cities of the Third World", in ODI Review, May 1976.

Lambert, D.: "L'urbanisation accélérée de l'Amérique latine et la formation d'un secteur tertiaire refuge", in Civilisation, No. 2, 1965.

Le Brun, Olivier and Gerry, Chris: "Petty producers and capitalism, in Review of African Political Economy, May-Oct. 1975.

Leys, Colin: Underdevelopment in Kenya: The political economy of neo-colonialism, 1964-71, 1975.

-- "The politics of redistribution with growth: The 'target group' approach", in Institute of Development Studies Bulletin, Aug. 1975.

Leys, C.: "Interpreting African underdevelopment: Reflections on the ILO report on employment, incomes and equality in Kenya", in Manpower and Unemployment Research in Africa, Nov. 1974.

Lubell, H., Singer, H., Souza, P.R., and Tokman, V.E.: Policies for the urban informal sector in Brazil, Paper presented at the Seminar on the Informal Sector in Brazilia, February 1976.

Lubell, H., and Sethuraman, S.V.: Income and employment generating policies for lower-income urban settlements, Paper prepared for an Ad Hoc Expert Group Meeting on Strategies for the Improvement of Different Types of Lower-Income Settlements, United Nations, New York, 1977.

Lubell, H., and McCallum, D.: "The urban informal sector", in Bogota: Urban development and employment (Geneva, ILO, 1978), Chapter 4.

Mabogunje, A.L., and Filani, M.O.: Absorption of migrants into Kano City, Nigeria (Geneva, ILO, 1977; mimeographed World Employment Programme research working paper; restricted).

Mac Ewan, Scott, A.: Capitalism and petty production in Peru (University of Essex, 1977, mimeographed).

Marga Institute: The informal sector of Colombo city (Sri Lanka) (Colombo, ILO, 1979) (published in 1978 under the same title; Geneva, ILO; mimeographed World Employment Programme research working paper; restricted).

Mazumdar, Dipak: "The urban informal sector", in World Development, No. 8, 1976.

McGee, T.G., and Yeung, Y.M.: Hawkers in South-East Asian cities: Planning for the bazaar economy (Ottawa, IDRC, 1977).

-- "Peasants in cities: A paradox, a paradox, a most ingenious paradox", in Human Organisation, No. 2.

Merrick, Thomas W.: Employment and earnings in the informal sector in Brazil: The case of Belo Horizonte, in Journal of Developing Areas, Apr. 1976, pp. 337-354.

Ministerio de Trabajo y Desarrollo Laboral, Dirección General de
    Empleo: Empleo en el sector informal de la ciudad de La Paz
    (La Paz (Venezuela), Mar. 1980).

Moir, Hazel: Jakarta informal sector (Jakarta, National Insitute of
    Economic and Social Research, Indonesian Institute of
    Sciences, 1978), published in 1978 as a mimeographed World
    Employment Programme research working paper; restricted).

Moser, Caroline, O.N.: "Informal sector or petty production: Dualism
    or dependence in urban development?", in The Urban Informal
    Sector: Critical Perspectives in World Development, Sep.-Oct.
    1978.

Mosley, P.: "Implicit models and policy recommendations: Policy
    towards the informal sector in Kenya", in Institute of
    Development Studies Bulletin, No. 3, 1978.

Nihan, Georges, and Jourdain, R.: "The modern informal sector in
    Nouakchott", in International Labour Review, Nov.-Dec. 1978.

Nihan, G., Demol, E., and Jondoh, C.: "The modern informal sector in
    Lomé", ibid., Sep.-Oct. 1979.

Nihan, Georges: "Le secteur non structuré: Signification, aire
    d'extension du concept et application expérimentale", in Revue
    Tiers Monde, Apr.-June 1980.

OFISEL Ltda.: El sector informal en la economía urbana de Bogotá
    (Geneva, ILO, 1977; mimeographed World Employment Programme
    research working paper; restricted).

Page Jr., and John, M.: Small enterprises in African development: A
    survey, World Bank Staff Working Paper No. 363 (Washington,
    1979).

Papanek, G.: "The poor of Jakarta" in Economic Development and
    Cultural Change, Oct. 1975.

Papola, T.S.: "Informal sector in an urban economy", in Nagarlok,
    Oct.-Dec. 1978.

Peattie, Lisa R.: "'Tertiarisation' and urban poverty in Latin
    America", in Cornelius, W., and Trueblood, F. (eds.):
    Urbanisation and inequality (London, 1975).

Penouil, Marc: "Activités de transition et activités informelles: 4
    études sectorielles à Abidjan et Yaoundé" (1979; unpublished
    manuscript).

Quijano, A.: "The marginal pole of the economy and the marginalised
    labour force", in Economy and Society, Nov. 1974.

Reichmuth, Markus: Dualism in Peru: An investigation into the inter-
    relationships between Lima's informal clothing industry and
    the formal sector (unpublished B. Litt. Thesis, University of
    Oxford, 1978).

Reynolds, Lloyd G.: "Economic development with surplus labour: Some
    complications", in Oxford Economic Papers (New Series), Mar.
    1969.

Rimmer, P.J.: "The future of trishaw enterprises in Penang", in P.J. Rimmer et al. (eds.): Food, shelter and transport in South-East Asia and the Pacific (Canberra, 1978).

Sánchez, C., Palmieri, H., and Ferrero, F.: Desarrollo industrial, urbanización y empleo en la ciudad de Córdoba (Argentina): Un caso de crecimiento desequilibrado (Geneva, ILO, 1977; mimeographed World Employment Programme research working paper; restricted).

Santos, M.: L'espace partagé (Paris, 1975).

Schaefer, K. (assisted by Spindel, C.R.): "The urban informal sector and non-formalised labour", in Sao Paulo: Urban development and employment (Geneva, ILO, 1976), Chapter 4.

Schreiber, José G.: Small business development in Brazil: A study of the UNC program (New York, ACCLON International, 1976).

Sethuraman, S.V.: "Towards a definition of the informal sector" (Geneva, ILO, 1974; unpublished manuscript).

-- "Survey instrument for a study of the urban informal sector: The case of Jakarta" (Geneva, idem, 1975; unpublished manuscript).

- "The urban informal sector", in Jakarta: Urban development and employment (Geneva, idem, 1976), Chapter 7.

-- "The urban informal sector in Africa", in International Labour Review, Nov.-Dec. 1977.

-- "The urban informal sector: Concept, measurement and policy", ibid., July-Aug. 1976.

-- "Urban poverty and the role of the informal sector in creating employment", in Khadija Haq (ed.): Equality of opportunity within and among nations (New York, 1977), Chapter 8.

-- Employment promotion in the informal sector in Ghana (Geneva, ILO, 1977; mimeographed World Employment Programme research working paper; restricted) (reproduced from ILO-JASPA: Employment promotion in the rural and informal sectors in Ghana (Addis Ababa, 1977)).

-- "The informal urban sector in developing countries: Some policy implications", in Social Action, July-Sep. 1977 (also reproduced in Alfred de Souza (ed.): The Indian city: Poverty, ecology and urban development (New Delhi, 1978), Chapter 1).

Silverio, Jr., and Simeon, G.: The neighbourhood sari-sari store, Institute of Philippine Culture, Research Series No. 2 (Quezon City, 1975).

Sit, Victor F.S., and Ng, S.H.: "Ambulatory labour in Hong Kong", in International Labour Review, July-Aug. 1980.

Souza, P.R., and Tokman, V.E.: "The informal urban sector in Latin America", ibid., Nov.-Dec. 1976.

-- "Distribución del ingreso, pobreza y empleo en áreas urbanas", in El Trimestre Económico, July-Sep. 1978.

Standing, G.: "Urban workers and patterns of employment", in Subbiah Kannappan (ed.): Studies of urban labour market behaviour in developing countries (Geneva, International Insitute for Labour Studies, 1977).

Steel, W.F.: Small-scale employment and production in developing countries: The evidence from Ghana (New York, 1977).

Tokman, V.F.: "Políticas para el sector informal urbano en América latina", in Revista Internacional del Trabajo, July-Sep. 1978.

-- "Urban poverty and employment in Latin America: Guidelines for action", ILO-PREALC Occasional Paper No. 1, 1977.

-- "An exploration into the nature of informal-formal sector relationships", in World Development, Sep.-Oct. 1978 (appeared in 1977 as ILO-PREALC Monógraph No. 2).

-- "Tecnología para el sector informal urbano", ILO-PREALC documento ocasional No. 1 (Santiago, 1978).

Watanabe, Susumu: Technological linkages between formal and informal sectors of manufacturing industries (Geneva, ILO, 1978; mimeographed World Employment Programme research working paper; restricted).

Weeks, J.: "Policies for expanding employment in the informal urban sector of developing countries", in International Labour Review, Jan. 1975.

-- "An exploration into the nature of the problem of urban imbalance in Africa, in Manpower and Unemployment Research, Nov. 1973.